SCHOLARS READING ROMANS 1
WITH DANIEL PATTE

SCHOLARS READING ROMANS 1 WITH DANIEL PATTE

Critique, Dialogue, and Pedagogy

Edited by
James P. Grimshaw

LONDON • NEW YORK • OXFORD • NEW DELHI • SYDNEY

T&T CLARK
Bloomsbury Publishing Plc
50 Bedford Square, London, WC1B 3DP, UK
1385 Broadway, New York, NY 10018, USA
29 Earlsfort Terrace, Dublin 2, Ireland

BLOOMSBURY, T&T CLARK and the T&T Clark logo are trademarks of
Bloomsbury Publishing Plc

First published in Great Britain 2023
Paperback edition published 2024

Copyright © James P. Grimshaw and contributors, 2023, 2024

James P. Grimshaw has asserted his right under the Copyright, Designs and Patents Act, 1988, to be identified as Editor of this work.

Cover design: Charlotte James
Cover image © *Escape* (detail) by Samuel Bak. Image Courtesy of Pucker Gallery

All rights reserved. No part of this publication may be reproduced or transmitted in any form or by any means, electronic or mechanical, including photocopying, recording, or any information storage or retrieval system, without prior permission in writing from the publishers.

Bloomsbury Publishing Plc does not have any control over, or responsibility for, any third-party websites referred to or in this book. All internet addresses given in this book were correct at the time of going to press. The author and publisher regret any inconvenience caused if addresses have changed or sites have ceased to exist, but can accept no responsibility for any such changes.

A catalogue record for this book is available from the British Library.

A catalog record for this book is available from the Library of Congress.

ISBN: HB: 978-0-5677-0398-9
PB: 978-0-5677-0402-3
ePDF: 978-0-5677-0399-6
ePub: 978-0-5677-0401-6

Typeset by Newgen KnowledgeWorks Pvt. Ltd., Chennai, India

To find out more about our authors and books visit www.bloomsbury.com and sign up for our newsletters.

CONTENTS

List of Figures   vii

INTRODUCTION   1
    James P. Grimshaw

Part I
OVERVIEW

Chapter 1
CAN ONE REALLY BE AN EXEGETE AND CLAIM THAT ALL EXEGESES
ARE EQUALLY LEGITIMATE?   13
    Timothy Gombis

Chapter 2
THREE COMMENTARIES, ONE AUTHOR: ONE AUTHOR SHAPED BY
HISTORY AND CULTURE   17
    Robert L. Brawley

Part II
METHODOLOGY AND ETHICAL RESPONSIBILITY

Chapter 3
ETHICAL RESPONSIBILITY AND THE NECESSITY TO CHOOSE
AMONG A PLURALITY OF EQUALLY LEGITIMATE AND PLAUSIBLE
INTERPRETATIONS   27
    Kathy Ehrensperger

Chapter 4
UNENDING INTERPRETATIONS: CONTINUING THE CONVERSATION   33
    Tat-siong Benny Liew

Chapter 5
THE COLLISION OF ADVERSE OPINIONS: A REFLECTION ON
DANIEL PATTE, JOHN STUART MILL, AND THE
ABSOLUTIZATION OF CERTAINTY   43
    Monya A. Stubbs

Chapter 6
CAN WE LIVE WITH ROMANS AFTER AUSCHWITZ? 53
  Gary A. Phillips

Part III
ROMANS 1:16-18 AND 1:26-27

Chapter 7
A CHINESE CROSS-CULTURAL READING OF "ΔΙΚΑΙΟΣΥΝΗ ΘΕΟΥ" IN ROMANS 1:17: A PLAUSIBLE FOURTH EXEGESIS IN CONVERSATION WITH DANIEL PATTE 81
  K. K. Yeo

Chapter 8
A HISTORICAL ANALYSIS OF DANIEL PATTE'S STRATEGIES AND ETHICS OF READING WITH A FOCUS ON ROMANS 1:16-18 AND 1:26-27 99
  Bernadette J. Brooten

Part IV
FUTURE APPLICATION AND PAST INFLUENCE

Chapter 9
PATTE'S *ROMANS* IN THE CLASSROOM: CAN THE INTRODUCTION AND CHAPTER 1 PROVIDE STUDENTS AN ENTRÉE INTO POSTMODERN HERMENEUTIC THEORY AND PRACTICE? 109
  John Jones

Chapter 10
THE TAPROOT OF MY PERCEPTION OF ROMANS AS NECESSARILY MULTIVALENT AND CONTEXTUAL 115
  Daniel Patte

References 149
Notes on Contributors 157
Index of Authors 161

FIGURES

6.1	*Escape/Flucht*, 1983	70
7.1	First plane of meaning-finding and producing process	85
7.2	Second plane of biblical exegesis	90
7.3	Third plane of cross-cultural interpretation	94
7.4	All three planes together form the whole reading process	95

INTRODUCTION

James P. Grimshaw

This is a book about a book. It is a creative collection of essays that introduces, critiques, dialogues with, and reimagines Daniel Patte's *Romans: Three Exegetical Interpretations and the History of Reception: Volume 1: Romans 1:1-32*. There is plenty to discuss about Patte's work, a grand achievement that follows two decades of work by Patte and other scholars through a seminar of the Society of Biblical Literature (SBL) titled "Romans Through History and Culture." This current collection of essays began as seven scholars gathered at the 2018 SBL Meeting in Denver for a Book Review Panel. And now, in this volume, there are nine scholars, from different cultural and methodological and disciplinary perspectives, who enter into a lively conversation with Patte. They introduce his volume, critique his methodology and ethic of interpretation, and provide alternative readings. To begin with a few highlights, the chapters in this collection include the insistence by Phillips that artwork, not academic arguments, should be used to address the interpretations of Rom 1 and suffering, and Yeo provides a Confucian Chinese reading that offers strikingly different views of God in Rom 1. Brooten calls for joint biblical and social-science research on the role of Romans in current public policy debates (e.g., gender, sexuality, violence), and Jones details the trial use of Patte's book in the classroom. Patte himself concludes this collection with a powerful and poignant description of how his life experiences, especially during World War II in France where his family helped Jews escape to freedom, shaped his reading of Romans. This book is a critical and communal conversation with Patte on the history of reception of Rom 1 and an example of the necessity of conversations among diverse interpreters that, as Patte says, "reflect the diversity of the modes of our human experience" (p. 148 in this volume).

 The chapters in this book are divided into four parts. The first part (Chapters 1–2) introduces the format of Patte's *Romans: Three Exegetical Interpretations* and the three historical interpretations he analyzes: forensic theological, inclusive covenantal community, and realized-apocalyptic/messianic vision. Timothy Gombis begins this first part by giving a concise but methodical review of *Romans: Three Exegetical Interpretations* that will help the reader became acquainted with the structure and substance of the book. He begins by acknowledging the early origins of the book—the "Romans Through History and Culture" Society of Biblical Literature seminar, which met for thirteen years. Gombis then summarizes the three parts of the book. Part 1 (Chapters 1 and 2) addresses the challenges of encountering the history of reception and how scholars often weigh in with veto power on the value of interpretations. Yet, Patte does not want to veto but to pay attention to the textual choices they make. In Part 2 (Chapters 3–5), the heart of the book, Patte takes on one historical approach to Rom 1:1-32 in each chapter, identifying different interpreters and commentaries that provide examples of that approach. Finally, in Part 3 (Chapters 6–7), Patte explores the contexts of these three approaches to Rom 1, a charitable understanding as Gombis puts it. And then he provides a guide in Chapter 7, with examples of various historic figures who have wrestled with Romans, to help the reader ethically evaluate the different readings. Gombis also mentions an appendix at the back of the book that provides a table summarizing the three approaches, for the more visually focused learners. Finally, he concludes by adding that Patte's book is clearly packed full with a lifetime of teaching experience, that Patte shares some of those teaching moments in the book, and that through the book the reader can catch a glimpse of the thirteen-year SBL seminar from which this book emerges.

Robert Brawley provides some helpful background to the research leading up to the book, gives a brief overview of the format of the book and then samples of the three interpretations, and offers alternative construals and dialogue with each interpretation. The core of his contribution are these three samples, which are an overview and conversation with the three interpretations. He begins the description of the first interpretation, the forensic theological perspective, by identifying the eleven historical interpreters Patte refers to that support this core perspective. This is a key part of each of the three interpretations, the grouping of key historical interpreters that support each framework. Brawley briefly describes the perspective, with its focus on the individual relationship with God, and then enters into some questions with Patte. He begins with Paul's discussion of his contested "apostleship" and then discusses the challenges of translating δικαιοσύνη θεοῦ with regard to both the options in Greek and English (as Yeo also discusses with Chinese translations). Finally, Brawley discusses the understanding of the Wrath of God in 1:16-18 (i.e., is God's wrath part of the revelation or is the human condition separate from that revelation) and natural revelation in 1:18-32.

In the second interpretation, the covenantal community perspective, which is moving away from the individual and toward a focus on establishing an inclusive community, Brawley again mentions the main interlocutors and then discusses some of the main themes. He highlights the covenantal aspects: God's election of Israel, the vocation of God's people, and the fulfillment of the law as in the love of neighbor. Then Brawley points out the inclusive community aspects, which must be understood in the context of the Roman imperial system, and includes a look at honor and shame in the imperial system. Finally, he finds quite persuasive Patte's discussion of the list of vices in this interpretation as not "sins to be avoided" but "people who are not to be excluded" (p. 20 in this volume).

The third perspective, realized-apocalyptic/messianic vision, focuses on thematic and figurative aspects, and Brawley lists the interlocutors here as well. He dialogues with Patte on Paul's name, and the "change" from Saul to Paul, and questions whether a transforming divine encounter relates to the change in name. He also recognizes Patte's discussion of intertextual and intratextual relationships but suggests Patte "misses an opportunity here to indicate covenantal promises that bleed through the intertextuality" between Rom 1 and 4 (pp. 21-2 in this volume). Finally, Brawley ponders Patte's translations and interpretations of "holding fast to the truth in unrighteousness" in 1:18. Like Brawley, Yeo also gives an overview of these three interpretations but focuses on the phrase δικαιοσύνη θεοῦ in Rom 1:17. And Brooten gives an overview of the translation of Rom 1:16-18 in the three interpretations.

In his concluding remarks, Brawley targets a few issues present throughout the book. He critiques Patte's use of the phrase "God's interventions" and wonders how that fits with a biblical or scientific worldview, then praises Patte's clarification of the concept of a figurative world that made more sense to Brawley than when he studied with Johan Christiaan Beker for his own doctoral work.

The second part of the book (Chapters 3-6) debates, affirms, and critiques Patte's methodology and his discussion of ethical responsibility. Kathy Ehrensperger locates the writing of the book within its larger context, emphasizes its focus on a relational dimension to interpretation, and highlights Patte's commitment to the impact of interpretation. First, she points out that Patte's approach is rooted in old Europe where diversity is always present through borders, languages, struggles, battles, and fruitful debates. Ehrensperger celebrates the interdisciplinarity that Patte and Grenholm encouraged, through the "Romans Through History and Culture" seminar, inviting systematic theologians, church historians, philosophers, gender critical, and postcolonial scholars to contribute to reading Romans. The seminar also journeyed through different eras, reading Romans in conjunction with patristic experts, Augustine scholars, and medieval scholars. Furthermore, the diversity in approaches and emphasis in current Romans interpretations may be indicative of those in Paul's context. Paul also theologized in a context of cultural diversity, in conversation with others, and in relation to everyday life issues, and thus he may be the ideal partner in theological and interreligious conversations today.

Second, Ehrensperger discusses the importance of frameworks in interpretation, recognizing a relational dimension of interpretation that includes ties to those in the present and indebtedness to those in the past. She quotes political theorist Seyla Benhabi on how understandings always happen within a particular framework. Patte recognizes this and emphasizes interpretation as a communal endeavor—the importance of acknowledging, respecting, and listening to other interpretations with modesty. Interpretations are done in the framework of conversations with others and with the text.

Finally, Ehrensperger weighs in on Patte's emphasis on ethics. Yes, many interpretations can be legitimate and plausible. And Patte does not just include critical scholars over against lay readers as possible contributors but also welcomes other past and present voices as he quotes Maya Angelou's "the collective wisdom of generations" (2004: 79). But, even so, interpretations can be dangerous. Ehrensperger points out that twenty years after the start of Patte's SBL seminar on "Romans Through History and Culture" was both the 2018 commemoration of the Reichskristallnacht and an attack on a Pittsburgh Synagogue just weeks apart—episodes of anti-Judaism even today. Interpretations have an impact, and Ehrensperger draws attention to Patte's emphasis that interpretations should integrate an ethical aspect. They are to promote life, build up communities, and empower others. All the while interpreters should recognize the limits of each of their attempts, always raising the question of power and authority in decision-making.

Tat-siong Benny Liew compliments Patte on the process and implications of interpretations but also questions him on his process of making ethical choices and on his scriptural criticism. Liew appreciates Patte's process that focuses on readers, which reminds Liew of Lynne St. Clair Darden's argument that Vincent Wimbush's term "scripturalization" be used to replace the term "biblical hermeneutics," as the former gives both better acknowledgment of the agency and greater expression to the complexity of readers. He commends Patte's insistence on not only scholarly readers but also student readers and those who possess "mother wit" or generational wisdom transmitted apart from formal educational channels (as Ehrensperger notes as well). And Patte's emphasis to highlight a multiplicity of legitimate and plausible interpretations does not allow "anything goes" and functions to promote rather than preclude engagement, judgment, and adjudication. Liew also affirms that Patte underscores the implications of interpretations. This reminds Liew of Jonathan Magonet's compelling story of Czech Jews fleeing the Soviets in Prague in the 1960s and their experience of living under a deceptive political regime with deceptive newspapers and understanding the importance of reading as if one's life depends on understanding what one is reading, whether it is a newspaper or the Bible.

Liew, however, first challenges Patte on the "entanglements in making a contextual ethical choice" (p. 35 in this volume). Patte claims that we should choose a reading that is best—that is, most ethical—within a given context. Yet, Liew wonders what is the best or most ethical reading—these are up for interpretations. And if it is up to the individual in his or her context, what about communal interpretive conflicts? Second, while "scriptural criticism" might be a helpful phrase for multiple interpretations, the reality of acknowledging multiple interpretations has been around for hundreds of years—is there a need for a new phrase? Finally, Liew finds the three categories of forensic theological, inclusive covenantal, and realized-apocalyptic/messianic vision artificial and somewhat "leaky" concepts that overlap with each other and may be too general.

Monya Stubbs compares Patte's description of scriptural criticism with John Stuart Mill's discussion of human freedom and censorship. Stubbs begins with a brief summary of a 2020 *Harper's Magazine* article (signed by numerous scholars, journalists, and artists) that argues against censorship and for openness to other ideas, against confusion and misinformation and for clarity and empowerment.

The quote sets the stage well for the chapter. Stubbs was teaching John Stuart Mill in a moral and political philosophy class at the United States Coast Guard Academy when Patte's book was released. She found "striking parallels between the basic principles of Mill's position on the government's limits on interference with an individual's thought and speech and the basic tenets of Patte's biblical interpretive process. The umbrella similarity is that both thinkers present the view that we cannot truly *know* or *understand* our own ideas/opinions absent the ideas/opinions of others" (p. 44 in this volume). The comparison of Patte with Mills helps elucidate Patte's argument and models the type of comparisons Patte himself is doing in his book.

Stubbs carefully goes through several similarities of Patte and Mills, thoroughly addressing their ideas point by point. Both challenge censorship and claim the importance of engaging views that you disagree with. Both acknowledge there may be fallibility with one's own and with other perspectives and the importance of listening to and recognizing differences between perspectives. For Patte, the goal is not to dismiss another interpretation but to make clear the choices we make in our interpretations, to hold ourselves accountable. Likewise, for Mill, there is freedom in expressing your opinion but also a responsibility to test your ideas with those different from your own. Both Mill and Patte are seeking truth but refute absolutism—for Mill, he is seeking a true opinion by testing it with others and refuting the absolutization of one's own certainty; for Patte, he is not seeking an absolute truth but, as Stubbs writes, is seeking an "interpretive truth that is the best interpretation in a given context" (p. 50 in this volume).

Concluding this second part, Gary Phillips gives a deep and detailed analysis of Patte's work with sustained attention to a particular context—the genocides in the twentieth and twenty-first centuries. K. K. Yeo takes a similarly thorough approach in the next chapter with a different context. Phillips primarily focuses on Patte's front matter, introduction, and opening chapter, and while he affirms Patte's work, he challenges Patte's utopian and optimistic approach. Phillips appreciates Patte's long teaching and writing career, which has consistently engaged the Holocaust and supercessionist thinking. He acknowledges Patte's sympathy to today's suffering and his effort to keep the destructive interpretations of biblical texts in the forefront of his work. And Phillips is grateful that Patte has highlighted Samuel Bak's artwork in this study.

But Phillips draws on Theodor Adorno's philosophy and Samuel Bak's artwork to question Patte's confidence in liberating the text from the sufferings of the past. Adorno is a philosopher who fled Nazi Germany in 1934, and Samuel Bak is a world-renowned artist and child Holocaust survivor. Philips argues that these two scholars want readers to be burdened by concrete suffering, that readers need to continue to recognize the material trauma and suffering linked to Romans. The proper response to Romans and its interpretations is not about liberation or healing but skepticism and doubt. Adorno and Bak, and Phillips himself, do not attempt to make suffering meaningful but to keep in front of the readers' eyes the paradoxes and contradictions of Romans and its interpretations. For Adorno, only art can move us forward, not discourse. The objective reality of suffering bodies must be shown in art not discussed in concepts. And this is what Bak wants to accomplish, according to Phillips, as he presents the fragmented physical bodies and disfigured material worlds that must be acknowledged in the present. As Phillips describes it, "Bak's art shows what Adorno describes" (p. 64 in this volume).

For Phillips, the focus should not be on the need for better interpretive methods or a different pedagogy but on a more far-reaching cultural analysis of the current concrete suffering of innocent children locked in cages, mass shootings, anti-Semitism, and the complex, systemic social problems today. While there may be survival after Auschwitz, there is no escape from the Holocaust and the suffering is not resolved or healed.

Phillips also includes Bak's image "Escape" in his chapter, the same image that is on the cover of Patte's book. The image, however, is not quite the same because Phillips shows the full image, compared with the cropped image on Patte's cover, and then gives a different interpretation of the image than Patte does. These two perspectives on Bak's image "Escape" provide a rich conversation for the reader to consider its meaning in relationship to Romans and suffering.

In the third part of the book (Chapters 7–8), Yeo and Brooten focus on a specific passage in Rom 1. Yeo analyses Rom 1:17 in both Patte's readings as well as a more detailed interpretation from his own Chinese context. Brooten offers a clear summary of Patte's investigation of Rom 1:16-18 and then calls for a cross-disciplinary study of 1:26-27 among religion and social science scholars.

K. K. Yeo focuses on the phrase δικαιοσύνη θεοῦ in Rom 1:17. His purpose is to briefly assess Patte's commentary on this crucial phrase and then bring his own Chinese cross-cultural approach in conversation with Patte's, similar to Phillips's more detailed reflection on a particular context. Yeo identifies and briefly explains how the three interpretations that Patte addresses read Rom 1:17 as "righteousness/uprightness of God" (forensic), "righteousness/justice of God" (covenantal community), and "righteousness of God" (realized-apocalyptic/messianic). Yeo then briefly assesses the work as a whole and further explains that Patte's work is an anti-commentary, not that Patte is against traditional commentaries but that he does not give his own commentary but assesses three others. Yeo wonders why Patte did not include more culturally diverse readings among the main three, as he has done before, but Yeo also realizes that this is a different kind of project and Patte does refer to many different cultural interpretive traditions throughout the book.

Yeo then brings Chinese cultural and Confucian philosophical ideas into conversation with Patte's commentary by laying out his own cross-cultural critical method, as a Chinese-Confucianist, in approaching δικαιοσύνη θεοῦ in Rom 1:17. Here are two examples related to language as Yeo argues that a different language (not just a different culture) has significant implications. First, on the view of God, Confucianism would find Paul's use of the Greek θεός in Rom 1 too harsh in judging humanity, while the Confucianist term for God, *Tian*, is both powerful and divine but also benevolent. Several words in Chinese for God offer a depth that is lacking in other languages. Second, on the word for "righteousness," the Chinese Bible translates δικαιοσύνη as *yi*. Confucius's teaching defines virtues that surround *yi*, such as caring for the poor and being trustworthy and calm, so that when a reader hears the word *yi* they would associate these other virtues with it. Yeo wishes that Paul would have given a list of virtues surrounding δικαιοσύνη. One of Yeo's larger points here is that interpreters should be aware of the limitation of their own language and consider other languages for a more expansive understanding. See also Brawley and Brooten for a discussion of translation.

Yeo concludes by suggesting Patte's approach is too cautious regarding multiple interpretations. He recommends being open to opposing voices and welcoming contradictions within Paul, that the Chinese culture is less interested in resolving those tensions. Yet, he also affirms Patte's focus on an ethic of biblical interpretation and wants to ensure that readings abide by the justice/righteousness of God, citing Kittel's TDNT and its association with the Nazi movement. Finally, Yeo calls for actively engaging other cultural interpretations and a humility in learning from them, which he relates to the open-endedness of the *Dao* (way) in the Chinese culture.

Bernadette Brooten situates Patte's study within the history of Christian reading strategies through the centuries and then explores in more depth Rom 1:16-18 and 1:26-27. She shows that there has always been a recognition of multiple meanings and of the Bible as an unstable text (see Liew for a similar point). She highlights the Antioch and Alexandria interpretive schools and their differences as well as the fourfold sense in the Middle Ages. It was then with the Enlightenment and Fundamentalism in the United States, much more modern movements, that interpretations focused on the one best, true interpretation—which has commonalities with the historical-critical method.

Brooten then refers to postmodernism, particularly postmodern architecture with its return to the past and use of both traditional and contemporary elements. She claims Patte is doing the same by going back before the Enlightenment, recognizing multiple interpretations, but also doing something new in reflecting on these three interpretations in his book and how they serve different communities.

Brooten, who practices and values historical criticism but with an appreciation of other readings, sees Patte's analysis of historical critics as a benefit, unlike others who have critiqued the focus on historical criticism (see especially Yeo). She equates his work with Eastern Orthodox Christians and Jewish interpreters who regularly and religiously consult earlier interpreters. Earlier interpretations, she argues, have often uncovered what contemporary interpreters incorrectly think they originally found—she gives two examples about the name Junia in Rom 16:7 and the debate about whether 1:26 refers to sex between women or another kind of unnatural sex.

With her focus on 1:16-18, she summarizes and adeptly compares Patte's three interpretations on this passage: forensic theological, covenantal community, and realized-apocalyptic/messianic vision (see also Brawley who gives a more general overview of the three interpretations for Rom 1 and Yeo who provides an overview of the three interpretations with attention to the phrase δικαιοσύνη θεοῦ in 1:17). She concludes this section with some implications of each of the three readings on 1:16-18. For example, the forensic theological reading is more individualistic and may disregard social justice while the covenantal community interpretation can promote a more inclusive society. The realized-apocalyptic/messianic vision might help contemporary readers acknowledge the cultural distance from Paul's very different worldview while also recognizing the apocalyptic thinking that is still in today's society. See also Brawley's discussion.

Finally Brooten examines Rom 1:26-27 on sex between women and sex between men and advocates for joint religious and social science research. Brooten, like Patte, finds it essential to consider how interpretations function in the world. She quotes a social-scientific research study that finds that the higher the level of fundamentalism in pastors or college students, the more they accept rape myths. In addition, verses from Rom 1:26-27 are the single most quoted verses in today's debates over public policy and law (i.e., regarding domestic violence). She challenges biblical scholars to join with social-science scholars to study some of these issues, for example, "female subordination, acceptance of LGBTQ individuals, and the like" (p. 106 in this volume), as a way of actualizing Patte's concerns about the dangerous effects of interpretations on certain groups of people.

In the fourth and final part of this book, John Jones takes a look into the future at how Patte's book might be used in the classroom while Patte takes an in-depth journey into his past to explain how his various life experiences shaped his reading of Romans. How might Patte's book on Rom 1 be used in a classroom in the future? John Jones completed an original case study of teaching the Introduction and chapter 1 of Patte's book at La Sierra University in Riverside, California. He first describes how the school chose Patte's book. It was selected for their master of divinity curriculum because it addresses "a broad accounting of the developments in hermeneutical theory that underlie and carry forward the paradigm shift hailed by Schüssler Fiorenza" (p. 110 in this volume). Patte's reading would supplement two other core readings in the curriculum: Krister Stendahl's classic "Biblical Theology" essay in 1962 and Elisabeth Schüssler Fiorenza's 1988 SBL presidential address on "The Ethics of Biblical Interpetation." Jones and his colleagues saw the book as helping students in several ways: to recognize the interpretive choices made by each reader, to see the act of reading as an ethical act and interpretation as one of many interpretations among equals, to prepare them for pastoral ministry so they can see interpretation with one's congregants as a fellow disciple, to acknowledge the role of theologians, church historians, and exegetes in the interpretation process, and to model "the author's own journey of insight in the company of fellow pilgrims" (p. 111 in this volume).

Jones then gives a glimpse of a trial run with the students. While chosen for the graduate curriculum, it was only possible to test the reading with a fourth-year undergraduate class in the history of early Christianity, with religious studies majors and general education students. The instructor took the first half of each of two 100-minute sessions to introduce Patte's issues, then discussion followed in the second half. While the reading was a stretch for some students, there was a lively engagement in the discussions for both majors and non-majors. The instructor expected more resistance to the hermeneutic of encounter between text and reader, but students mostly accepted the model. Some pre-seminary students were concerned that there would be backlash from their congregations over the idea of multiple interpretations, but this may have been more of the students' own unease than a pastoral concern. Jones concluded that more practical examples may have helped.

Going forward, the faculty may use shorter portions of Patte's reading at the undergraduate level, along with consulting the English literature faculty for ideas. But the main thrust will be the MTS and MDiv programs, including not only the biblical department but also the theology, history, and ethics departments.

As Jones looks to the future on using *Romans: Three Exegetical Interpretations* in the classroom, in the last chapter Daniel Patte looks to his past to reflect on how he arrived at the acceptance of multiple, legitimate interpretations of Romans. The reader might expect Patte to respond here to each contributor in this book, but he has chosen to reflect on his own experience growing up in France that led to the origins of his book, and it is an intriguing story that could serve as one model for how interpreters make explicit the context that shapes their readings.

Patte begins this reflection when he was four years old with his friend Patrick, his Catholic friend whom his parents forbade him to play with, because Protestant Huguenots believe in salvation by faith not salvation by good works. Demonization of those with different interpretations started at a young age. He then details the visitors his family had in France at their family farmhouse in 1943-4 during World War II, visitors that included Jewish refugees who stayed at their farmhouse as his parents and others risked their lives to help Jews find their way through the Alps mountains to Switzerland to escape persecution. This was at age five, and helping Jews (who were staying in his bedroom) contradicted what he had learned from his parents about how Paul described Jews as doing works of the law to gain salvation. Does Patte the young child avoid those who believe differently, or does he help them? This was his first awareness of the contradiction that came into his family's life as Protestants who read Rom 1:16-17 and 3:21-24, the contradiction between their belief that one is justified by faith in Jesus Christ and living it out differently. Understanding how to resolve this and future contradictions have been critical to Patte's current perspectives.

These experiences and contradictions as a young child faded for Patte for a decade, but they came back full force as a teenager, in part through two experiences that he identifies as the taproot of his interpretation of Rom 1 as multivalent. The first took place at the age of thirteen, around a big fireplace in his schoolhouse, where a conversation was taking place among the Protestant Huguenot Pastor Louis Dallière, a Jewish scholar André Chouraqui, and several students, including Patte. Dallière was also dealing with the contradiction of his own experience of helping to rescue Jewish refugees and his reading of Paul that Jews who did not believe in Jesus would not be saved. In order to resolve it, Dallière described the theology of the mystery of Israel based on Rom 11, insisting that Jews will come to believe in Jesus and therefore eventually be saved, even if it is a mystery. The Jewish scholar Chouraqui, however, did not buy this. He insisted that Jews will not be saved because they will come to believe in Jesus but will be saved because of God's eternal covenant with the people of Israel. And what Chouraqui said next is what made an impact on Patte as a thirteen-year-old, that there are contradictions between our convictions and our practices, that we try to resolve, but one must not hold on too tight or absolutize our interpretations. And with those different interpretations that are based on convictions, people must make ethical choices between these interpretations, choices that come out of their contexts.

In the next four years, a second experience continued to shape Patte as he participated in a Lycée student group that was composed of Protestants from different backgrounds as well as Catholics. As they discussed biblical texts, alongside novels and plays by Camus and Sartre, they would inevitably come up with different interpretations but they would also ask "What is the 'problem' in the believers' life this particular interpretation helps the believers to address?" This made sense to Patte, with what he learned from Chouraqui, that different interpretations might address different contexts and that absolutizing interpretations was dangerous.

Patte drew on these early experiences as he continued his career as a scholar and participated with his colleagues in the SBL seminar "Romans Through History and Culture" from 1997 to 2011 and then later as he wrote *Romans: Three Exegetical Interpretations.*

Those are the ten responses that make up this eclectic collection. There are many ways a reader might use this book, and we hope you will consider various options. On one level, this collection will help the reader better understand Daniel Patte's book and decide how to approach his larger study—the first two chapters by Gombis and Brawley provide a good start and each of the ten chapters provides a distinctive lens. On another level, there are many ways to engage in certain themes in this collection and how it dialogues with Patte's work. If you would like to use Patte's volume in the classroom, see what Jones has tried. One could focus on methodology and/or ethical responsibility (part 2) or on particular passages (part 3). The theme of language and translation appears in Brawley (Greek and English), Yeo (Greek, English, and Chinese), and Brooten (Rom 1:16-18). The messiness of interpretation is especially tackled by Liew (in communal contexts), Phillips (regarding suffering) and Yeo and Brawley (with the view of God). Discussions of the longer history and plurality of interpretation, as well as the importance of interdisciplinarity, are seen in Ehrensperger and Brooten. Stubbs has a unique discussion on philosophy, freedom, and censorship. And Patte's conclusion is an excellent example of how to reflect on your own context when interpreting the Bible and would be instructive for both students and seasoned scholars. Finally, we hope this collection will serve as a model of how to engage in deeper conversations—with other readers, about critical issues around Romans, and on how biblical interpretation must take seriously methodology, ethics, interdisciplinary study, and the cultural impact of interpretation.

Part I

OVERVIEW

Chapter 1

CAN ONE REALLY BE AN EXEGETE AND CLAIM THAT ALL EXEGESES ARE EQUALLY LEGITIMATE?

Timothy Gombis

Daniel Patte presents alongside each other three critical interpretations of Romans in commentary form in order to "demonstrate that, despite their marked differences, each is equally legitimate (critical) and plausible (making hermeneutical sense)" (Patte 2018: xiii).[1] The work flows from Patte's participation in the "Romans Through History and Cultures" Society of Biblical Literature seminar, which has brought together exegetes, theologians, and church historians over the last two decades or so.

Patte's project immediately appears to run against the grain of the training of most exegetes—those who likely make up a large percentage of the SBL. While he admits that he is arguing "against the common practice in the guild," he points to "the multiplicity of critical exegetical studies" and receptions of Romans to buttress his claim that exegetes ought to "acknowledge that Paul's text offers a plurality of interpretive choices" (1–2). The aforementioned seminar's focus on the range of receptions of Romans revealed that the genre of critical commentary was especially Eurocentric and that interpreters needed to engage critical commentaries, especially the form of that sort of literature, critically (7–8, 46–67). Further, the experience of the seminar led members to wonder whether divergent and competing critical interpretations "were in fact *equally legitimate*—that is, appropriately grounded in Paul's text" (8; emphasis original).

In the bulk of the work, Patte provides commentary on Rom 1:1-32 from three critical interpretive angles of approach. The first focuses on Paul's theological argument, attending to linguistic details in the letter and its epistolary style. The second gives special attention to the letter's sociorhetorical features, along with the manner in which Paul rhetorically shapes his audiences' ideology and practice. A third reading is that which involves Romans as a "religious text for its religious content," seeking to understand how Romans speaks of religious experience and vision through figurative language (8).

---

1. This review was first published in *Review of Biblical Literature* (www.bookreviews.org). © Society of Biblical Literature. Reprinted by permission.

Before he carries out this triple-commentary in chapters 3–5, Patte first lays the hermeneutical groundwork for the remainder of this monograph in the opening two chapters. The first chapter describes the challenging encounter of exegesis and the history of reception. Critical exegesis proceeds on the assumption that there is a singular meaning to Paul's letter to the Romans and that this can be recovered through historical study. Indeed, from the beginning of the seminar's project, Patte recounts that among theologians, church historians, and exegetes, there was the assumption that biblical exegetes had "veto power"—prerogative to weigh in finally on the appropriateness of interpretations (16). Proceeding on this assumption, however, would have halted the project from the start, so participants agreed on an approach, which Patte carries through, called "scriptural criticism." According to this notion, any interpretation of a biblical text—that is, of a text that believers read as scripture—is the result of an interpretive process that necessarily includes the three types of interpretive choices: "*analytic textual choices, hermeneutical theological choices,* and *contextual choices*" (18; emphasis original).

This approach led to a charitable mode of encounter with other interpretations: they would not be presumed illegitimate until proven otherwise but presumed legitimate until proven otherwise (19).

Rather than endorsing any and all interpretations as legitimate, this approach recognizes that faith communities read Romans as scripture, listening to it as teaching upon which they wager their lives (31). Interpretive differences may be seen as arising from the various life contexts and ethical challenges believing communities face (34). Further, Paul's instruction in Rom 14:1–15:13 to competing factions among the Roman Christians to welcome one another without quarreling over differing opinions provides scope for regarding divergent interpretations with charity so long as they lead to healthy Christian community dynamics (31).

In his second chapter, Patte argues that any critical interpretation of Romans that claims to be the one and only correct interpretation of the letter inevitably chooses from one of a number of approaches to the text. An immediate problem arises because of the ambiguities and perceived inconsistencies within Paul's presentation. Any singular interpretation inevitably follows a line of thought that weaves together a number of textual details throughout the letter while leaving unexplained those that do not fit. Such an interpretation cannot account for the reality that Paul's letter contains a theological argument while being "undergirded by another meaning-producing dimension … that conveys an existential or coherent convictional horizon of faith reflecting Paul's religious experiences" (52).

Because of this reality, most critical commentaries are hybrid in character. Each new commentary follows a chosen line of interpretation—one of three surveyed by Patte in part 2—while also incorporating exegetical insights from previous critical commentaries (57). Patte's contribution in this volume is to display commentary from three critical exegetical methodologies: (1) "the *theological logic* of Paul's way of thinking studied by *behind-the-text exegetical methodologies*"; (2) "the *rhetoric and ideological logic* of Paul's discourse framed by the presumed cultural perspectives of its intended readers studied by *in-front-of-the-text exegetical methodologies*"; and (3) "the *thematic and figurative logic* of the letter as an Other-centered religious discourse that readers are invited to enter so as to share in its religious vision (a realized-apocalyptic/messianic vision) studied by *within-the-text exegetical methodologies*" (55; emphases in original).

Part 2, as indicated above, consists of three chapters in which Patte provides commentary on Rom 1:1-32 according to these three critical methodologies. In chapter 3, he draws on the commentaries and works of Moo, Schreiner, Bultmann, and Fitzmyer, along with others, to provide a "forensic theological" reading of the passage. It is forensic because it regards God as judge of individual sinners (77–8). While there is a good bit of variety among individual interpreters, this general angle of approach understands Paul as describing the culpability of each individual as humans stand condemned for sin and in need of justification by faith.

The fourth chapter contains commentary from what he calls an "inclusive covenantal community" perspective, which covers the diversity of readings known more or less as "new perspective" and "beyond the new perspective" approaches (121). Patte's designation of this approach as community-centered rather than theological may rankle interpreters who discern Paul's theology as centered around community. In any case, his exposition engages such commentators as Wright, Dunn, Nanos, and Jewett, among others, and is characterized by attention to the rhetorical features and dimensions of Romans (137).

Finally, Patte comments on the Romans passage from a "realized-apocalyptic/Messianic vision," which includes interpreters such as Beker, Keck, Gaventa, and Campbell, rooted in the work of Käsemann. Patte finds himself among this group, which may be why this chapter is the lengthiest commentary of the three lines of interpretation.

Patte's treatment of Rom 1:1-32 from these divergent lines of interpretation in the three chapters of part 2 is commendable in that proponents of each will find little with which to quibble. Indeed, Patte represents the charitable posture of the seminar toward other interpretations in that his exposition of each is genuinely sympathetic.

In part 3, made up of two chapters, Patte relates the critical exegeses to the history of reception. In chapter 6 he excavates the situational and convictional contexts that produce each of the preceding lines of interpretation. This is an exercise in charitable understanding of others, reckoning with the concerns of communities of interpretation that seek to hear from scripture a "Word-to-live-by" (338). Patte then surveys, in chapter 7, several receptions of Romans to discern how to evaluate divergent readings ethically. He examines various figures who have wrestled with Romans according to the foregoing interpretations, finding in each ethical good and bad fruit. The volume concludes with an appendix in which Patte lays out side by side the three interpretations in a three-column summary table.

In one sense, Patte's offering has a narrow point, which ought to make the task of reviewing fairly simple: he aims to "demonstrate that, despite their marked differences, each [line of interpretation] is equally legitimate (critical) and plausible (making hermeneutical sense)" (xiii). One can hardly argue that he has not succeeded, though scholars and commentators will surely continue to claim that Paul does not mean that but this, that Romans cannot be read in that way but must be interpreted this way.

In another sense, there is just so much packed into this volume, gathering the fruit of a lifetime studying and teaching Romans. Patte covers exegetical problems and theological implications but also shares experiences in teaching Romans. What is more, he provides a way forward for engaging with the reception history of Paul's letter. Further, readers are let in on the flavor of the SBL seminar from which the volume springs. Finally, for such a large volume, Patte's writing is winsome and conversational. This is a commendable addition to the growing body of literature produced by the "Romans Through History and Cultures" seminar.

Chapter 2

THREE COMMENTARIES, ONE AUTHOR: ONE AUTHOR SHAPED BY HISTORY AND CULTURE

Robert L. Brawley

Introductory Survey

This volume forms the capstone for a mammoth project undertaken by Daniel Patte spanning more than two decades. The groundwork was laid by a seminar of the Society of Biblical Literature titled "Romans Through History and Culture," which itself has a history that covered thirteen years and has produced ten volumes in the Romans Through History and Culture series. As the title implies, the seminar was necessarily interdisciplinary, and many of its corporate decisions influence Patte's approaches and conclusions. The volume is shaped primarily first by an oft-stated axiom that all interpretations should be considered legitimate and plausible (based on textual evidence) and second by the determination of three interpretive frameworks that characterize interpretations of Romans through history and cultures: reading Romans for (i) its *forensic* theological thought, or (ii) its call to an inclusive *covenantal community*, or (iii) its *realized-apocalyptic/ messianic* vision.

The heart of this volume is Patte's three commentaries themselves, but as the title of the seminar implies, these are necessarily located in Patte's own historical and cultural contexts. His discussion is divided into three major parts. The first is a thoroughgoing account for the legitimacy and plausibility of interpretations according to his three frameworks. Patte then establishes the historical and cultural context for each of his commentaries by critical research focused on prominent interpreters who are supplemented by an array of additional commentators. The second part is Patte's three distinct, coherent commentaries for each of the three frameworks, always in critical conversation with interpreters who represent the frameworks. Given the space for introducing readers to these methodological issues, Patte's three commentaries in this volume are each confined to Rom 1:1-32. To be sure, like other commentaries this volume requires consideration of the entire structure of Romans, the addressees, as well as rhetorical features and the logic of the argument.

Part 3 adds challenging research on the evidence of these three interpretive frameworks in the history of the interpretation of Romans. Patte correlates each approach to extended historical and cultural contexts. Then, he describes milestones in the history of interpretation for each: Augustine and Luther for the forensic approach; Clement of Alexandria, Abelard, and liberation theologians for community-centered receptions; and John Chrysostom, Eastern Orthodox interpreters, and Pentecostals/Charismatics for the realized-apocalyptic/messianic vision. Finally, a comprehensive appendix outlines thirty-one theological terms and ethical themes in Rom 1:1-32 for each of the approaches.

The front matter includes a note on Samuel Bak's painting "Escape" on the cover, a preface, and a foreword, all of which are rich in indicating (i) Patte's own context in current political and cultural history; (ii) his perspective against turning scripture into an exclusivist, authoritative weapon against neighbors; and (iii) his establishment of three primary types of interpretation, each of which according to his mantra is equally legitimate and plausible. The latter does come with the caveat "until proven otherwise." The positive evaluation of multiple interpretations is supported by a postmodern worldview, which is axiomatically anti-foundational and which undermines absolutism. Parallel to this is a turn toward what I consider to be philosophical constructivism with its perception that all reality must be construed by processes in human brains, which self-evidently involve multiple construals. To be noted here is that Romans itself is Paul's own construct of reality, so that any interpretation of the epistle is a second-order construct of reality. Accordingly, even Patte's caveat of "until proven otherwise" could be problematic: one person's poison (construal) may be another's proof (construal). Significantly, this includes challenges among interpreters themselves. An ultimate test for various interpretations remains, however—namely, ethics, that is, who is helped and who is hurt by an interpretation. Needless to say, although justice has a transcendent character, this too is debatable (see McIntyre 1988).

Before turning to his commentaries, Patte introduces rationales for and the perspectives of the three interpretive approaches using the categories of "behind the text," "in front of the text," and "within the text." Further, each of the three approaches exhibits different ways of construing sin, the human predicament, and how resolution of the human predicament comes about. For example, forensic approaches to sin are individually centered, whereas community approaches are corporately centered. Of course, these necessarily involve privileging certain features of the text over others, and yet the categories bleed over into each other producing what the author calls a hybrid, a mixture of methodologies. In my view, such hybridity already challenges the separate categorization of three approaches itself inasmuch as most interpreters today are eclectic; they embrace interpretations far beyond what can be analyzed as a category. A case in point involves social identity theory, according to which individuals are members of groups in which there is always a dialectical relationship between individuals and groups to which they belong, and optimal distinctiveness means that these two poles are balanced as if individual and communal aspects are two dimensions of one entity. Thus, an individual over against a communal approach comes under scrutiny. Further,

Patte's own emphasis on legitimacy and plausibility leads to yet another quasi-definition of sin that overlaps all three categories. For him, "absolutizing" any one approach is deadly.

This volume is so richly complicated that the only possibility I see for a review is to give samples of Patte's interpretations, which inevitably involve accepting alternative construals, with the latter of which I occasionally dialogue.

Forensic Commentary

The first of Patte's own commentaries assumes a forensic theological framework in conjunction with eleven interpreters who support this core perspective as the most significant element for rendering the epistle coherent. The roster is impressive, including C. H. Dodd, C. K. Barrett, F. Leenhardt, J. Dunn, and D. Moo. This framework addresses, as of first importance, predicaments and their resolutions *for individuals*, particularly with respect to the problem of evil, God's judgment (including God's wrath), and salvation. This virtually compels discussion of forensic terms such as δικαιοσύνη, ὀργή, πίστις, and σωτηρία.

From the beginning Patte discusses Paul's contested "apostleship," and I also contest the implication that the reference to his call is about the *authority* of a position "apostleship." Does the Greek not rather indicate the *function* of being called as one who is sent by God? Moreover, with respect to authority, do Paul and the epistle itself carry any weight beyond the power of persuasion? Consideration of the promises of God in scripture (Rom 1:2) involves perspectives on continuity between Israel and Christians but also on believers as God's new chosen people, and therefore on the issue of supersession. On the other hand, this occurs only in the context of Patte's previous establishment in part 1 of a post-Holocaust perspective in which he appropriately repudiates supersessionism.

According to forensic interpretations, the theme of Romans in 1:16-17/18 is a summary of Paul's theology as a whole—justification by faith, although Patte points out that terminology for justification does not occur here. Even among interpreters following this approach there is debate about appropriate grammatical and philological construals of Paul's text, especially syntax (e.g., objective-subjective genitives) and "appropriate translations" into English. Such is the case with δικαιοσύνη θεοῦ (1:17). In my opinion this is problematic in that as necessary as translations are, they *always* choose among syntactical and lexical options from *both* languages and consequently say both too much and too little (nevertheless, see Patte's discussion of double entendre [2018: 237]). Therefore, the Greek always surpasses any argument based on translations.

One focus of the discussion on 1:16-18 is the understanding of the wrath of God. As expected, this too occasions diversity of opinions. Does the revelation of God's δικαιοσύνη in the gospel implicate God's wrath as a part of the gospel? Or is God's wrath the human condition apart from the good news of the revelation of God's δικαιοσύνη? Are God's δικαιοσύνη and wrath complementary, or do they stand in contrast?

For the remaining section of 1:18-32, forensic interpreters also have distinct views on natural revelation, either that it alone is inadequate for salvation or that a natural knowledge of God is rejected. In any case, God hands humans over to themselves. When humans reject God, God allows them to do so. Thus, all are without excuse. Homoerotic behavior is then highlighted, which according to Jewish mores is something that is against nature. Even though the commentary in this volume ends at 1:32, forensic interpreters anticipate chapter 2 as a trap for Jewish Christ believers so that with respect to sin all human beings are in the same boat.

Covenantal Community Commentary

Patte's second commentary follows a framework that focuses on Paul's efforts to persuade the Romans to support his *mission* to include gentiles as far as Spain. The commentary according to this category dialogues especially with R. Jewett although Elsa Támez and N. Elliott (and many others) are also interlocutors. This approach moves away from concentrating on the individual and highlights interpretations that center on establishing an inclusive community. Emphasis falls on Paul's Jewishness and the continuity of Christianity with Israel, and thus the inclusive community is covenantal. Further, the human predicament is a corporate matter of disruption of social relationships based on ideologies that segregate people, and the resolution is God's justice realized by the power of the gospel unto salvation. As Paul is trying to win over the Romans to support the mission, the methodology includes rhetorical studies concerning persuasion as well as establishing solidarity in place of division.

Covenantal aspects as a basis for community life are especially God's election of Israel, the vocation of God's people, and the fulfillment of the law as in the love of neighbor (Rom 13:8). The clearest case for believers as a covenantal community is Paul's attempt to convince his audience that Abraham is the father of us all (Rom 4).

The inclusive covenantal community is a matter of social life that must be understood in the context of Roman imperial systems. Consequently Patte interprets Paul's exordium as a countercultural parody of imperial systems. In this line of thought Paul is called and sent as God's ambassador to the gentiles (Rom 1:1, 5)—Patte states that this occurs only in Romans (Patte 2018: 159) but see Gal 1:16 and 2:8-9. Or when Paul declares that he is a debtor to barbarians and the foolish; he eviscerates social honor and shame in imperial systems. Further, the thesis statement in 1:16-17/18 that the gospel embodies God's justice controverts imperial claims to justice.

Patte's interpretation of 1:18-32 from this perspective views the rhetorical trap not as directed at Jewish Christ believers, as in the forensic category, but quite the opposite. The list of vices is not to identify sins to be avoided but to identify people who are not to be excluded. For myself, I consider this dramatic inversion of the forensic perspective formidable and rhetorically persuasive. This view also values what can be known of God in other religions, and the suppression of truth is the denial of truth that others have received. But then those who have received such truth fail to glorify God because improper interhuman relationships make them incapable of honoring God as God.

Apocalyptic/Messianic Commentary

Patte describes his framework for his third commentary as a "realized apocalyptic/messianic vision," which focuses on thematic and figurative aspects. The latter are discovered by startling language that pushes interpretation to figurative levels, which Michael Riffaterre calls "ungrammaticalities." A case in point is Paul's figure of himself as Christ's slave (1:1). This figurative world is both the result of Paul's religious experience and the source for comparable experiences for his audience. Patte's commentary in this vein proceeds only with a careful definition of apocalyptic as repetitive "empowering divine interventions" (Patte 2018: 221) in believers' experiences. The headliner interlocutors in this section are E. Käsemann, J. Christiaan Beker, and D. Campbell but also philosophers such as J. Taubes, G. Agamben, A. Badiou, and S. Žižek. Patte relies heavily on Beker who recognizes that Paul himself interprets scripture and the gospel within the framework of the figurative world shaped by his own faith/vision. With this, the entire perspective shifts from conceptual accounts of Paul's thought to experiences that are mediated through the figurative world. Patte's perspective is nevertheless that the text contains its own structure whereas according to constructivism interpreters must superimpose structures onto texts in order to understand them. Significantly the apocalyptic/messianic perspective increases the continuity between Israel and Christianity in that the experiential encounters are part of an ongoing fulfillment of scriptural typologies of divine intervention.

Patte's apocalyptic/messianic commentary has an extensive discussion on the name "Paul" (1:1-6) as a figuration that involves both linguistic issues of the name as Latin but adapted to Greek, as well as the account in Acts of a "change" in the name from Saul to Paul as an adaptation from an Israelite perspective. At this point, however, I raise the question of legitimacy and plausibility in that textually Paul speaks of a change in orientation ("called to be an apostle," "set apart for God's gospel," 1:1; compare Gal 1:15), but I see no indication from Paul of a change in name. His calling assuredly alludes to a transforming divine encounter, but does identifying himself by name in Rom 1 create a figuration of an encounter that changed his name? What can be said, however, is that Patte obviously enters into a figurative world in which he experiences the figuration.

Further, the figurative world builds on intertextual and intratextual relationships. For example, what has been promised beforehand clearly alludes to scripture as an intertext (1:2), which is itself a figuration and which reflects the designation of the "son of God" from the seed of David (1:3). Further the "obedience of faith" among all the nations (1:5) is an intratextual counterpart to Paul's reference to himself as Christ's slave (1:1). In my view, Patte misses an opportunity here to indicate covenantal promises that bleed through the intertextuality, such as the confirmation of Abrahamic promises that become obvious in Rom 4.

Even though Patte is working within the apocalyptic/messianic framework, he makes an innovative reading of 1:18 by means of an analytical philological argument. First, the case that the participle κατεχόντων means "holding fast to the truth in unrighteousness" is so strong that he is able to judge translations such as the NRSV's "suppress the truth" as implausible. Is he making this judgment at the expense of valuing multiple interpretations, or has he proven that in this case on the basis of the text such interpretations are illegitimate? Second, on the basis of "holding fast to the truth in unrighteousness," he determines that "idolatry is a religious fanaticism that absolutizes a true but partial revelation" (Patte 2018: 311), along with an appeal for recognition of such partial truth on the part of others. He persuades me to accept his appeal to value manifestations of the truth from a variety of religions, and yet the notion of idolatry as absolutizing raises the question: Was Greco-Roman idolatry not always incomplete rather than absolute? There always had to be other gods, unless of course it is the multiplicity that is absolute.

The problem of absolutizing also puts its stamp on the list of vices in 1:22-31. The argument is a bit subtle here. From the framework of the figurative evocation of experiences in the apocalyptic/messianic approach, the naming of vices is not meant to correct actual practices. Rather, Paul chooses stereotypes that together presume that his audience will automatically assume that something has gone wrong with it all. The vice list is not to be parsed for detailed description, because as a whole it is a figuration that evokes the experience of a world in which the truth about God has been distorted into a lie. Granted, in Paul's list, space and position highlight human sexuality, but Paul's qualification of what is "unnatural" also makes this a metaphor of the problem of idolatry, that is, the unnatural perversion of the truth about God into a lie.

Tying Up Loose Ends

Throughout the book, Patte refers to acts of God as "interventions." I take this to be unfortunate in that it reflects the development of methods of the natural sciences that presuppose "closed systems" for scientific experiments. "Intervention" implies that God, who ordinarily occupies some other dimension of reality, penetrates the closed system of human existence. This is superimposed onto a prescientific biblical worldview according to which rather than step into human reality with interventions, divine reality permeates all reality (panentheism?). If divine reality permeates all reality, the issue is to perceive instances of how God is always active. Things are quite different when Patte refers to a transformative encounter with a "Christic-event" (Patte 2018: 259) rather than a "Christic-intervention" (268). I can only add that this kind of transformative encounter presumably results in an ongoing Christic-relationship.

Perhaps a personal reference best shows my high evaluation of Patte's work. I happened to be on the ground floor, so to speak, in my doctoral work at Princeton

Theological Seminary when Beker wrote *Paul the Apostle* (1980). Even though he was on sabbatical one year when he was writing the book, he met with me one day and talked about his basic concept of "contingency and coherence." The following year I was in his seminar on Paul, which was the highpoint of all my studies. But when I read Patte's clarification of a figurative world, I understood Beker's surface and deep structure better than when I sat at his feet.

Although generally very well written, the volume is characteristically repetitive. This is likely a necessity inasmuch as few readers will read it from beginning to end. Ordinarily I would not comment on matters of copy editing, but there are an egregious number of typos. A startling one is a dangling participle (Patte 2018: 263). Another is the repeated misspelling of Fitzmyer as Fitzmier (108, 110). The volume shifts back and forth between transliterating Greek and using the Greek alphabet. Why not one or the other? But in one case a word is incomprehensible because it is written partially in the Greek alphabet and partially in the Latin (96). Repeatedly Greek terms are printed with a grave accent on the ultima when they stand alone. Copy editors working with Greek should know that accents have to do with pronounciation, and Greek words with an acute accent on the ultima change to a grave accent only when followed by *another Greek word* that is not an enclitic. Even if, therefore, a word has a grave accent in the full Greek text from which it is taken, when it stands on its own, the accent should be acute. Otherwise, misuse of Greek accents appears to betray unfamiliarity with Greek.

To sum up, anyone who has ever interpreted Romans will assuredly find affirmation in Patte's insistence on the legitimacy and plausibility of all interpretations, although to be sure this is always qualified by other interpretations that are equally legitimate and plausible. Last but not least, this project is also so insightfully challenging that no serious article or commentary on Romans should ever be undertaken without this book.

Part II

METHODOLOGY AND ETHICAL RESPONSIBILITY

Chapter 3

ETHICAL RESPONSIBILITY AND THE NECESSITY TO CHOOSE AMONG A PLURALITY OF EQUALLY LEGITIMATE AND PLAUSIBLE INTERPRETATIONS

Kathy Ehrensperger

Daniel Patte has taken many of us on a journey to reading Romans through history and cultures. Romans is the text to which faith communities have turned again and again to find guidance, comfort, and support in their struggles in times when the ground under their feet was shaking. It has been commented on, analyzed, cited, torn apart, and lived by over centuries by millions of people. Readings of Romans have had enormous impacts in history, constructive and destructive, well beyond what the one who wrote it could ever had imagined.

Diverse and divergent readings of Romans should be taken seriously and respected as legitimate and plausible not only by literary critics but also by those for whom this letter is a Word-to-live-by, that is, scripture. This is the template of the magisterial volume of Daniel Patte's commentary on Romans. His approach is rooted in good old Europe where diversity could never be escaped over its long history as we know it, as borders, languages, self-perceptions, and struggles around and about this area triggered horrific battles and creatively fruitful debates. It led Daniel Patte to initiate, together with Cristina Grenholm, the "Romans Through History and Cultures" seminars in 1997, which involved an ever-widening circle of scholars (i.e., ninety-three active via publication but many more involved in the discussions) as it grew in depth and breadth until its conclusion in 2011. In the introduction to this volume and to the opening of the series *Reading Israel in Romans: Legitimacy and Plausibility of Divergent Interpretations* (2000), called "Overture," Patte and Grenholm emphasized that each and every interpretation, be it scholarly, creative, spiritual, or any other, relates to and is shaped by text, context, and hermeneutical presuppositions.

The Plurality and Intersectionality of Biblical Interpretation

Patte frequently reminded the seminar participants to abandon the language of right or wrong in their interpretative endeavors. He referred to interpretations that one did not share as nevertheless legitimate and plausible, opening doors and passageways to conversations across many borders. Thus, systematic theologians, church historians, philosophers, gender critical and postcolonial scholars, and biblical scholars engaged with each other and with their different approaches, their diverse hermeneutical presuppositions, and the various methodologies of their different disciplines—all of which contribute to the endeavor of reading Romans. This was interdisciplinarity not only in theory but clearly in practice! It led to astonishing interactions and conversations in a community of scholars from different fields gathered around the letter to the Romans. Together we heard and saw an inspiring text resonate in various ways leading to hearing sounds from Romans possibly not picked up before and breaking the spectrum of light into shades of colors possibly not noticed before. The goal of biblical interpretation is not to find the one and only true and correct meaning of Romans; there is a plurality of legitimate and plausible interpretations of this letter that became crucial for Christian self-understanding over the centuries and in diverse cultural contexts. With emphasis on the practice of interdisciplinary work and on conversations across disciplinary borders, the door for real encounter was opened—in the sense of Emmanuel Levinas, the doors for an encounter between the same and the o/Other opened. Differences and different presuppositions are not to be deplored but are actually what render conversation and encounter possible. Pluralism is constitutive not only of any society but also of academic discourses. As interlocutors necessarily have to be and remain different, any discourse presupposes plurality. Discourses over scriptural tradition thus cannot but reflect this pluralism. Multiple readings, expressions, and commentaries then are not mere or unfortunate ambiguities but the necessary "manner" and way of biblical interpretation.

It is striking that Romans is at the heart of most significant contemporary interpretative debates, as it was throughout the history of interpretation, of the churches, and of interreligious relations. The current debates and diverse approaches are of course as contextual as any before, and the specific contexts in which they emerge significantly influence the respective hermeneutical presuppositions of the diverse readings. Hermeneutical presuppositions, rather than being regarded as a problem or even as illegitimate, are, like plurality, part of the business of interpretation and therefore should not be deplored but recognized as part of interpretive conversations. The diversity in approaches and emphases that is prevalent in current interpretations of Romans may actually be indicative of some characteristics shared between Paul's context and today.

Paul lived and theologized in a context of cultural diversity; he theologized in conversation with others, in relation to concrete everyday life issues in his communities. Despite the differences in contemporary contexts and perceptions of diversity, there may be some analogies between Paul's context and the contexts of contemporary biblical interpreters, which could render the apostle an ideal partner in theological and interreligious conversations today. Particularly, the aspect of doing theology in conversation with scriptures as well as with others in all their diversity rather than in isolation may prove more relevant for today than ever before. This is not dispensing the interpreter and the practitioner from his/

her responsibility for the outcomes of their readings of Romans. Rather it invites all into open conversations about the issues of living together in open societies in search of common ground for peaceful cooperation.

Daniel Patte had initiated a journey among scholars across disciplines. This journey has led travelers in different directions, including to the awareness of the limitations of Western contextualized interpretations and of the limitations of a discipline exclusively dominated by men for centuries. Thus the book series "Romans Through History and Cultures" included different eras: Romans read in conjunction with patristic experts, with Augustine experts, with medieval scholars, with philosophers, with feminist scholars (i.e., through gender critical eyes), with non-Western colleagues (i.e., through postcolonial eyes) and in conversation with colleagues rooted in Greek Orthodox traditions.

On Hermeneutical Frameworks

Significantly, the first volume of this book series, published in 2000, had focused on the theme of the people Israel in Romans, whereas the most recent volume (2013) came back *full circle* to this beginning—or better in a *spiral movement* dealing with some interpreters of the twentieth and early twenty-first centuries and their attempts at overcoming the caricature of Judaism in New Testament interpretation. This diversity and respect for the other is not something that remained on paper in Daniel Patte's work. If the diversity is really respected, then this must go along with overcoming the domineering power imbalances in the discipline. The aim has to be to work toward conditions where all in the conversation meet as equals and where respect is truly mutual. The recognition of the relational dimension of interpretation both synchronically, in the recognition that this business is a collective one, and diachronically, in the recognition that interpreters are indebted and tied to those who were in the business before them, has been brought to the forefront of the discipline by Daniel Patte through his work in the "Romans Through History and Cultures" series. In that it resonates with gender critical stances who for decades have advocated the relational and collective dimension of interpretation. They were at the forefront of challenging the exclusivist Western, male-dominated perspectives in biblical interpretation and thus pioneered what has come to fruition also in Daniel Patte's projects—that hermeneutical presuppositions frame all approaches. Feminist theologians such as Elisabeth Schüssler Fiorenza have been pioneers in emphasizing the social location and embeddedness of each approach (not just women's) to biblical texts and hence challenging the notion of detached objectivity in academic discourse. As the political theorist Seyla Benhabib (1996: xxxiv) has formulated, "Understanding always means understanding from within a framework that makes sense for us, from where we stand today. In this sense, learning the questions of the past involves posing questions to the past in light of our present preoccupations … Every interpretation is a conversation, with all the joys and dangers that conversations usually involve."

Daniel Patte has contributed to the development of approaches in biblical studies that have tried to be true to this perception of the endeavor of interpretation as a conversation in which all participants not only apply historical and literary critical methods to the texts studied but as important critically reflect on their own hermeneutical presuppositions. He has done this not only at SBL seminars initiated by him but also in the classroom. This decade-long engagement is now coming to fruition in the magisterial work of this commentary on Romans where Daniel Patte draws together the strings of divergent interpretations and demonstrates what this means when applied consistently to the first chapter of Paul's letter. He is deeply concerned with overcoming the self-centeredness that pervades many approaches that are at risk of forgetting that interpretation is a communal enterprise and that, inasmuch as we might be convinced of our own approach and findings, none of us are in possession of the ultimate correct meaning and the truth of the text. This is not a pathway to anything goes, as Daniel Patte frequently had to clarify, but a warning against hiding behind so-called textual facts. Legitimate readings are defined by Daniel Patte as legitimate until proven otherwise; they have to be grounded in the text by following particular critical methods; plausible readings are defined as making sense although by different coherent interpretive lines of reasoning. Within these parameters Daniel Patte asks for the acknowledgment of and respect for divergent interpretations as legitimate and plausible. This means that really listening to each other is tantamount in interpretive conversations. The dichotomy of right or wrong can lead to walls that hinder hearing each other's voices. The constructivist recognition that "whatever view one has of reality, one's presentation of this reality is through a partisan prism: this discourse is both factual and effectual" (Patte 2018: xxi) could lead to modesty on all parts, scholarly modesty that recognizes the limitations of one's own perspective. This means that interpretation involves choices—choices rooted in our contexts, which render that particular interpretation ring true in particular circumstances and convincing because they affect our lives in the here and now. To pretend that there is no choice in interpretation is not innocent but often a matter of life and death for our neighbors. Thus, the discourse requires the inclusion of questions concerning the well-being of those who might be affected by choices of interpretation.

The Ethical Responsibility of Interpretation

All of this indicates that at the heart of Daniel Patte's approach lies a deep concern for the impact of any interpretation. The emphasis on the contextuality, and thus on issues of contemporary life as part of the recognition of the hermeneutical presuppositions and interpretive choices, keeps at the forefront the fact that interpretations are not merely theoretical abstractions. Particularly since the texts interpreted, here Romans, are scripture, that is, Word-to-live-by for faith communities all over the world, interpretive choices matter, they have an impact. And although it is difficult to anticipate the afterlife of texts that theologians and biblical scholars write, Daniel Patte has always emphasized that any interpretation, as legitimate and as plausible as it may be, includes ethical responsibility for its impact/effect.

It is no coincidence that the first sessions of the SBL seminar "Romans Through History and Cultures" in 1998 focused, as mentioned, on Israel in Romans. The 2018 commemoration of the so-called Reichskristallnacht (i.e., the pogroms that destroyed and severely damaged half of all synagogues in Germany and the horrors of the Shoah after that) that followed just by a few weeks by the attack on the Tree of Life Synagogue in Pittsburgh demonstrate that interpretations that explicitly or implicitly promote anti-Judaism are not innocent. Other interpretative choices can be made! And not only as far as anti-Judaism in interpretation is concerned. In the case of anti-Judaism, it is intrinsically intertwined with a Christian self-understanding built on contempt for the exemplary other, who in Christian discourse throughout the centuries were the Jews. Similarly, the contemptuous exemplary other who is denigrated includes women, and those who do not fit into some declared Christian norms. Interpretive choices have to be made, always trying to do justice to the text. But any denigration of the other for whatever reasons should act as a red flag. The ethical dimension in interpretive choices cannot be left out of the equation. Admittedly, this is not a straightforward affair—we often look through a glass dimly when trying to elucidate which is the responsible choice of interpretation in a given situation and context. There cannot be a one for all—and one for all times—answer to the ethical question. Thus, the ethical question must be asked—again and again in each context—even as the legitimacy and plausibility of divergent interpretations have to be respected. Interpretations do not have the same value in each situation, and context, even if they are legitimate and plausible—they might be helpful, but they can also be dangerous. However, the distinction Daniel Patte makes is not between learned/literate readings of critical biblical scholars and illiterate readings of pre-Enlightenment readers, or lay readers today. All those at the table around the text have a voice to be heard—past and present as "the collective wisdom of generations" (Angelou 2004, as cited in Patte 2018: 1). This is a treasure trove that we cannot afford to dismiss. Respect is not tolerance. Tolerance is based on power imbalance while respect is based on power balance. It requires that those involved in the conversation stand on equal par in order for true mutuality to be possible.

The distinction that Daniel Patte makes concerns the ethical responsibility of all those at the table around the text: Is the legitimate and plausible interpretation that is presented exclusivist, and does it render itself prone to bringing exclusion, contempt, destruction, even death? Or is it open to the voice of others, promoting and supporting hope and life in diversity in the here and now, even if it is troubling and puzzling? The call for ethical responsibility in interpretation raises the delicate question of who sets the standards of the criteria in a given situation and context. The question of power and authority sneaks in whether we like it or not. I consider it part of the communal process of interpretation to integrate this ethical aspect, even though it is a fine line, taking the risk of getting on one's high horse, making us behave as if we know more or are better than anyone else.

In his presentation of three interpretations of Romans (chapters 3–7), Daniel Patte tries to take into account the fact that interpretation of scripture serves to build-up communities; hence, its first and foremost role is empowerment. However, empowerment can never happen at the expense, contempt, or denigration of others, within or outside our own communities, if it is true empowerment.

Since the here and now is contingent, so are interpretations. The sincerity in the search for legitimate and plausible interpretations and the ethical responsibility for the effect on our communities and neighbors that go with it are a call to be answered in the humble recognition of the limitation of each and every one of our attempts.

Daniel Patte's volume on Romans is an attempt in this direction. It demonstrates in chapters 3, 4, and 5 how three different interpretations, although based on different hermeneutical presuppositions and therefore coming to different conclusions, can be legitimate and plausible within the frame in which they argue. Setting them alongside each other demonstrates that there are values and limitations in all of them. The question of right or wrong is obsolete as the question at the forefront is which one is appropriate and ethically justifiable in a given context. Thus, this threefold approach is to join the conversation of interpretation and also an invitation to continue to work on a place to live collectively, together and for all, out of interpretations that can only be "the almost-true," "the sometimes-true," and "the half-true" (Chamoiseau 1992, as cited in Patte 2018: 472–4).

Chapter 4

UNENDING INTERPRETATIONS: CONTINUING THE CONVERSATION

Tat-siong Benny Liew

First of all, I need to thank Professor Patte for these five hundred pages of scholarship. I do not know how long it took him to write it, but it certainly took me a while to get through this thick volume. Because of its length and complexity, it also took me a while to think through its strengths and shortcomings. For the sake of scholarly engagement and development, I will focus more on what I see to be the book's potential pitfalls. However, let me begin briefly with what I appreciate about Patte's book: namely, Patte's helpful reflection on and explication of not only the interpretive process but also the implications of an interpretation. As I said in my written endorsement of Patte's book: "The book will make you think—and think again—about what happens *when* we interpret and *after* we interpret as scholars and teachers of the Bible" (Patte 2018: back cover).

What I Appreciate

As Patte states, this volume, as a practice of "scriptural criticism," is the result of the decade-long project on "Romans Through History and Culture," a project that involved ninety-three scholars of various specialization, including not only biblical scholars with expertise in Pauline studies but also theologians and church historians (Patte 2018: xvi). By "scriptural criticism," Patte refers to the understanding that interpretation of text *as scripture* must always involve "three types of interpretive choices: *analytical textual choices, hermeneutical theological choices,* and *contextual choices*" (18; emphasis original).

Process of Interpretation

This emphasis on reception and interpretive choices, and hence by implication the inevitability and reality of multiple interpretations, makes sense. Every reading is inevitably selective not only because different interpreters approach a text with their respective presuppositions and in various contexts but also because no interpreter can literally attend to every single piece of information or data in a given passage. In my view, this is true of any reading of any text and not only applicable to text that is recognized and read as scripture, especially if one removes the word "theological" or replaces it with "ideological" in Patte's typology of interpretive choices.

This reminds me of the late Lynne St. Clair Darden's (2015) argument for replacing the term "biblical hermeneutics" with one coined by Vincent L. Wimbush: namely, "scripturalization" (cf. Wimbush 2012). For Darden, "scripturalization" gives both better acknowledgment of the agency and greater expression to the complexity of (African American) readers, because, in Darden's understanding, "scripturalization" focuses on what readers make of texts that they read *as scriptures* and rejects the traditional emphasis that biblical hermeneutics tends to place on exegeting authorial intentions (2015: 7, 13–15, 24–43).[1] This shift in both terminology and focus further functions then, for Darden, to expose and exhibit power differentials that are often at play in interpretation in general and in interpretation of *scriptures* in particular. As the participation in the Romans Seminar of not only biblical scholars but also theologians and church historians showed, power differentials in biblical interpretation exist on the basis of not only race, class, and gender but also disciplinary expertise. I appreciate, therefore, Patte's insistence on not only readers'—including his student readers' (2018: 40)—reception and interpretive choices but also their possession of "mother wit" or generational wisdom transmitted apart from formal educational channels (1). Such insistence has the potential to help level the interpretive playing field by acknowledging the agency and legitimacy of different readers.

While insisting on having a single, definitive interpretation is definitely a problem,[2] allowing for multiple interpretations can also fall into a meaningless relativism if our attitude concerning other people's interpretations is one of indifference or disengagement. As Patte writes, "Verifying any assertion against counterclaims is still needed … an *anything goes* attitude is to be rejected; the legitimacy and plausibility of receptions can be challenged by being proven otherwise" (2018: 8, 31; emphasis original). It is important to realize that Patte's emphasis on and acknowledgment of a multiplicity of legitimate and plausible interpretations function to promote rather than preclude engagement, judgment, and adjudication.

---

1. One may well question here if Darden's understanding of "scripturalization" is the same as Wimbush's, since Wimbush (2017), as his later work makes clear, says that "scripturalization" is for him a short hand for language games that humans make and play (Wimbush 2012, 2017), so the term, for Wimbush, is not narrowly restricted to how one reads or uses the Bible as a collection of sacred or religiously authoritative writings.

2. Human desire for certainty is understandable though not necessarily desirable. Even Origen's allegorical interpretation of the Bible has having truth and certainty at its core. See Harrill (2017).

Implications of Interpretation

It is not surprising, then, that Patte's "scriptural criticism" involves pedagogical and ethical considerations (2018: 6, 14). These considerations are particularly important if not exactly unique to readings of the Bible. As Pierre Bourdieu suggests, "Utterances are not only (save in exceptional circumstances) signs to be understood and deciphered, they are also … *signs of authority*, intended to be believed and obeyed" (1991: 66; emphasis original). There are arguably no truer or older "signs of authority" to be "believed and obeyed" in many societies, cultures, and churches than the words of the Bible, and our utterances or our rhetoric about the Bible, given its status as a cultural icon or religious authority, certainly carry ethical implications and perhaps even, in the words of Patte (2018: 69), life or death implications.

In his book *A Rabbi Reads the Bible* (2004), Jonathan Magonet talks about his experience of working with a group of young Czech Jews who, having escaped to Great Britain after the liberal reform movement in Prague was crushed in 1968 by Soviet troops, compared reading the Bible to reading a newspaper in the then Czechoslovakia. According to Magonet, these young people demonstrated well that one needs to read between and behind the lines of the Bible. In fact, these young people's experience of living under a manipulative and deceptive political regime taught them that one needs to read as if one's life depends on understanding what one is reading, whether the text in question is the newspaper or the Bible.[3]

We have, of course, seen from history how certain readings of the Bible—especially when coupled with an assumption and insistence that a biblical text must have a single, definitive meaning—have led to the literal demise of many, including indigenous peoples, enslaved peoples, gender-nonconforming peoples, those of non-Christian faiths, and Christians with so-called heretical ideas. Patte's goal for this volume to contribute to not only the exegetical but also the ethical and pedagogical tasks (2018: 6) is, therefore, both understandable and admirable. I would go so far as to say this should be the goal for any and all books about the Bible. If a piece of writing is always an act—and an art—of persuasion, it inevitably has ethical implications.

What I Wonder About

Let me turn now, however, to some questions I have after reading Patte's book.

Entanglements in Making a Contextual Ethical Choice

First, I wonder if the thought about how we should choose among what Patte calls "equally legitimate and plausible" readings (2018: xxiii, 9, 32, 73, 220) needs to be better nuanced. According to Patte, this should be done as a "contextual ethical

---

3. I am indebted to Dana Nolan Fewell for introducing me to Magonet's book.

choice" (xxiv, 121, 389), meaning we should choose a reading that is best—that is, most ethical—within a given context. That certainly sounds good and reasonable, especially since scholars from different generations have talked about the need to produce biblical interpretation that causes less if not no harm. Krister Stendahl in his article "Ancient Scripture in the Modern World," for example, talks about how his scholarship about women and Jews in the Bible has to do with what he calls a "public health" concern (1982: 205). A couple of decades later, Ken Stone (2005) would write an entire book with "practicing safer texts" as its title.

What I want to point out, however, is the simple but by no means simplistic fact that people also interpret and understand words such as "best," "ethical," "health," and "safety" differently. Centuries ago Augustine already proposed "love" as the criterion to adjudicate different meanings or interpretations of scripture (*De doctrina christiana* 3.33-34, 55; cf. Patte 2018: 42). What precisely is the "loving" act or practice at a given moment, however, is very much subject to interpretations. There are, therefore, even more layers of interpretation that we have to think about than what Patte has given us. Interpretation does not stop at the moment of one's recognition that a "contextual ethical choice" has to be made among "equally legitimate and plausible" readings. That recognition, in turn, requires one to interpret not only the meaning of "ethical" but also one's context(s). I am emphasizing the pluralization of context here because understanding and using context in the singular is common though, in my view, erroneous. After all, the reality of interpretive contexts being plural can be easily shown in the scholarship on Paul's Romans. This history of scholarship has shown that what Paul wrote can come across to readers very differently if readers read Romans within the context of Christianity (e.g., Käsemann 1980), within that of Judaism (e.g., Nanos 2017, 2018), or within that of the Roman Empire (e.g., Elliott 2010). Interpretation is required all the way through. In other words, there is no end to interpretive struggles—and I have not even mentioned here the contexts of the readers. Note that even if we singularize a reader's context, this context (be it a classroom, a club, a church, a clan, or a country) is, more likely than not, occupied or shared by a number of persons. Patte's surprising address to his reader in the singular as if she is an individual making a singular decision in isolation—"it is up to you, my patient *reader*, to make a choice for *your own context*" (Patte 2018: 472; emphasis on "reader" is mine)—bypasses and obscures the messy reality of *communal* interpretive conflict.

Necessity of "Scriptural Criticism"

My reference to Augustine brings me to my second question. Do we really need "scriptural criticism" to appreciate or even just acknowledge the legitimacy, plausibility, and reality of multiple interpretations? Interpreters of the Bible in the Middle Ages already talked about it with what they called the literal, allegorical, moral, and anagogic meanings of a biblical passage (e.g., Grant and Tracy 2005: 83–91). When I was a graduate student studying with Professor Patte (!) at Vanderbilt and *before* the beginning of the Romans seminar, biblical scholars were already talking about multiple interpretations because of reader-response criticism, particularly the branch of it that emphasizes more the agency and decisions of readers (e.g., Detweiler 1985; Fowler 2001). What then does "scriptural criticism" really have to offer?

Artificiality of the Schema

What "scriptural criticism" does seem to offer is a categorization—or, using a term that is familiar within biblical studies, a typology—of different camps or "families" of readings (Patte 2018: 8), but I wonder—here is my third question—if what it offers is actually too neat, tidy, and artificial. We have, according to Patte, in the case of Romans (i) forensic theological readings that focus on behind-the-text concerns, center on individuals, and are about justification by faith; (ii) sociorhetorical readings that focus on in-front-of-the-text concerns, center on collectives, and are about an inclusive covenantal community; and (iii) religious or realized apocalyptic/messianic vision readings that focus on within-the-text concerns, center on other, and are about the power of God for salvation (8, 36–7, 46–56). These are, however, such leaky terminologies and concepts. I know many in the academy like to separate theological studies and religious studies, but I myself cannot really figure out how theological readings are not also religious readings, for instance, or how justification by faith and the creation of inclusive covenantal communities are not about God's power for salvation. After all, I do not see how the theological or the religious are separable from the sociorhetorical, especially when we are talking about reading and writing. In fact, this third category reads like a catch-all category for anything that does not fall within the well-known debates between Lutheran and "New Perspective" or "Radical New Perspective" readings of Paul (e.g., Dunn 2005; Nanos 2017). For these religious or realized apocalyptic/messianic vision readings, Patte highlights their interpretive expectation of and attention to what he calls "puzzling" or "surprising" features of a text. "We need to allow the text to *surprise* us," he writes (Patte 2018: 214; emphasis original). However, is it not the case that, despite the method we use to begin our research and where we end up with it, we often proceed to study precisely because we find something puzzling, surprising, or interesting in a passage or in a book in the first place? In other words, how is this characteristic not true of most if not all interpretations?

Since Patte specifies Paul's self-identification as "a slave of Christ Jesus" as an example for this third type of reading (214–15), I immediately think of Dale Martin's book *Slavery as Salvation: The Metaphor of Slavery in Pauline Christianity* (1990) and wonder if it would fall into this religious or realized apocalyptic/messianic vision type of readings, even though it focuses on 1 Corinthians rather than on Romans. That is to ask, is Patte's threefold schema applicable to interpretations of books beyond Paul's letter to the Romans to other letters and even other genres of writing within the New Testament? A long time ago, a wise person told me that generalization is helpful because it provides orientation, but generalization is always false because there will be a lot of details that do not fit. Is this the case here?

Let me give a more specific example to help drive home this point. Cynthia Briggs Kittredge has floated, albeit briefly, a feminist reading that foregrounds Rom 16:1-16 in the study of the entire letter and sees the letter as "Paul's commendation of Phoebe," who carried with her Paul's letter to Rome (2012: 121). Briggs Kittredge's suggestion brings up for me not only the restrictions of the genre of commentary (with Patte's volume focusing *only* on the first thirty-two verses of Romans)[4] but also the limitations of Patte's threefold scheme. Let me explain.

After the conventional beginning of a New Testament letter (Rom 1:1-7), Paul explains why he has not visited the Romans (Rom 1:8-17) and how the Gentiles' idolatrous practices and moral failures result from their refusal to acknowledge God despite God's self-revelation through creation itself (Rom 1:18-32). Then Paul proceeds to argue in the rest of his letter that this God of Israel, without abandoning God's covenant to save "all Israel" (Rom 11:26), has also redeemed, accepted—indeed, adopted—the Gentiles through Jesus Christ (whose life and death also signal the dawning of the end time). What if, however, all of this, as Briggs Kittredge suggests, is only a setup to recommend Phoebe? Can we not interpret Paul's argument about the coming together of Jews and Gentiles as his subtle argument also for the equality and interdependence between women and men, especially given, as Briggs Kittredge points out, the number of women being featured by Paul in his closing greetings—besides Phoebe, there are, for example, Prisca, Mary, Junia, Trypheana and Tryphosa, Persis, Rufus's mother, Julia, Nereus's sister, and sisters in Asyncritus's sisters? More importantly for my purposes here, this reading would be using an emphasis on collectives (the coming together of Jews and Gentiles; the interdependence between males and females) for Paul's goal of recommending an individual (Phoebe) to the Romans. In other words, it deconstructs Patte's separation of readings with an individual focus (forensic theological) from those with a communal focus (sociorhetorical).

After all, if the three types of reading are neatly separable, why does Patte adopt the commentary genre for his own threefold interpretation of Rom 1 in this book, especially in light of his earlier faulting of the commentary genre for causing scholars to incorporate insights from other types of reading and end up with a kind of hybrid product that mixes together the forensic theological readings, the sociorhetorical readings, and the religious realized apocalyptic/messianic vision readings (2018: 56–62)? Patte's very attempt to identify these three camps or "families" always already involves, as he himself realizes and admits, *his* interpretive choices (76, 123–4, 220). That is to say, others who look at existing

---

4. Scot McKnight has recently argued that "reading Romans backwards" (i.e., not reading Romans sequentially from the letter's beginning) is better and more conducive for understanding the occasional and ecclesial nature of Paul's letter, and McKnight does that by starting the first chapter of his book with Phoebe (Rom 16:1-2), including the need for the Roman church or churches to encounter Phoebe's female body before they could hear what Paul had to say in his letter to them. See McKnight (2019).

readings of Romans may well come up with an entirely different schema with a different number of interpretive camps or "families."

Rationale for the Threefold Emphasis

I wonder, therefore, why there are so many sets of three in Patte's volume. I have already mentioned the book's threefold task and its suggestion of a threefold choice for any interpreter. There are also three types of reading, with each having three characteristics. Given not only the name ("scriptural criticism") and the subject (Paul's letter to the Romans in the Christian Testament) but also Patte's regular reference to "believers" in the volume (e.g., Patte 2018: 240, 307, 338, 380, 391, 452, 473), is the number a reflection of Patte's own trinitarian commitment? Since Patte also quotes approvingly Daniel Boyarin's statement that "responsible preaching is the model for responsible scholarship and not its stepchild"[5] three times (5, 6, 339) and equates theological argument with homiletic argument in a footnote (73 n. 1),[6] is the number three chosen as an imitation of a three-point sermon? Alternatively, is the number three a mere matter of convenience, since it conveniently functions to avoid not only a dualistic setup but also an even lengthier manuscript with more camps or "families" of reading? If the latter, I would love to hear what other types of readings Patte has been able to identify among the many scholarly publications on Romans besides the three types that he has given us as examples in this book.

Importance of Factual Data

I do not quite agree with the comparison Patte makes in the "Foreword" between multiple interpretations and Trump's claim of "fake news" and "alternative facts." This comparison comes across as if facts really do not matter in our work of interpretation. However, as Patte repeatedly states, a reading is legitimate *only if* it is "grounded in the text" (2018: xv, xxiii, 129, 151, 395). For example, while there are variant readings among numerous manuscripts of Mark as well as different translations and multiple interpretations of this Gospel, one cannot say that there is a birth story of Jesus in Mark's Gospel, just as one cannot follow Trump and say that his so-called favorite biblical verse in Proverbs, "never bend to envy," is in the Bible. What Trump often does is a dismissal of facts, clear and simple. Trumpism has nothing to do with honoring multiple legitimate and plausible readings. I hope I am not being too strong with my words here, but to compare or connect the two is, I think, problematic and perhaps even insulting to what we do as biblical scholars who embrace multiple interpretations of the same text. After

---

5. Boyarin (2000: 246–50).
6. Stephen D. Moore has also made a connection between biblical scholarship and the sermon instead of seeing the sermon as the "constitutive other" of scholarship, though he limits his comparison to what he calls the "exiled" or "contextual hermeneutics" of primarily the Global South; see Moore (2018: 286–7).

all, Patte is clear that a reading can be proven wrong and that he does not believe in "anything goes" (2018: 19, 31). The reason why some of us cannot change the mind of fundamentalists is not necessarily because they believe in Trump's "alternative facts" or "fake news"; it has to do with the fact that they have a whole different approach to reading the Bible. Since we are talking about Trumpism, both Erin Runions (2014) and Adam Kotsko (2018) have provided some very helpful analysis of Trumpian interpretive approach to the Bible. Kotsko points out that Trump is in the eyes of his Bible-believing supporters similar to Nebuchadnezzar and Cyrus in the Bible:

> An ignorant pagan ruler [who] makes the divine agency *unmistakable* ... [and] whose impulsive and blasphemous ways ... [make] his declarations of divine power and authority all the more meaningful when they do come, because they are so obviously contrary to his inclinations ... What looks like hypocrisy, or at least deep irony, from the outside appears from within ... as the surest possible evidence that God is in control. (2018: n.p.; emphasis original)

Runions tellingly calls this approach to the Bible "literalist allegory," which she grosses as the "allegorization of present events by way of the text" so "texts, geographical locations, and events described in the Bible are understood as saying something about contemporary events in the light of ultimate truths" (2014: 151, 157). Notice the oxymoron: "literalist allegory"; these people take what is and what is not in the Bible so seriously that they take the words literally—and, yes, problematically—as happening in their own lives and times.

What Trump's Bible-believing supporters think about his so-called alternative facts and fake news, I do not really know and I do not really care to know. I am adamant, however, that when it comes to the Bible, these Bible believers do not make up facts or verses in the Bible. The key is how they interpret what they read in the Bible with a particular set of—yes, in my view, skewed and twisted—logic. While we may talk about multiple interpretations of the Bible, including interpretations that might have led people to support Trump, because of multiple interpretive logics, systems, or approaches, we cannot—and should not—confuse or connect multiple interpretations of the Bible with Trump's claim about "fake news" or "alternative facts."

Affects of Biblical Interpretation

Having said that, I do want to register my appreciation for Patte's clear explanation of discourse in his discussion of Trump's claims. Referring to the work of J. L. Austin and John R. Searle, Patte breaks down speech act as having two components: "(1) a 'propositional content,' which is often a 'factual content,' and (2) 'effectual features' or 'illocutionary force'" (2018: xviii). While Patte hopes that highlighting the "effectual dimensions" of a discourse for people to see the "problematic effects of ... words ... and behaviors" will change their interpretive choices, recent events— such as news report regarding how the policies of the Trump administration result in cruel treatment of migrant children under custody in the United States—have shown that knowledge of effects or consequences do not necessarily dissuade people from their views or choices. Rather than equating the "effectual dimensions" of a discourse with interpretive effects as Patte does, I am reminded of what rhetorical criticism within biblical studies has always emphasized: namely, the roles and significance of logos, ethos, and pathos in ancient rhetoric (e.g., Mack 1990: 35–6). Given not only the affective turn in the humanities in general (e.g., Ticineto Clough 2007; Gregg and Seigworth 2000) and the study of religion/theology (e.g., Schaefer 2015; Bray and Moore 2019) and of the Bible in particular (e.g., Koosed and Moore 2014: Kotrosits 2015; Black and Koosed 2019) but also the understanding of biblical interpretation itself as a form of rhetoric, I cannot help but wonder at the same time how Patte's book would be different—even fuller, perhaps?—if he had paid greater attention in his own analysis to the "illocutionary force" or the emotive power of other scholars' reading of Romans. Attending to this affective dimension of discourse may not dissuade others from following Trump's "alternative facts" or from embracing particular interpretations of the Bible, but it will help us better understand not only the influence of Trump's rhetoric but also why "two centuries of sophisticated exegetical studies failed to convince fundamentalists to abandon their 'wrong' interpretations" (Patte 2018: xix).

Conclusion

Let me close by affirming with Patte the importance of not only acknowledging but also engaging multiple interpretations, because how we read texts may imply how we treat others and navigate the world. Since Patte chose a painting of a Holocaust survivor (Samuel Bak's "Escape") as the cover art of his book as a way to underscore the life-and-death implications of biblical interpretation and the value of "scriptural criticism," I am wondering, after more than five hundred pages of Professor Patte's "scriptural criticism" and more than five hundred years after Luther's *sola scriptura*, if we cannot perhaps also return and learn from the rabbis: not only Rabbi Magonet and his book *A Rabbi Reads the Bible* but also those who were much closer to Paul's time than to ours. They knew how to converse with scriptural texts and with each other without insisting on a single reading or meaning. They knew that texts, like people and the world, are all much richer and much more complex than any one person or any single reading can grasp.

The scenario that Kenneth Burke provides to illustrate the dynamics of language—what he calls "the unending conversation"—is applicable to not only our work of biblical interpretation but also the unfolding drama of life. Burke writes:

> Imagine that you enter a parlor. You come late. When you arrive, others have long preceded you, and they are engaged in a heated discussion, a discussion too heated for them to pause and tell you exactly what it is about. In fact, the discussion had already begun long before any of them got there, so that no

one present is qualified to retrace for you all the steps that had gone before. You listen for a while, until you decide that you have caught the tenor of the argument; then you put in your oar. Someone answers; you answer him [sic]; another comes to your defense; another aligns himself [sic] against you, to either the embarrassment or gratification of your opponent, depending upon the quality of your ally's assistance. However, the discussion is interminable. The hour grows late, you must depart. And you do depart, with the discussion still vigorously in progress. (1941: 110–11)

Interpretation and scholarship, biblical or otherwise, are all about participating in the give-and-take of discussion and deliberation that can at times get, yes, heated, passionate, and emotional. I certainly agree with Patte's concluding suggestion that "being ethically responsible involves participating with other interpreters in the constant to-and-fro movement from one interpretation to another of the (almost-true, sometimes-true, half-true) interpretations" (2018: 474), even if I am not as optimistic as Patte is that the "true-true" (473–4) will come to life out of these conversations.

Chapter 5

THE COLLISION OF ADVERSE OPINIONS: A REFLECTION ON DANIEL PATTE, JOHN STUART MILL, AND THE ABSOLUTIZATION OF CERTAINTY

Monya A. Stubbs

Personal Point of Departure: Intentional Communicative Chaos

On July 7, 2020, *Harper's Magazine* published an online thought-piece entitled "A Letter on Justice and Open Debate." Signed by a chorus of scholars, authors, journalist, artists, musicians, and entertainers, the letter applauds the current demands for social reform. It also warns against a rise in moral attitudes and political commitments that favor ideological conformity over open debate and an appreciation of difference. The letter's signatories argue against censorship and maintain: "The way to defeat bad ideas is by exposure, argument, and persuasion, not by trying to silence or wish them away" ("A Letter on Justice and Open Debate"). The challenge, however, facing American citizens (world citizens) at this historic moment of human unrest is more subtle and insidious. The article fails to understand that we have not entered a moral moment that is trying to silence ideas. On the contrary, we are at a time in history where we are seemingly trapped in a world defined by intentional communicative chaos. Humanity is bombarded with competing information and ideas.

However, the abundance of competing information and ideas does not seem to create a clarity that defends one position over/against the other. Instead, mass-information and miscommunication have been weaponized. In this current historical moment, the purpose of debate or the collision of adverse ideas is not to give people the tools to make an informed decision or choice but to normalize chaos and confusion. The goal is not to empower people with clear and nuanced information so that we are better able to discern, understand, and determine where we stand on issues that affect our ability to create a world *all* have reason to value. Rather, those in positions of public authority use competing ideas as a means to further complicate (rather than clarify) the fundamental issues on which our common existence rests. The result is that people are left intellectually paralyzed, emotionally numbed, and spiritually depleted. We are forced into a zero-sum-game where truth rests in a shallow brand of coercion and dogma.

Moreover, the absence of public debates that seek to clarify rather than convolute the pressing issues of our time leave human beings stymied in our capacity to reflect on and bring to critical consciousness the presuppositions that ground our actions. We are forced to remain trapped in the world of our own opinions; or even more troubling, we become an uncritical, passive repository for the ideas of others, which, when enacted, might advance policies, procedures, and behaviors that diminish our collective aptitude for justice and our commitment to freedom. Speech that seeks to confuse rather than clarify is simply a siren call and must be tuned out at all cost. However, speech that offers itself up for public scrutiny, invites engagement and critique, and is open to transition and transformation is necessary for one's personal growth as an autonomous human being, for one's social development as a world citizen, and for the continued development of American democracy. It is with this social context in mind that I explore Daniel Patte's commentary on Romans.

Introduction: Disciplinary Intersections and Mutual Indebtedness

My reflection on Patte's commentary focuses on his reading paradigm, scriptural criticism. I develop the analysis by offering basic similarities I find between Patte's description of scriptural criticism and John Stuart Mill's discussion on "Of the Liberty of Thought and Discussion" in the second chapter of *On Liberty*. While I am not an expert on Mill's political philosophy, as a biblical scholar I am profoundly interested in the intersections of disciplines and how they shape patterns of human relating. Due to a particularly high number of enrollees at my current assignment,[1] my theological and ethical background, and my work in equity-minded leadership, I was asked to teach a core class on moral and political philosophy. I readily accepted the challenge. Of course, Mill was one of the featured philosophers. Patte's book was released during the time the class was studying Mill. As I reviewed Patte's book, I noticed striking parallels between the basic principles of Mill's position on the government's limits on interference with an individual's thought and speech and the basic tenets of Patte's biblical interpretive process. The umbrella similarity is that both thinkers present the view that we cannot truly *know* or *understand* our own ideas/opinions absent the ideas/opinions of others.

In order to demonstrate this basic similarity between the two thinkers and to highlight the basic interpretive dimensions that anchor scriptural criticism, I make three interrelated movements. The first section of my reflection outlines Mill's response to the question of a government's limits on censoring a person's liberty (on thought and speech) and teases out intersecting points with Patte's scriptural criticism. The second section looks closely at the concept of fallibility, an idea both Mill and Patte feature as significant to the human experience, and for Patte, central to ethical biblical interpretation. I conclude by exploring the

---

1. At the time I wrote this chapter, I served at the United States Coast Guard Academy.

relationship Patte establishes between biblical interpretation, freedom, and the contextual character of our human experience. My hope is that through exploring the intersections between Mill's discussion on censorship and Patte's position on biblical interpretation, we are better able to appreciate our mutual indebtedness—an indebtedness that enables us to grow more fully into our individual self, while simultaneously accepting responsibility for the social/communal well-being of our shared existence (Stubbs 2013, 2007).

Daniel M. Patte, John Stuart Mill, and the Question of Censorship

Daniel Patte's *Romans: Three Exegetical Interpretations and the History of Reception: Volume 1: Romans 1:1-32* reminds me of the second chapter of John Stuart Mill's *On Liberty*. For instance, Mill begins the chapter with a type of thought experiment on the issue of human freedom and censorship. Mill writes, "What if all humankind minus one, were of one opinion, and only one person of the contrary opinion, humankind would be no more justified in silencing that one person, than he, if he had the power, would be justified in silencing humankind" (2015: 19). Mill presents the view that a government's censorship of ideas (or another individual's censorship of a person's ideas) is an infraction on its citizens' individual liberty. Moreover, censorship is a moral corruption because ultimately the censorship of an idea denies people the improvement of their mental well-being. To support his position, Mill posits one overarching reason, with two distinctive hypotheses. The "peculiar evil of silencing the expression of an opinion is that it is robbing the human race, posterity as well as the existing generation—those who dissent from the opinion, still more than those who hold it" (19). He further hypothesizes about the opinion that might be censored: "If the opinion is right, they are deprived of the opportunity of exchanging error for truth; if wrong, they lose, what is almost as great a benefit, the clearer perception and livelier impression of truth produced by its collision with error" (19). In summation, Mill argues that the majority is never justified in suppressing the opinion of the minority because (i) the minority's opinion might be true; (ii) the minority's opinion might have a kernel of truth in it that we need to find by refuting it; and (iii) even if it is false, we will gain a better appreciation of the true opinion by letting that opinion be heard and then refuting it. For Mill, a person's individual liberty is preserved and humanity is best served through the "testing" of ideas.

Patte also begins his commentary with a type of thought experiment about censorship. For him, the issue centers on traditional biblical scholarship's tendency to demonstrate one biblical interpretation of a text (here a Romans interpretation) as more legitimate and plausible than all others—and in the process, stated negatively, delegitimize and thus, in essence, silence all other interpretations. Patte refers to this interpretive goal/posture as "a self-centered denial of the learned scholarship of other exegetes" (2018: 15). The central concern then is not that "other" interpretations are rendered implausible or illegitimate through a process of critical engagement. The issue is not that any and every interpretation is valid. Rather, as we will discuss below, like Mill, Patte challenges the morality of censorship and its accompanying predisposition, the assumption of human infallibility.[2]

Mill, Patte, and the Benefits of Difference

Mill and the Collision of Adverse Opinions

Moreover, there is considerable benefit to engaging an opinion with which you disagree. Even false opinions often contain a modicum of truth. By the very act of silencing it, argues Mill, "we lose the opportunity of discussion, and 'the collision of adverse opinions' that could and often does, expose the remainder of the truth" (2015: 52). But suppose the received opinion is not only true but entirely true, asks Mill. Even then, Mill maintains, contrary opinions must not be prohibited because without them we easily forget the rational basis of the opinion. It is, as Socrates would say, an opinion not tied down by knowing the reason *why*. The opinion, then, becomes dogma without real impact on "the growth of any real heart-felt conviction" (52). One might deduce from Mill's argument that this is a type of compulsion because we are forced to remain imprisoned in our personal opinion (even if it is a right opinion). We are not given the *opportunity* to break out of the world of our personal opinions to examine other opinions.

Scriptural Criticism, Fallibility, and the Collision of Adverse Opinions

Patte seeks this sense of freedom for biblical scholars and argues that it is achievable through the practice of scriptural criticism, which follows a certain methodological logic. Every biblical interpretation moves on three levels: an analytical level that emphasizes the methodological approaches used to ground a reading in textual evidence; a hermeneutical/theological level that constitutes the themes used to circumscribe one's dialogue with the text; and finally a contextual level through which one relates life and text. Patte maintains that biblical interpreters commonly make explicit their choices on the analytical level. However, they are less inclined to make explicit the hermeneutical/theological and contextual choices they employ to make sense of a biblical text. Scriptural criticism claims that *responsible* biblical interpretations must make each of these levels explicit (even though a reading might emphasize one over the other two).

Patte's call for biblical scholars to make explicit all three levels of their interpretive choices is a necessary and compelling move in the critical analysis of texts. It prevents us from making positivistic claims about our respective *readings*.

---

2. Mill highlights the benefits of human fallibility. He reasons that opinions should not be censored because those who would silence an opinion they believe is false presume infallibility. What is false, according to Mill, is that anyone is beyond being wrong. I will discuss this point later in my analysis. See also Mill (2015: 19–20).

Scriptural criticism asks biblical scholars to presume *fallibility*—not first and foremost on the part of other interpretations; rather, for our own interpretation. A responsible biblical analysis liberates us from the trap of our own opinion and affords us the opportunity to examine other opinions. But, according to scriptural criticism, we can only make explicit our interpretive choices by comparing them, as well as our ultimate interpretive claim(s), with those of other interpreters. The goal, then, is not to demean and/or diminish another reading; rather it is to show how different foci yield dynamic meanings and implications for a given text. A person interested in salvation, righteousness, and God will ask different questions than one interested in Paul's view of indebtedness and Jesus's view of women. Moreover, the questions we ask and the *meanings* we find are influenced by our social location.[3] However, this is not to say that every interpretation is valid. It does suggest though that an interpretation should not be ignored or presumed invalid (both forms of censorship) simply because it does not align with one's own interpretive questions and conclusions. In fact, according to Patte, the focus on differences (adverse opinions) is essential: "it is only when we recognize the differences between our interpretations and those of others that we learn from them, and thus truly respect them—rather than co-opting them, by pretending they are the same as ours, or rejecting them as meaningless" (2004: xxxvi n1). Each of these responses is a form of censorship, and it impedes the improvement of the person's mental well-being.

Combating a Peculiar Evil: Human Freedom, Moral
Credibility, and Ethical Responsibility

Yet, to impede upon the improvement of a person's mental well-being (even if the person is oneself) is not simply a practice of intellectual injustice. As mentioned above, Mill categorizes it as a peculiar evil. Patte makes an equally radical claim. He challenges the moral credibility and the ethical responsibility of biblical interpretations that fail to make explicit their interpretive choices. Additionally, he challenges the moral credibility and ethical responsibility of biblical interpreters that presume that they have sufficient assurance that they are correct in their *particular* interpretive conclusions and exegetical approaches by refusing to acknowledge/engage adverse opinions. But Patte's call for biblical scholars to bring

---

3. See Stubbs (2013). I discuss how Harriet Tubman's explanation about her move from enslavement to freedom functions as a part of my personal context as an interpreter of Paul's letter to the Romans. Her words and experience help bring to light the presuppositions I bring to my reading of Romans. Tubman functions as an illuminating agent. The particular constellation of themes (subjection-reflection-transformation) that form the vantage point from which I analyze Romans was formulated as a result of my taking the lived experience of Harriet Tubman as normative. In other words, my analysis of Romans grants epistemological privilege to the lived everyday realities of Harriet Tubman and the difficult and often ignored issues they confront.

our readings to *critical consciousness* is not an altruistic exercise. Rather, it is an autonomous act that serves as a way to honor biblical interpretation as scripture—as a word by which we live. Bringing our readings to critical consciousness is the means by which we sharpen our own perception of what we hold as truth.

Mill says it this way: there is a great difference in "presuming an opinion to be true, because with every opportunity for contesting it, it has not been refuted, and presuming its truth for the purpose of not permitting its refutation" (2015: 21). Moreover, he adds:

> Complete liberty of contradicting and disproving our opinion, is the very condition which justifies us in assuming its truth ... to call any proposition certain, while there is anyone who would deny its certainty is permitted, but who is not permitted, is to assume that we ourselves, and those who agree with us are the judges of certainty, and judges without hearing the other side. (21)

Mill argues that the prohibition of censorship and the *collision of adverse ideas* privileges individual liberty. According to him, human freedom, on the one hand, is manifest in our ability to openly express our opinions/ideas. But equally important, human freedom requires we take responsibility for those ideas. And one can only take responsibility for her opinions when the "certainty" she holds in a position is tested by opinions/ideas that present a different aspect of "certainty" than the position she holds as truth. We are *free* to engage in the expression of ideas and through this engagement we sharpen our understanding of the opinions we hold, expand our understanding of the opinions others hold, and ultimately improve our mental well-being (34). In other words, diversity of opinion is in one's self-interest.

Yes, biblical scholars must make explicit the exegetical method(s) used to focus their analysis of the text, clarify the theological categories presumed most relevant in their analysis of the text, and highlight the ideological presuppositions that color their interpretive gaze. Each of these "revelations" is an essential part of the interpretive process and open to the critique of others. So, is Patte suggesting that truth is merely measured by the explicitness of the interpretive process? For instance, as we have emphasized throughout the chapter, Mill maintains that a "true opinion" tied down by the reason why improves humanity's mental well-being. We find this truth not by censoring ideas/opinions but through the testing of our ideas by other purported truths. Patte views interpretive *discourse* as a central feature in the exegetical process, but he measures the moral/ethical credibility of the interpretation by an additional factor.

Patte begins his commentary with a discussion on the importance of recognizing and appreciating discourses grounded in both facts and alternative facts—truths and alternative truths. His rehearsal of the political discourse surrounding the 2016 presidential campaign/election highlights the ambiguity and power dynamics involved in determining meaning. However, Patte's point is not to defend speeches or interpreters that intentionally misrepresent historical events or present interpretations of, for instance, Romans that are not grounded in the text. Rather, he employs this historical analysis to demonstrate the nature of discourses as a "speech act." Every speech act necessarily contains a propositional content that is often based on "factual content," and an *effectual* (or illocutionary) force. The effectual or illocutionary force of a speech act may be absent of facts (it may even be grounded in lies). But, the absence of factual truths does not, for many, diminish the presence of truth. A speech act that prioritizes the effectual or illocutionary feature obtains its truth-power from the way it affects our lives. It is, as the dictionary describes, an act of speaking or writing that in itself effects or constitutes the intended action. So not only does Patte suggest an idea or biblical interpretation must be open to discussion or, as Mill would say, open to a collision with adverse opinions. According to Patte's scriptural criticism, there is yet an additional interpretive feature that undergirds the validity of our interpretive conclusions. Biblical interpreters must be open to determining and challenging the effects of ideas/interpretations—the effectual dimension (illocutionary force) of interpretations and the behavior they promote in a particular contextual situation (Patte 2018: xv–xxv).

Patte argues that biblical scholars take responsibility for our interpretation by giving attention to the *effectual dimensions* of our interpretive conclusions. The true measure of the opinions we hold and the true purpose of the interpretive debates in which we engage are determined by our focus on ethical questions:

> Who is helped and who is hurt when one chooses one interpretation rather than another? How, in the concreteness of their lives, are people affected when one advocates a particular view of facts (opinions/certainty of truth) and a particular ideological perspective ... What are the consequences of holding to a particular interpretation as if it were the only true one? ... We are estranged from neighbors, without the possibility of truly considering the ethical/moral value of both their statements/interpretations and ours. (xxv)

In this light, responsible and ethical biblical interpretation is not only about the process employed to determine meaning but also about the complex levels of human relationships that are affirmed and/or denied as we reflect, execute, and implement these meanings in our lived experiences. For biblical interpretation, both the *means* and the *ends* matter.

Until Proven Otherwise: Freedom as the Refutation of Absolutization

The central tenet of Patte's scriptural criticism reminds me of the presumption of innocence, the legal principle that argues one is considered innocent until proven guilty. Patte writes, "When one encounters interpretations that are different from ours ... these should *not* be presumed illegitimate (until proven otherwise) ... but rather they *should be* presumed *legitimate* (until proven otherwise)" (2018: 19; emphasis original). I noted earlier that scriptural criticism's goal is not to demean or diminish a biblical interpretation that is different from my/our own. Rather, it is to clarify and make explicit the interpretive choices that frame our conclusions.

We often come across a "plurality of legitimate interpretations." What scriptural criticism reveals most about the interpretive process—the collision of adverse opinions—is that it is inherently conflictual. Consider the key parenthetical phrase Patte places within his "presumption of legitimacy" clause: An interpretation that is different from our own should not be presumed illegitimate and should be presumed legitimate, *until proven otherwise*. So, after a closer reading, where I thought scriptural criticism departed from Mill's posture against censorship may actually be where the alignment is strongest.

Recall Mill's second and third reasons for not silencing a minority opinion: the minority's opinion might have a kernel of truth in it that we need to find by *refuting* it; and even if it is false, we will gain a better appreciation of the true opinion by letting that opinion be heard and then *refuting* it. While one's initial posture is fallibility (and so we recognize an opposing position may be true), this posture is always married to the goal of refutation. In our analysis and encounter with other interpretive choices and conclusions, we are not simply seeking to clarify our own position. Patte, like Mill, implies that our encounter also looks to *prove* the legitimacy or illegitimacy of other interpretive choices/conclusions. For Patte the most pronounced site of conflict does not, however, rest in our exegetical choices. Certainly, as Patte explains, "*not everything goes*" (2018: 393; emphasis original)! But beyond the strange ideas that Paul, for instance, might be talking about "walking on the moon or about driverless cars" (393), more often than not, our exegetical choices yield equally plausible interpretations. Therefore, the refutation represents a struggle for authority, not legitimacy.

An interpretation may prove exegetically legitimate but morally/ethically irresponsible—and therefore lack authority. In this sense, Patte's scriptural criticism and his commentary on Romans is an exercise in *refuting* absolutism. We are never seeking the absolute truth; we are seeking an interpretive truth that is the best interpretation in a given context. As Patte writes at the close of this volume: "Any of these interpretations/receptions becomes very destructive—and often in tragic ways—when it is absolutized, that is when it claims that one does not have any real choice" (2018: 472). He reminds us that his work is an exercise in preventing absolutized conclusions about Romans. Instead, he writes that his work on Romans "strove to avoid this pitfall by laying out alternative interpretive choices that any reader of Romans as Scripture has and also the benefits that each kind of interpretation has in particular contexts" (472). Patte further notes that he cannot and should not propose "the best" interpretation/reception of Romans (1:1-32). Rather,

> the best interpretation/receptions is necessarily contextual. And therefore, it is up to *you*, my patient reader, to make a choice for *your own context*—carefully acknowledging that those interpretations/receptions of Romans, which are the most familiar to you, might not be "the best" in a new situation ... we have the freedom to interpret and appropriate the multiple meanings of the biblical texts. This is a much-needed freedom, as our contextual situations are constantly changing. (472–3; emphasis original)

In this sense, Patte's scriptural criticism aligns with Mill in advancing a type of utilitarian ethical paradigm for biblical interpretation. There is no universal positivistic interpretation of a given text. There is no absolute interpretation that warrants interpretive authority at all times, under all circumstances. The authoritative interpretation—the "best interpretation"—is dependent not on the most familiar interpretation or on the interpretation of the majority. Instead, it is the interpretation that addresses "contextual issues, problems, joys, tragedies that believers encounter in their life in a particular contextual situation" (473). The "best interpretation" is the one that maximizes the overall "happiness" (best state of affairs) of those impacted in their lives in concrete socioeconomic, religious, and cultural contexts. Biblical interpretation, as outlined by Patte's scriptural criticism, is ultimately an exercise of one's individual freedom, which he calls "ethical responsibility." He writes:

> Being ethically responsible involves participating with other interpreters in the constant to-and-fro from one interpretation to another ... Being ethically responsible involves using one of these interpretations (helpful in a particular context), while cooperating with other interpreters who use other interpretations according to the demands of other contexts. (474)

Biblical interpretation as an exercise in freedom means a reader is free to consciously identify the realities of her existence, acknowledge the areas that are life-giving and/or life-diminishing, bring those determinations to a conversation with the biblical text (and with other interpreters) so as to discern an appropriate behavior and/or mindset that reflects, according to Patte, a love of God and a love of neighbor. However, and most importantly, we are only able to experience such freedom when we refute, as Mill reminds us, the *absolutization* of our own certainty.

Chapter 6

CAN WE LIVE WITH ROMANS AFTER AUSCHWITZ?

Gary A. Phillips

The need to let suffering speak is a condition of all truth.

—Adorno (1992: 17–18)

[My art] protects the sensitive scar of an ancient wound while still remaining true to [the] knowledge of the wound itself.

—Bak (interviewed by and qtd in Raskin 2004: 154)

The Reader's Challenge

Daniel Patte's commentary (2018) on the Letter to the Romans makes an important contribution to the critical and ethical engagement with a biblical text whose interpretations have been a source of life and hope for so many and of suffering and death for very many others; it is a timely challenge to the scourge of biblical interpretive violence linked to this influential Pauline letter. At the same time, his commentary shows the need for an analysis of the connections between violence and history, biblical interpretation and culture, and Holocaust art and suffering that his hermeneutical approach does not adequately provide; ironically, hermeneutical readings like his contribute to the damage Patte seeks to end. Still, if the measure of a biblical criticism that matters is its capacity to challenge readers to think and to act as if another person's life or death depended upon their interpretations, by this standard Daniel Patte's commentary matters a great deal.

Patte's discussion of Romans' reception history and the three exegetical readings of the first chapter of Romans that he showcases fills most of the commentary's 531 pages, and it testifies to the scope of the impact of Romans, for better and for worse, across ages and cultures. I leave discussion of those materials to others for comment. Instead, his brief "Note on Cover Artwork" (xii), "Foreword" (xv–xxv), "Introduction" (1–9), and opening chapter, "The Reception of Romans Through History and Cultures: A Challenge for Exegesis, Theology, and Ethics" (13–45) are the primary focus of my response. In these pages Patte is highly self-reflective about the central concerns and concepts that shape his commentary: Romans' damaging interpretive effects, especially anti-Jewish supercessionist readings; the conflict between and about plausible and legitimate interpretations; the importance of the Shoah and the artwork of Holocaust survivor Samuel Bak; the critical and ethical urgency of a proposed hermeneutic of "cause no harm to others"; the utopian hope of liberating Romans and its readers from violent and suffering history, to name key ones. These pages lay out the gist of Patte's view of biblical interpretive violence, its causes, and the critical and ethical remedy to the suffering and violence as he sees it.

In a nutshell, Patte views the plague of biblical interpretive violence at root to be a hermeneutical problem demanding a change of discourse and guiding ethical questions that lead to the liberation of Romans, its readers, and history of reception. Throughout history Romans has been read in ways that have resulted in "death, exclusion, and destruction," including, especially, to justify the Holocaust (Patte 2018: 9). Reading Romans is literally a matter of life and death: interpreters make life and death ethical decisions for themselves and others when they read, and must bear responsibility for the consequences of their interpretations. Patte pinpoints the central cause of interpretive violence as "exclusive" readings. Exclusive readings and their readers cause suffering and injustice to "others" because they are committed to "One and Only" true reading (68). Exclusive readings of Romans—not the biblical text itself Patte insists—are responsible for inflicting "catastrophe upon catastrophe" on others. Ironically, exclusive readers are self-damaging, imprisoned themselves by the violence and "self-inflicted brokenness" of their own dehumanizing and harmful interpretations. Patte's remedy is a hermeneutic of "cause no harm to others."

It makes possible a pedagogy of *reading with* as opposed to *reading for* others (39) that affirms all plausible and legitimate readings of Romans, categories readers familiar with Patte's writings will recognize. To employ a medicinal metaphor, a hermeneutics of "cause no harm to others" works as a critical and ethical pharmakon to counteract poisonous, exclusive readings of Romans. Inclusive readings are curative: they heal biblical text, its readers, and history. To reject others' readings on the basis of a "One and Only" true reading is absolutist, dangerous, and damaging. The way to liberate Romans, its readers, and its history of interpretation from this plague of violence then amounts to changing the discourse and forefronting ethical questions (xxv). Patte's utopian solution is predicated upon rational decision making and deontological ethical choice: when readers opt for a discourse that questions who is harmed and who is helped by their interpretations, a liberative, nonviolent interpretation presumably follows.

The contrasting view I argue is that the problem of biblical interpretive violence and suffering is culturally more far-reaching and structurally pernicious than Patte's hermeneutical remedy can explain or repair. Hermeneutical thinking that begins by privileging a certain discourse and ethical questions proves insufficient for critically addressing and ethically redressing the material realities that structure and sustain biblically inspired cultural violence today; ironically, a hermeneutics of "cause no harm to others" exacerbates the interpretive violence. Paradoxically,

Patte's cure is equally deadly. As Derrida (1981) reminds us, the pharmakon is both remedy and poison.

After Auschwitz ours is an age of ongoing atrocity, a barbaric cultural time that implicates all aspects of modern thinking and living from the metaphysics that undergirds our concepts of truth and self, to the aesthetics that shape our appreciation of style and beauty, to the ethics that enliven our values and actions. The experience of a disastrous twentieth century—national socialism, Stalinism, Viet Nam, normative mass murder, the nuclear threat, and now the ecological devastation sweeping the globe—suggests that "the prospect for catastrophe has become truly total" (Adorno 2005b: 268). Much more than "One and Only" true reading is required to explain interpretive violence; the material fabric of genocidal culture grounds the problem and that demands an alternative critical, ethical, and aesthetic analysis. In the shadow of the Shoah, readers face the daunting, if not impossible, challenge, in Theodor Adorno's words, of "arranging their thoughts and actions so that Auschwitz will not repeat itself, so that nothing similar will happen" (1992: 365). Nothing short of a tectonic transformation of barbaric modern culture and the wholesale ways we are given to think and act (including interpret biblical texts) is required to alleviate the suffering of others. Given the ubiquity of genocide and other forms of systemic violence that condition life today, liberation from violence and suffering is not a present option; and yet, paradoxically, we are obliged to seek a way to end the barbarity, as artist Samuel Bak imagines, to effect a *tikkun olam*, the rabbinic ethical obligation to heal the world.

The aesthetic philosophy of Theodor Adorno and surrealist artwork of Samuel Bak offer resources that show what a cultural transformation of this magnitude entails.[1] Their efforts challenge readers to be burdened by the weight of concrete suffering and to think in contradictions without becoming ethically immobilized and politically discouraged. Both insist upon coming to terms with the aporetic and traumatic character of post-Holocaust life, the futility of consoling narratives of liberation, and the unremitting ethical demand to keep the concrete and particular suffering of individual victims immediately before our eyes: theirs is a "skeptically utopic"[2] critical, ethical, and aesthetic response to barbaric culture. For readers of Romans, the foremost critical and ethical responsibility must be first to the many silent and faceless victims of biblically inspired violence, not to the liberatory status of a revered biblical text and its damaging interpreters and interpretations. The reader's challenge at this barbarous time is to sustain ways to hear the suffering of particular voices and see their concrete faces, a tall order given the interpretive penchant for abstraction and conceptualization. The

---

1. With few exceptions Adorno and critical theory have been ignored by biblical critics although see the works of Roland Boers (2009) and John Rogers (2000). The journal *Bible and Critical Theory* explores the intersection of critical theory and biblical studies.

2. I use this expression to signal the contradiction for both Adorno and Bak of a this-worldly future reconciliation and justice that is not negated by present-day, material suffering.

necessary first step in rearranging thoughts and actions so that Auschwitz will not be repeated is to confront the material suffering linked to Romans.

The Shoah's Challenge

Striking from the outset is the attention Patte gives to the Holocaust and its significance for interpreting Romans today. He situates his commentary, our reading of Romans, and the text's reception history squarely in the shadow of the Shoah: after Auschwitz, we read Romans in the wake of the incomprehensible suffering and unspeakable violence of the Nazi death camps.[3] Patte asks his readers to face the sobering fact that Romans and its supercessionist interpreters are implicated in a long history of anti-Jewish violence and suffering that culminated in the murder of six million Jews, including a million and a half children, and the near total destruction of European Jewish culture. But this pivotal Christian text's damaging impact is hardly limited to Jewish suffering; Romans is shamefully tied to the suffering of "women, gays and lesbians, less educated, barbarians" and those who fall into the category Patte describes as "other" (2018: xii). Patte laments the difficult truth that a biblical text meant for Christians to live and hope by is also a text that Jews and others suffer and die from. This leads him to conclude that readers have an interpretive and ethical duty—we might think of it as the hermeneutical equivalent of the Hippocratic Oath—to read Romans henceforth in ways that cause no harm to others. Invoking the Apostle Paul's words, Patte "hopes against hope" that a hermeneutic of "cause no harm to others" will liberate letter, reader, and reception history from its barbaric past and, presumably, still damaging present.

To conjure an image from another commentator, Patte asks us to hold up Romans in one hand and the reality of Jewish genocide in the other.[4] Instead of the newspaper that Karl Barth implored, Patte lifts up a painting by Holocaust child survivor Samuel Bak to place in tension with Romans and his own commentary (see Figure 6.1). A child art prodigy, Bak was one of only two hundred Jews to survive the liquidation of the Vilna ghetto's eighty thousand inhabitants that included his father and grandparents. His stunning, surrealist artwork bears powerful testimony to his experience of barbaric suffering and loss and the need for a critical, aesthetic, and ethical response to the Shoah that acknowledges the truth of personal and cultural disaster and seeks to end the violence. By strategically positioning Bak's

---

3. "After Auschwitz" is a phrase closely associated with Theodor Adorno's statement, "To write poetry after Auschwitz is barbaric" (1981: 34). On the dispute over its meaning and Adorno's revision of the statement, see Steiner (1967) and Nosthoff (2014).

4. Attributed to Karl Barth is the saying "*We must hold the Bible in one hand and the newspaper in the other*," but the original quote may have been "Take your Bible and take your newspaper, and read both. But interpret newspapers from your Bible" ("Barth in Retirement"; emphasis added).

Escape/Flucht (1983, hereafter *Escape*) on his book cover, Patte witnesses to Holocaust suffering and asks his readers to do the same (see Figure 6.1).

Escape features a lone and forlorn bird whose tattered and tallit-drawn body is nested in a tree branch, its wings in pieces and impaled with wood. Flight seems an impossibility, inviting viewers to contemplate the irony of Bak's title. In his opening note, Patte explains that this painting "illustrates the overall vision that guided the writing" of this commentary (2018: xii). For Patte, *Escape* visually represents the world's deep brokenness and a hoped-for liberation from its violence and suffering. By extension, Bak's painting serves as a visual metaphor for the violence and suffering that has imprisoned Romans, its readers, and its reception history, and the possibility of their hoped-for deliverance. This consoling comparison sustains Patte's hope that one day Romans, too, "might still 'escape,' still flying with damaged wings, still being inspiring, still faithfully wrapped in the remains of its Jewish prayer shawl" (xii). Given Romans' damaging history, in particular its link to the catastrophic destruction of European Jews, the picture of this Christian text "wrapped in the remains of its Jewish prayer shawl" that doubles as death-camp clothing creates an irony impossible to ignore. Patte is acutely aware of the connection of Romans to the Shoah, but what about future destruction? What confidence can we place in a changed discourse and set of ethical questions that Patte prescribes as a cure for the harm of Romans to others, especially Jews, after Auschwitz? And to what and to whom will this text be "faithful"? To Christians who seek to live well by it? To Jews and others who suffer horribly from it? To a violent modern culture and interpretive tradition that finds novel ways to damage others with it? Patte's conditional wording ("might still escape") hints at an ambivalence about what that future might bring. After all, why would "hope against hope" be needed if the path to liberation of Romans and its readers is assured by a hermeneutic of cause no harm and secured by a different discourse and ethical questions? Patte may harbor doubt and, given Romans' interpretive history, so should we.

Skepticism is an appropriate response to this barbarous text and Patte's proposal. Doubt fosters a different take on Romans' barbaric history and Bak's vision in *Escape*, one that acknowledges the impossibility of escape from history and of utopian liberation from suffering. This perspective recognizes the brutally violent, genocide-ridden twentieth and twenty-first centuries and a warranted critical and ethical suspicion about liberatory narratives of material and moral progress, consoling readings of biblical texts and comforting theological applications of Holocaust victims' art. As I explain in greater detail below, Bak's artwork voices a skeptical perspective though the use of visual irony, paradox, and contradiction—but hardly consolation—to reflect and reflect upon the conundrum of a skeptical utopic, post-Holocaust life that affords past victims no prospect of escape from suffering.

As Larry Langer (1991) has shown from his analysis of Holocaust testimonies, past suffering maintains an ongoing presence in the deep memory of Shoah victims that resists all efforts to control or erase it. The suffering associated with deep memory persists long after the trauma is first experienced, which explains why past victims depend on a lexicon of "disruption, absence, and irreversible loss" (xi) to tell the truth of their ongoing Shoah experiences. When hearing or seeing Holocaust testimonies, we must resist the impulse to impose "bracing pieties" (2) of liberation, redemption, or salvation that rely upon discourse that favors chronology, conjunction, and coherence (xi). We must also resist equating survival *after* Auschwitz with escape *from* Holocaust suffering and violence. For "former victims, the Holocaust is a communal wound that cannot heal" (204).[5] Bak affirms this when he says his art safeguards the painful scar of past suffering so that it can remain true to the knowledge of that suffering in the present. Far from fleeing suffering history, as Patte envisions Bak to be saying, his artwork preserves memory of the trauma and pictures the impossibility of escape from it. Like the dour bird he beautifully paints, Bak is arrested and pierced by suffering injustice, incapable of flying away from it.

Patte's comparison of Bak's *Escape* with Romans' escape is fraught for several reasons. First, Patte's brief description of the canvas does not address the formal contradictions and ruptures, ironies and incoherencies—the syntax and semantics of deep memory—of the composition itself. This contrasts with the detailed grammatical and syntactic attention Patte gives to the Romans text and its interpretations. The particularities of this painting and Bak's experience are generalized in ways that hold Bak's actual suffering experience at a distance from Patte and his commentary readers. Patte's eyes and ears are attuned to a syntax of consolation, chronology, and coherence—a reading *with others* (2018: 39)—that grounds interpretive truth in a salvific narrative and Enlightenment discourse of liberation at the expense of the suffering truth Bak labors to paint. Bak's vision for his painting and Patte's vision for his commentary are fundamentally incommensurate notwithstanding Patte's claim to the contrary (xii).

More concerning still is the comparison Patte establishes between a particular Jewish child's suffering at the hands of Nazis and their murderous collaborators and an innocent biblical text imagined metaphorically to suffer from harmful readings imposed upon it (9). Anthropomorphizing Romans this way varnishes the horror of Bak's suffering experience through abstraction. Just how does one conceptualize, much less compare, the sufferings of a child/adult past victim? What ideas and words can possibly suffice to communicate the reality of genocide? More specifically, what can anyone know from their own experience about the sufferings of Bak as a child, or the million and a half children murdered by the Nazis? Not only must we resist attempts to abstract and compare sufferings, but we must oppose efforts to enlist Holocaust art and past victims' discourse about their suffering in service to consoling interpretive ends.[6] When those ends are Christian and theological, the effort to construe a past victim's suffering as meaningful only exacerbates the violence by making suffering hermeneutically useful. As

---

5. Langer (1991: xi) prefers the terminology "former victim" to "survivor" because the latter is too often burdened with the presumption that suffering is a thing of the past.

6. See especially Langer (2006: 48–63).

Emmanuel Levinas (1982) argues, suffering is useless and meaningless. Adorno characterizes all such writing and interpretation as barbaric.

These cautions about Patte's reading and use of Bak's art give pause; however, they do not lessen the importance of Patte's effort in the commentary and throughout a long teaching and writing career to remember the Holocaust and to contest supercessionist interpretive violence. That Patte's hermeneutical effort is arguably barbarous and damaging only confirms the impossibility of extracting biblical critic and commentary from a post-Shoah damaged and violent culture that tarnishes everything: choice of discourse and ethical questions cannot extricate and restore text or reader from this world of suffering violence. It is a contradictory reality that is not resolvable or comforting. Still, Patte's Shoah focus sets him apart from many New Testament exegetes for whom the constellation of Holocaust, anti-Semitism, violence, and the ethics of interpretation continue at best to be subordinate concerns.[7] Whatever the methodological, theological, and ethical reasons for this, and they are complex, we must take seriously Patte's pronouncement that we read Romans in the shadow of the Shoah as well as the damaging complications of his hermeneutical approach. His commentary amounts to a critical and ethical challenge to readers to interrogate the cultural factors that make possible not just his but our own harmful readings of Romans today, theologically well-intentioned and methodologically sophisticated though they may be. Patte himself gestures in this direction with his discussion of the post-2016 Trump election distortions of language, fabrication of facts, indifference to truth, and denial of reality. He even asks if this is a "return to barbarism" (2018: xx). But such analysis requires altogether different resources to identify nonconsoling, skeptically utopic ways to pierce the methodological, interpretive, and ethical categories that shield readers from the real faces and voices of actual suffering and the truth they speak about their suffering experience and our contributions to it.

The Challenge of the Caged Children

Reading in the shadow of the Shoah today means critically understanding the historical connections between and the contradictions of deeply ingrained cultural anti-Semitism in nineteenth- and twentieth-century German society, the dominating power of philosophical idealism and romantic aesthetics, the liberatory ideals of Enlightenment thought, and the vaunted German biblical and theological commitment to Nazi genocidal goals.[8] Past Jewish suffering and anti-Semitic violence were socially conditioned, biblically grounded, and

---

7. Linafelt (2000, 2002) and Kelley (2002, 2015) are two notable exceptions. It remains to be seen whether the emergence of the Black Lives Matter movement will affect theological and biblical awareness of systemic violence.

8. For discussion of German cultural anti-Semitism, see Baranowski (1996: 527–9) and Bergen (1996). On anti-Semitic biblical scholarship, see Casey (1999: 282–5).

philosophically justified. The violence was facilitated by the most respected universities, scholarly and religious organizations, and educated Christian biblical scholars and theologians, many of them avid Nazis, who actively promoted Jewish suffering and violence. The names Kittel, Kuhn, Althaus, Dibelius, and Hirsch, among others, stand out as a sobering reminder that critically faithful readers of the Bible were catastrophically fateful for Jews and others. And so interpreters of Romans today must ask: Given this past constellation, what is the fabric of present-day American society, and does a culture of biblical violence exist, now more than seventy-five years after the death camps were first liberated, that enables interpretive and physical violence aimed at Jews and others? Importantly, in what ways does contemporary biblical scholarship exacerbate the violence and suffering of others?

Consider the appalling images of caged immigrant children incarcerated by Trump administration officials at the Ursula Immigrant Processing Center in McAllen, Texas; the biblical justifications offered in support of their maltreatment; and the critical responses of biblical scholars to the children's suffering. Many of these children were barely toddlers. They were forcibly separated from their families and confined in unsanitary holding pens largely deprived of health, legal, and educational care. These actions were strongly defended by Attorney General Jeff Sessions in June 2018 by direct appeal to Romans: "I would cite you the Apostle Paul and his clear and wise command in Romans 13, to obey the laws of the government because God has ordained them for the purpose of order" (Mullen 2018).[9] In defense of Trump's nativist immigration policy that ripped apart families, the White House press secretary opined, "It is very biblical to enforce the law" (Mullen 2018). Session's Orwellian explanation that the incarceration of toddlers actually "protects the weak" rhetorically transformed the reality of suffering children and state violence into an act of divinely sanctioned protection. The children's suffering was ideological and theological abstracted.

Unfortunately, this is not an isolated instance of culturally conditioned and biblically approved violence directed against Jews and others in the United States today. The Anti-defamation League has documented a record rise in the number of anti-Semitic and immigrant-directed hate crimes—some involving mass murder, and many claiming biblical inspiration—since the 2016 presidential election (Anti-Defamation League 2020).[10] The frequency and intensity of discursive and physical violence has increased owing in part to Trump's repeated stoking of racial, ethnic, and religious fears, hostilities, and grievances, with the Bible playing both

---

9. Amnesty International estimates the Trump administration has removed as many as six thousand children from family units, far more than is publicly acknowledged, and continues to incarcerate children despite a 2017 court injunction halting its rupture and incarceration actions. See Bochenek (2018).

10. Applying the FBI definition of mass murder (three or more persons killed excluding the perpetrator/s in one event), the United States experienced seventeen mass murders in 2019.

a confirming and a catalyzing role. His June 2020 Bible photo-op at St. John's Episcopal Church in Washington, DC, is a case in point. Trump's brandishing of the Bible on one hand and the use of state violence directed at peaceful, law-abiding citizens protesting the police killing of George Floyd and systemic racism on the other reflect a dynamic and deadly connection between scripture, political ideology, and state-sponsored violence. We live at a time, Patte acknowledges, marked by ideological and political warfare and the subversion of facts and truth whose effect is to enflame violence against others, and the Bible spurs that on. But a hermeneutic of "cause no harm to others" does not expose the constellation of social factors that effectively weaponize Rom 13 to justify the teargassing of peaceful demonstrators and incarceration of defenseless children. To argue that the remedy for this complex social problem is a discourse that raises ethical questions is ultimately reductive, obscures the actual suffering, and arguably contributes to the violence.

To understand why a changed discourse and ethical questions is critically and ethically insufficient, consider the example of influential Nazi New Testament scholar K. G. Kuhn. Philosophically trained and admired for his historical acumen, Kuhn was steeped in humanistic values and Enlightenment principles that privileged ideals of liberty, community, and self. Along with other anti-Semites, notably Gerhard Kittel,[11] Kuhn was consumed by a driving ethical question, namely the "Jewish question" (*Die Judenfrage*). Biblical anti-Semites like Kuhn critically read their scriptures in order to redress the damage they believed Jews and Judaism inflicted on world culture, especially the racial and religious purity of the German Volk: Jews were a biological and spiritual menace to the nation's cultural health and well-being. German idealism and romantic aesthetics offered critical and aesthetic categories for constructing Jews as an historical and theological danger that legitimated a violent remedy. Their thoroughly reasoned pursuit of the Jewish Question helped pave the way to Auschwitz and the murder of children deemed a peril to all German life.

The barbarism of German biblical criticism did not end with the liberation of Auschwitz. Kuhn's anti-Semitic scholarship has continued to influence biblical scholarship and theological reflection reliant upon his historical construction of Jewish identity and Jewish self-hatred (Casey 1999: 284–5). His anti-Semitic ideas were preserved in the much-revered Kittel-edited *Theological Dictionary of the New Testament* (*TDNT*), a text Patte references, archived in leading theological research and seminary libraries across the world, and now available digitally to a worldwide reading audience deaf to Kittel's Nazi distortions. Scholarly and pedagogical dependence upon his discredited ideas, along with other anti-Semitic entries in the *TDNT*, has largely gone uncontested: Nazi discourse and questions

---

11. Concerning Kittel, William Albright wrote, "In view of the terrible viciousness of his attacks on Judaism and the Jews, which continues at least until 1943, Gerhard Kittel must bear the guilt of having contributed more, perhaps, than any other Christian theologian to the mass murder of Jews by Nazis" (1947: 165).

continue to percolate in subtle ways through the critical literature and culture largely unchallenged. The central point here is that Nazis, too, reasoned and raised ethical questions about who should live and who should die when they read biblical texts. Their racialized discourse grounded in idealist philosophical and romantic aesthetic assumptions protected Aryan children by incarcerating and eliminating Jewish children categorized as nonhuman "others." Along with the rise of overt neo-Nazi political ideology and violence in American society today, Nazi scholarly discourse and questions morph their way through post-Holocaust biblical scholarship and teaching, furthering the barbarism of culture.

Why has the Romans-justified incarceration of innocents not prompted a great critical outcry from biblical scholars and theologians to the suffering of children? Why have the Charleston Church mass shooting of nine African Americans, and the Pittsburgh Tree of Life and California Chabad of Poway synagogue mass murders not energized biblical scholars to marshal the critical resources required to confront culturally enabled, biblically inspired, and politically enacted anti-Semitic and racist violence in the way George Floyd's murder has motivated Black Lives Matter advocates to take on policing practices and forms of systemic racism?

The paltry response of American biblical scholars and their religious and scholarly organizations to the Trump administration's deployment of the Bible to justify and incur violence shows how the barbarity continues after Auschwitz in a different way.[12] Except for a meager handful of opinion essays and letters to editors, scholars and their professional societies have remained largely silent in the face of the caged children[13]; the initial interest in speaking out after Sessions's public comments has all but dissipated with internet images of incarcerated children replaced by pictures of violent street protests in Portland, Louisville, and other places. Those scholars who first responded to the children framed the issue as a problem of interpretation: Sessions misread Paul's argument; he failed to comprehend the letter form and its historical context; he showed little grasp of Rom 13's complex, interpretive history; and so forth. Interpretive method, not the suffering of innocent children, was the critical and ethical focus. Responsibility to the text and an aesthetic of historical reading method dominated; the children's suffering was subordinated to the right discourse and questions. Notably lacking was any sort of cultural analysis that attempted to account for the constellation of historical and structural links between Sessions's reading of Romans, philosophical idealism, romantic aesthetics, anti-Semitism, social media, and nativist ideology responsible for the barbarism of the Ursula Detention Center. A text-centric, idealist hermeneutics concerned with the correct discourse or method minimized the need to theorize the conditions and effects of public biblical criticism. As a result, the ties between the reality of the children's suffering, state violence, and the

---

12. The American Academy of Religion's recent support for a scholars' strike to promote racial justice is an isolated counter example. See "AAR Calls on Institutions to Support Faculty in #ScholarStrike."

13. Two examples are Aymer and Nasrallah (2018), and Scott (2018).

violent use of biblical texts as ideological weapons and Rom 13 were diminished or, worse, severed from the hermeneutical consideration.

What explains this disconnect? In his discussion of the origins of modern biblical hermeneutics and its limits in responding to genocidal violence, Shawn Kelley (2015) argues that a critical engagement with political violence in the form of fascism, genocide, and Enlightenment instrumental rationality was pivotal in shaping the twentieth-century hermeneutical project and its critique of modernity. In his words, the "philosophical and the political side of the hermeneutical project [were] deeply intertwined, which is why hermeneutical theory can claim to identify the conditions that make textual interpretation possible and, in the same step, free us from the ill effects of modernity" (8). While postwar biblical scholarship embraced the hermeneutical project's interest in textual interpretation and liberation from historical ignorance, the links to political violence and larger cultural realities were largely ignored. This depoliticization, reinforced by an idealist preoccupation with "proper categories" for reasoning and a romantic aesthetics that subjectivized truth and the reading experience, succeeded in distancing biblical criticism from material political, racial, economic, ideological, and other sociocultural forms of violence. This move had the cumulative effect of rendering suffering "an abstraction rather than identifying its facticity" (8). As it concerns the Holocaust and other forms of genocidal violence, Kelley concludes that hermeneutical theory shorn of its originating political response to violence effectively "diverts our attention away from the Holocaust itself without creating a dialogue with the Holocaust's reality" (9).[14] In other words, the *idea* of the Holocaust and suffering supersedes the *fact* of unfathomable suffering. The particularity and concreteness of incomprehensible suffering and unspeakable violence that Shoah victims attest recedes from view and is replaced by concern for discourse, ideals of validity and truth, and correct interpretive categories. Viewed through this lens, Patte's hermeneutical preoccupation—with categories of interpretive plausibility, validity, and legitimacy; with a pedagogy of "reading with"; with the liberation of Romans, its readers, and its reception history—inevitably diverts attention away from the facticity of Jewish suffering. The barbarous treatment of caged immigrant children cannot compete with the interpretive harm done to the biblical text, its readers, and history of reception notwithstanding Patte's deeply held, other-motivated concern to end biblical interpretive violence.

This leaves us with a thicket of questions and concerns: What if escape from barbaric history is not an option not only for past victims of Shoah violence such as Bak, but also for interpreters of Romans such as Patte committed to ending violent interpretations of Romans? What if all critical discourse, all hermeneutical readings including Patte's hermeneutics of cause no harm, are barbarous and implicated in this age of atrocity? If so, how is it possible in the shadow of the

---

14. Kelley does make room for a hermeneutical approach to genocide if it is complemented by sociocultural analysis that seeks to explain the connections among racial, economic, and ideological factors.

Shoah for criticism of Romans ever to avoid exacerbating the suffering of others through its interpretive strategies, discourse, and questions? In Adorno's terms, how can we make the unspeakable suffering and incomprehensible violence of the Shoah determinative of critical thought and ethical action so that Auschwitz is never repeated?

This last question orients the balance of my response where I explore Adorno's philosophical aesthetics and Bak's artwork in more detail. Adorno's historical and aesthetic analysis exposes the aporetic condition of living responsibly in a deeply barbarous world after Auschwitz. Ours is an historical time after Hiroshima, after Viet Nam, after genocides in Bosnia and the Sudan, after mass shootings in Orlando and Sandy Hook Elementary School, after the caging of immigrant children in McAllen, Texas. In the face of this suffering history Adorno identifies the role that certain art—in particular nonconsoling modern art—can play in negatively showing the truth of suffering as a condition for exposing and ending the violence.

I turn next to Samuel Bak's aporetic artistic style as an instance of nonconsoling art and the way his visual syntax of aporia, paradox, and irony enables him to voice the truth of his suffering experience: simply put, Bak's art shows what Adorno describes. I follow with an aporetic reading of *Escape* that searches out the contradictions at work in his composition in contrast to Patte's hermeneutical reading. I argue that the particularity of Bak's suffering and the paradoxical and aporetic experience of *escape/nonescape* after Auschwitz is pivotal for understanding not only his life but ours as well, and this becomes a central fact of damaged life lived today in the shadow of the Shoah. I hold up Bak's suffering *voice* in dialectical tension to Patte's consoling hermeneutical *vision* of liberation from destructive history to underscore the insufficiency of a utopian liberatory remedy to suffering that privileges categories and concepts of inclusion, legitimacy, and plausibility over the concrete, material expressions of violence.

This brings me to the obvious final question: Can we live with Romans after Auschwitz? Dare we? My answer is a tenuous "maybe." I argue that Patte's answer is also tenuous, more wavering than his confident assertions admit. His repetition of Charles Simic's "*La vie est plus belle que les ideés*" complicates his rationalist ideals and deontological ethics leaving his confident, utopian hermeneutical answer asking. His engagement with Simic and Bak exposes a tension, an aporia, in his thinking that the idea of changed discourse and ethical questions supersedes the violent reality. Ironically, despite his impressive hermeneutical effort Patte shows the truth of Bak's and Adorno's tenuous, skeptical utopic position, namely that in the shadow of the Shoah all interpretations of Romans must be burdened by the weight of the empirical and thought in contradictions with no certainty of success and no escape from the trying.

Adorno and the Challenge of Barbaric History

For aesthetic philosopher, noted musicologist, and public intellectual Theodor Adorno, Auschwitz has altered everything: philosophy, theology, aesthetics, ethics, culture, individual life—nothing will ever be the same after Auschwitz. In incomparable ways Auschwitz the event has revealed the barbarity of modern existence and our inadequacies in grasping its causes and remedies; Auschwitz the aesthetic shapes the way culture employs violence at all costs to control and to eliminate life (Kemp 2020). Adorno dedicated himself to the task of diagnosing the roots of barbarous history, the cultural conditions that make suffering pervasive, and the importance of art in telling this truth. The son of a Christian mother and Jewish father, Adorno fled Nazi Germany in 1934 in the exodus of Jewish academics following Hitler's appointment as chancellor and the growing Nazification of German society. After pursuing a degree at Oxford, Adorno immigrated to New York and soon thereafter joined members of the Frankfurt Critical Theory group at Princeton. In 1941 he moved to California with Max Horkheimer, his coauthor on several, significant research projects that applied Marxist critique most famously to Enlightenment rationality and the American culture industry. Following the war Adorno returned to Frankfurt where he took up a long and influential teaching and writing career as an important public intellectual intent upon educating postwar German citizenry about the barbarism of history and the horrors of the Holocaust and fascism. He suffered a fatal heart attack in 1969 at the height of student protests over educational and political reform sweeping Europe at the time.

Adorno's view of barbaric history owes in large measure to his personal experience of anti-Semitism, exile, and escape from Nazi imprisonment, torture, and industrial death that has come to signify Auschwitz. Material reality anchors and orients his critique of modern Enlightenment thought. Indebted to the Hegelian and Marxist critique of idealism,[15] Adorno is an iconoclastic, antifoundational thinker who is deeply suspicious of the preference given to the whole or the concept at the expense of the particular or the material: the "preponderance of the object" (1992: 183) is Adorno's rejoinder to a Western intellectual tradition enthralled by totalities (hence the fatal attraction to fascism and authoritarianism instead of freedom) and the notion of the thinking subject independent of the material world. As a response to a philosophical tradition that privileges discourse and conceptual categories, Adorno anchors his ethical and aesthetic critique in the objective reality of suffering bodies. We live in catastrophic history, he argues, in which Western humanistic thought and values, despite all utopian hope for freedom, have failed to reduce human and animal suffering: "The whole thing is truly barbarous," Adorno concluded (2005a: 107). What has been realized instead is the unprecedented barbarism of industrialized murder sustained by instrumental reason that commodifies death and unfreedom; this unfreedom is perpetuated by today's culture industry. The incomprehensible suffering of the Nazi death camps exemplifies this wider barbaric history, at once its culmination and continuation. Because barbarism so pervasively conditions

---

15. Adorno nurtured a "negative dialectic" in contradistinction to Hegel's positive-oriented dialectic that resolved contradiction.

life in today's social world—"damaged life" or "wrong life" as he calls it—Adorno wonders if "one can live after Auschwitz" (2003: 435).

Adorno's answer to this question exposes the aporia in his thinking about escape from barbaric history and the nature of the critical, aesthetic, and ethical response to actual suffering: "A new categorical imperative has been imposed by Hitler on unfree mankind: to arrange their thoughts and actions so that Auschwitz will not repeat itself, so that nothing similar will happen" (1992: 365). The reality of Auschwitz demands a materialist inversion of the Kantian ethical imperative: a different critical and ethical response is needed if we are to find "our way out of barbarism" (2005b: 268) and to "restore an unbarbaric condition" (2005a: 50) Although rendering justice to Auschwitz's past victims is an impossibility, we are nonetheless obliged never to forget the suffering nature of "damaged life" and to seek an end to the barbarity that makes it possible. Quietism is not acceptable: we dare "not surrender to cynicism merely by existing after Auschwitz," Adorno insists (2004b: 252). But ideology or theology that offers utopian consolation is not an option either.

Because modern society is so effective in blinding us to suffering reality and in deafening us to the voices of those who suffer—to make suffering "mute and inconsequential" (Adorno 1997: 18)—Adorno finds it is left to art and art alone to show us the critical and ethical way forward into an unbarbaric future: "It is now virtually in art alone that suffering can still find its own voice, consolation, without immediately being betrayed by it. The most important artists of the age have realized this" (2004b: 252).[16] However, only certain forms of art enable the suffering voice to be heard on its own truthful terms, namely art that is "burdened by the weight of the empirical" (1997: 19) and "thinks in contradictions" (1992: 145); such negating art actively resists conceptualizations and consolations of suffering and injustice. Adorno singles out the surrealist paintings of Paul Klee, the atonal musical compositions of Arnold Schoenberg, the dramaturgy of Samuel Beckett, and the lacunae-rich poetry of Paul Celan as examples of artists and art that effectively employ contradiction to negatively image suffering. Contradiction and negation enable the expression of art's truth content because it both shows and does not show damaged life for what it is. But the conundrum facing ethically responsive art, even by Adorno's rigorous negative standard, is that in the process of enabling suffering to find its voice through aporetic strategies, art nonetheless renders suffering and injustice into meaningful, albeit negative, images.[17] Adorno acknowledges this aporia with the qualification that suffering is not *immediately* betrayed by such art: the betrayal of suffering is only deferred.

---

16. See Phillips (2017) for a fuller discussion of Adorno's aesthetics and its relationship to Bak's art.

17. Margaret Bourke-White's iconic photographs of the Buchenwald camp liberation are an example of a brutal images transformed into meaningful, aesthetic objects. Langer acknowledges art's central paradox: "art signals its limited success through ultimate failure" (1991: 81). Gibbs calls this the "Janus face of art" (2002: 31).

It is against this backdrop then that we should hear Adorno's much misunderstood statement "Writing poetry after Auschwitz is barbaric." Readers who have taken the statement to be a blanket prohibition of all art after Auschwitz fail to understand Adorno's historical and aesthetic point about the aporetic condition of modern life (Nosthoff 2014). The whole thing is truly barbarism; there is no utopian way out of the vicissitudes of history after the event and aesthetics of Auschwitz, including even ethically responsive art. And yet, paradoxically, after Auschwitz there is no escape either from the ethical obligation to make the world unbarbaric by enabling the voice of suffering injustice to be heard. Samuel Bak's paintings respond to this suffering reality; he is one of those artists who paints the aporetic nature of post-Shoah life and in whose artwork suffering injustice finds its distinctive voice.

Bak and the Challenge of Escape/Nonescape

Escape marks Bak's experience as a child Holocaust survivor and world-renowned artist.[18] Born into a secular Jewish professional family, Bak was an art prodigy whose first exhibition at age nine took place in the Vilna ghetto. With the exception of his mother, all of his immediate and extended family were murdered in the Ponary Woods, a Nazi experimental site for the Final Solution. Bak was miraculously spirited out of the HKP forced labor camp by his father days before his execution. After Soviet forces liberated Vilna in July 1944, Bak fled with his mother to Łódź, Poland, eventually arriving at the Landsberg Displaced Persons Camp near Munich, Germany, where they stayed for two years before immigrating to Israel. There he attended high school, received his first formal art training, and performed his compulsory national service. As an itinerant adult artist, Bak moved about to different European cities, developing his painting style and finding his voice. In 1984 Bak relocated outside of Boston where today, at age eighty-eight, he presently resides and actively paints ("Samuel Bak").

Across more than seven decades Bak has painted testimonies to his experience of personal and communal suffering and loss. His preoccupation with physical bodies and material worlds—frequently presented in fragmented and disfigured, impermanent and provisionally reconstructed forms like the bird in *Escape*—concentrates critical, aesthetic, and ethical attention upon the particularity of suffering and the corresponding obligation never to forget the injustice (Phillips 2017: 4–7). The beauty of his artwork stands in stark contrast to the barbarity of its subject matter; it is a pervasive contradiction that reflects and refracts deep memory of the ruptured worlds of his childhood and as an adult after Auschwitz. As Bak readily admits, he is unable to escape the contradictions that "dwell" within him (Bak 2019a).

---

18. See Bak (2002) for a fuller account of his life and artistic development.

Escape/Flucht, the image Patte uses on his commentary cover, has an itinerant history as well. It was first exhibited publicly in 1994 at the Joseph Gallery Hebrew Union College-Jewish Institute of Religion in a show entitled "Flight: Escape, Hope, Redemption." In 2006 Bak included the work in another exhibition, "Samuel Bak Life Thereafter. Leben danach," in Osnabrück, Germany, at the Felix-Nussbaum-Haus. We can reasonably infer from the title of both exhibitions that Bak links escape to both life and hope but, as we will see, in tensive, aporetic ways.[19] Bak (2019b) has used "Escape," or its variations, as a title for at least eight different works produced over a seven-decade period (in 1944, 1962, 1963, 1965, 1983, and 2010) in artistic styles ranging from abstract to realist to surrealist and executed variously in oil, charcoal, and pen on diverse media. Notably, he produced his first "Escape" at age ten or eleven around the time he and his mother fled Vilna for Łódź. Bak (2019a) strongly associates this first drawing with the paradoxical experience of his father saving his life only then to lose his own. The experienced juxtaposition of death and life, imprisonment and freedom, exile and home, escape and nonescape imprinted his early childhood experience and the tensions of these contradictions surface repeatedly in his choice of compositional content.

"Escape/nonescape" better names the ongoing experience that infuses Bak's artistic life as several of his titles intimate: *Ongoing Escape* (2017), *Escape Emerging* (1965), and *For Another Escape* (2017) are three examples. He revisits this aporetic trope, which serves as a metonym for a life shaped by continuing suffering and injustice. Bak (2019a) writes: "Although I consider myself as a non-believer, I believe in the instinct of life. A permanent readiness for escape, which nurtures our fantasies, imaginations, hopes, survival, etc.—is part of being human. And sometimes, when life is unbearable, it might inspire the escape from life itself. There is no way I could escape the contradictions that dwell in me." The permanent readiness for escape/nonescape has been a wellspring of artistic creativity that has enabled him to voice trauma. The visual aporia that mark his canvases reflect and refract this life/death contradiction; it is what enables him to protect "the sensitive scar of an ancient wound while still remaining true to [the] knowledge of the wound itself" (Raskin 2004: 154).

Bak's titles are consistently, and self-consciously, ironic. About "Escape" and other works he writes, "Having created several thousands of works that needed titles, inevitably, I repeated myself, again and again ... The titles I give come a long, long time after the creation of the artworks. I hope the beholders will pay attention to a presence of irony that offers a better perspective" (Bak 2019a). The ironic iteration of "Escape" in its various formulations as a title and trope signals Bak's inability to free himself from or get beyond his personal history as a child survivor and the continuing experience of escape/nonescape lived in the wake of personal and cultural disaster. Lawrence Langer, a perceptive commentator of Bak's art, offers the expression "death/life" as a way to capture the ongoing, aporetic experience of

---

19. Bak has painted a series entitled *Hope* (2014) and *Still Life* (2005) where the irony and contradictions play out visually and with the play on words.

past suffering lived in the present; Adorno speaks of it as "life that does not live" (2005a: 19) or "damaged life" (2005a). Viewed through a Freudian lens, we might see Bak's iteration of escape/nonescape as that fraught process of remembering, repeating, and continuously working through his ongoing suffering experiences of multiple exiles, displacements, and the trauma of family loss that continue to haunt but also, paradoxically, to heal. It is a suffering experience that demands a syntax of rupture and incoherence rather than that of coherence and continuity to convey. The working through on canvas after canvas, year after year, means that the task of addressing suffering remains a perpetually unfinished, unsettling business. In Freudian terms, Bak's artwork is an expression both of mourning and melancholia, a conscious and unconscious response to suffering loss that both resolves and fails to resolve the suffering (Fewell and Phillips 2008). With this tension in mind, let us turn to Bak's painting to see how visual aporia, paradox, and irony communicate the ongoing suffering experience of escape/nonescape in ways that meet Adorno's strenuous demand for truthful, nonconsoling art.

The Challenge of Escape/Nonescape

We spy a bird soaring high up in a cloud-dappled sky strangely nested in a tree branch as if cradled by a skeletal hand. Its wings are spread apart simulating full flight, or we might imagine in preparation for lift off. Both readings seem possible. The two wings are multiply pierced by the tree branch that extends from beyond the right edge of the image frame and outside our field of vision. The truncated picture contributes to the effect of the fragmented tree branch either free-floating, or anchored, or even carried away with the bird in flight. Again, each reading seems possible. Taken together, however, they contradict each other, a visual interpretive incoherence that invites us to consider the irony of Bak's title.

In the full painting, not the abbreviated detail that Patte uses on his book cover, we confront a larger incongruous picture. A close inspection reveals the bird's body to be a mélange, a patchwork, of ill-fitting cloth strips that spurs doubt about the integrity of the bird's form and the viability of flight and real escape. Any initial assumptions of pictorial realism are perturbed by a patched-together bird that looks more like a child's pieced-together balsa wood model than a living creature cable of flight. The creature is garbed in the familiar striped pattern of the Jewish prayer shawl, one of the two specific features Patte mentions; it is also the fabric of the death camp inmate's uniform. Jewish holiness and Nazi horror collide in a troubling tension. Bak's deep memory visualizes the irony of a Nazi compulsion to erase all things Jewish by employing a Jewish aesthetic to dress others not deigned to be human and who never should have existed in the first place. But the Nazi effort to erase all things Jewish, and then to erase the erasure of all from memory and history failed. It is ironic to think that the perpetrators' hope of forgetting Jews required that their victims be remembered precisely

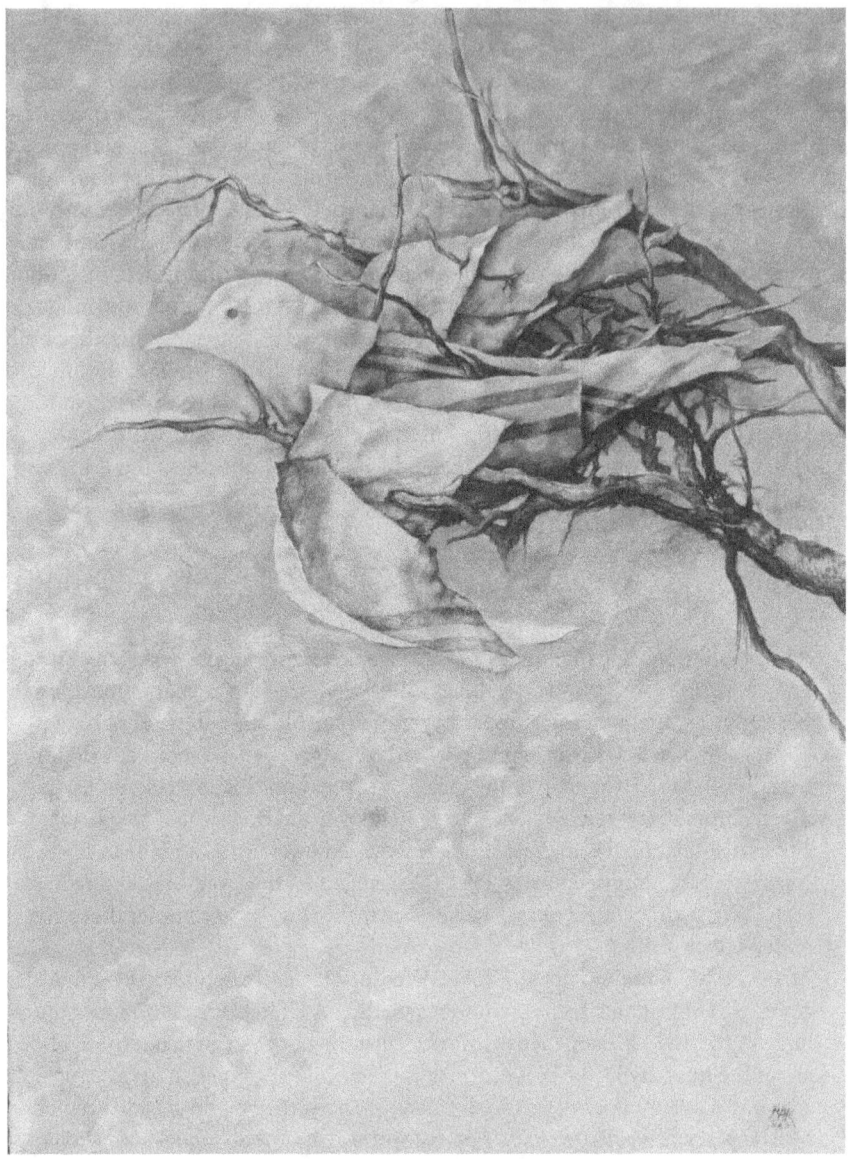

Figure 6.1 *Escape/Flucht*, 1983. Mixed media on paper, 30 × 20.5 in. Courtesy of Pucker Gallery (Bak 1983).

on Jewish terms. The murderers were imprisoned by their own pathology of forgetting and remembering, unable to escape it.

Compositionally, bird and tree dominate the upper half of Bak's image frame leaving an expanse of empty sky below, an important feature Patte's detail also omits. The scale of emptiness accentuates the solitariness of the bird and the contradictory predicament of bird in flight, bird nested, bird ensnared. This aporetic picture of escape/nonescape may defy reason, logic, and interpretation but not Bak's bodily and creative experience of death/life. If we take Bak at his word, his titles are meant ironically to provide a better perspective to the viewer. But what is the perspective if not incoherence? Better than what if not coherence? It is the vision of an ongoing experience of escape that is perpetually frustrated, deferred, and yet to arrive; it is also the perspective of a nonescape that remains constant. Bak shows us both. He shows us the negative: his failed escape and failed nonescape—an escape/nonescape—by way of perceptual, logical, and interpretative aporia. No image of escape can ever exhaust Bak's experience of suffering, and so he repeatedly and necessarily fails to paint it; and yet, remarkably, his artwork shows us this failure through the aporia that energizes his artwork and truth telling.[20]

My alternative aporetic reading of "Escape" contrasts with Patte's in important ways. Unlike Patte's choice of detail, the full image is vital to my reading and Bak's visual statement. Patte describes the painting as a "poignant figure illustrating Bak's personal experience as a Holocaust survivor" (2018: xii). But only damaged wings and tallit are mentioned leaving unmentioned other distinctive compositional elements, structure, and material features—the syntax and semantics of Bak's visual statement. There is no mention of the contradictions and ironies, and that levels out the timber and pitch of Bak's voice especially when Patte enlists and subordinates Bak's vision to the purposes of the commentary and his larger writing project. Whose voice, whose vision, whose experience, we may ask, does Patte hear and see? That of the Jewish nonbelieving survivor/artist for whom escape/nonescape from suffering is never possible, or that of the Christian believing biblical scholar for whom a biblical text's escape from the prison house of damaging biblical interpretations and the "vicissitudes of history" remain a utopian dream verging on a certainty? Patte gives us his answer when he says that "Escape" illustrates the overall vision that guided the writing of this book on Romans (xii); it is a coherent picture and plan that employs Bak's suffering art to make consoling interpretive sense of Romans and its sufferings. But Patte's confidence in Bak's ability to escape—"How does one escape this quagmire in a productive way? Indeed we need to and can 'escape'—see Samuel Bak's image on the cover" (xxv)—is not only in tension with Bak's compositional statement but also at odds with Patte's own hesitations over Romans' escape that he qualifies with "barely" and "might still" (xxv). Might this hesitation indicate an aporia in Patte's thinking that raises doubts about the critical and ethical viability of inclusive readings that do no harm?

Even though Bak shows and tells us he has escaped and not escaped the vicissitudes and violence of history, Patte confidently insists that readers can

---

20. In Judith Butler's terms, in the effort to give "critical image" and statement to his suffering, Bak's artwork "must not only fail to capture its referent but show its failure" (2004: 146).

escape once they elect a "type of [critical] discourse" that "focus[es] on ethical questions: Who is helped and who is hurt when one chooses one interpretation rather than another?" (xxv). Right discourse, right questions assure liberation grounded in a reasoned response to the catastrophe of damaging readings of Romans and the sufferings it has caused. Adorno, much like Levinas, sharply rebukes idealist philosophy for its confidence in discursive rationality and deontological ethics that effectively diminishes the facticity of bodily suffering: "Dealing discursively with [Auschwitz]," Adorno insists, "would be an outrage, for the new imperative gives us a bodily sensation of the moral addendum—bodily, because it is now the practical abhorrence of the unbearable physical agony to which individuals are exposed even with individuality about to vanish as a form of mental reflection. It is in the unvarnished materialistic motive only that morality survives" (1992: 365). The horror of bodily agony, not outrageous reasoned discourse, motivates the critical and ethical response.[21]

We can extend Adorno's rebuke to idealist biblical criticism preoccupied with methodology and discourse. The sheer facticity of another's suffering should instigate critical reading before discourse about concepts of good and evil, right and true, legitimate and plausible interpretations that Patte appeals to as a way to categorize reality and reason our way to an ethical response. Adorno rejects all such interpretive efforts—philosophical, theological, and hermeneutical—that attempt to make suffering meaningful. He describes it as "squeezing any kind of sense, however bleached, out of the victims' fate" (Adorno 1992: 361). Biblical interpretation that squeezes sense from past victims "removes us from things as they are" (364).

Whether or not he would accept Adorno's view of barbaric history, the negative functioning of art, or the aporia of thinking, Patte is clearly sympathetic to the vastness of today's suffering and the catastrophic role biblical texts play in that suffering. After Auschwitz, in the United States in 2022, we have witnessed the detention of immigrant ("other") children in euphemistically labeled "summer camps"; the forcible removal of nursing infants from their mothers' breasts; ICE raids that have left children abandoned and compelled to suffer the loss of family members who are made to "disappear"; the forced, unaccompanied transport of small children across the country; the concentration of extended families compelled to live in squalor and disease, exposed to the corona virus; and worse, the documented death of children held in custody. American political authorities, religious leaders, courts, and press on the left and right pursue ideological and theological discourse and raise their questions about these children. They victimize the victims all over again by turning their suffering experience into a political or biblical argument, into statements that make the children's suffering serve some larger purpose and greater end. They make suffering useful and interpretively meaningful. We have encountered such barbaric, instrumental

---

21. This is the same revulsion Primo Levi associates with images of the Muselmänner, the "living dead" (1996: 88–90).

reasoning and aesthetic in the past century in the heart of enlightened, biblically faithful, Christian Europe.

Bak, too, recognizes the barbaric continuities with the past in the ways children are treated today. "After Auschwitz" is not merely a reference to time; the phrase names a style, as in to "take after" someone or something. "To take after Auschwitz" is to adopt an aesthetics of harm that makes the suffering of innocents normative, acceptable, and even beautiful. Bak's artwork questions and rejects that aesthetic not only for the millions of Jewish children swallowed up in the Nazi abyss but also for the suffering children of Myanmar and Mississippi today who live abbreviated, damaged lives. For this reason "Holocaust painter" and "surrealist artist" descriptors fail to capture the scope and amplitude of Bak's critical, aesthetic, and ethical sensibilities and vision. In reflecting on his reworking of the iconic photograph of the Warsaw Ghetto Boy, Bak speaks most directly about the suffering of today's children and his obligation to paint it (Fewell and Phillips 2009). His various constructions of the Ghetto Boy in fragmented and damaged shapes "is no dream world," he says, "but rather reality experienced and expressed through metaphor. If you look at what happens on my canvases, if you focus your eyes onto the decomposed image of the Warsaw boy, you will discover what I feel about the destructured world in which we live, our troubled times, the contradictions and losses that we must face" (Raskin 2004: 76). There is no turning away from the contradictions and the suffering.

Patte, too, acknowledges this present destructured and contradictory world. He hopes against hope that the reader who lives in a Trump-inspired "fake news," "alternative facts," "conspiracy theory," and polarized country can escape "the quagmire in a productive way" (Patte 2018: xxiv–xxv). But for Patte, his readers should pin their hope on right discourse, questions, concepts, logic, and an inclusive hermeneutical "do no harm to others" praxis. Adorno and Bak, however, present an aporetic alternative. Even though the event and aesthetics of Auschwitz show us there is no escape from barbarous history, we are nonetheless obliged to find ways to make this world unbarbaric, to effect *tikkun olam*. Art that shows us the contradictions—the aporia of Bak's escape/nonescape—offers a better perspective on the truth of suffering and the ethical demand not to rest until we end it.

The Challenge of Living with Romans after Auschwitz

We must face a last question, a variation of one Adorno poses: Can we live with Romans after Auschwitz (2003: 435)? For a lover of Christian scripture this is Patte's frightening question that he answers with a mostly confident "yes": a hermeneutic of "cause no harm to others" cures the damage and changes the history. Yet, despite his confident assurances, Patte also seems aware at some level that idealist and deontological ethical assumptions are less than convincing. I find evidence of this wavering when he discusses the challenge to exegesis, theology, and ethics. Multiple times he repeats Charles Simic's "*La vie est plus belle que les ideés*" (46, 68,

69): "Life is more beautiful than ideas." Ideas to the idealist are supreme; ideas are more foundational, more permanent, more real, and more beautiful than material reality, a poor second. But if with Simic Patte understands *life* to mean more than the *idea of life*—something akin to the *experience of life* that one has before one can formulate a coherent and logical idea about the facticity and materiality of life—then arguably he moves in Adorno's and Bak's (and my) direction away from the primacy of the idea and subjective toward the material and objective. The *idea* of living is incommensurate with material life, and the *idea* of suffering is incommensurate with material suffering. Living and suffering are more than, other than, terms or ideas or discourse about life and suffering and cannot be reduced to or equated with them. This recognition—better this skeptical reaction—is a movement of thought toward enabling the material suffering experience of death/life to determine how to think and to act; it begins to alter the conditions that make history barbarous and the event and aesthetic of Auschwitz inevitable.

Moreover, we might even see the repetition of Simic's phrase as symptomatic of Patte's effort to work through the catastrophe of a damaging Romans text as well as the erosion of total confidence in the idea that a hermeneutic of "cause no harm to others" brings an end to death and suffering. I am imagining a Freudian-style, therapeutic working through that labors to bring insight and leads to change analogous to Bak's visual working through the trauma of escape/nonescape. Importantly, the comparison here is not between Patte's trauma and Bak's trauma: to compare one suffering with another this way is barbaric and useless. What I am comparing is the *ethical motivation* and the *aporetic thinking* that occur in response to material suffering. Perhaps what the multiple citations of Simic's "*La vie est plus belle que les ideés*" indicate is the painful realization that escape from the damage of weaponized biblical texts cannot be assured despite all hope and hope against hope. Patte's admission in his Note on Cover Artwork that Romans might "barely escape" and "might still 'escape'" indicates that ambivalence (2018: xii).

The reality of barbaric/beautiful life exceeds all ideas about barbarity and beauty; it exceeds all ideas of freedom, discursive critical strategies, and hermeneutical theory and methodology. But biblical scholars are a methodology-driven, Enlightenment-grounded, reason-based, discourse-prioritizing, not-very-comfortable-with-aporia professional lot too often caught up in settling for—which too often means settling scores with—the one right interpretation, idea, method, or truth at the expense of the readings' material effects. On this score Patte has it entirely right. This is in part what motivates the commentary: for Patte, ethical consequences are vital to consider when we interpret. But it is his (nearly) confident assertion that we can escape the violence (xxv) and suffering that proves ultimately unconvincing and wavering, and the aporias in his argument signal that. An aporetic reading of his repetition of Simic's words suggests there is more to living and dying with Romans than even Patte's own ideas, discursive interpretive strategies, or multiple volumes can possibly account for.

Patte turns to Simic in support of his view that the search for the "One and Only Truth" (2018: 69) in the interpretation of Romans or any scriptural text is dangerous, and here Patte wavers once again but is back in an idealist and deontological direction. According to Patte, the search for "One and Only Truth" (his capitalization) turns deadly when one interpretation excludes another, when it is absolutized, in Levinas's terms "totalized," or in Adorno's made "the whole." Patte confidently asserts that each and every interpretation of Romans is "life-giving when it humbly acknowledges that it is merely only one among other equally legitimate and plausible interpretations" (69). But "life-giving" for whom or for what? For interpreter, interpretation, or the "other" person who suffers interpretive harm? The anthropomorphic language puts him in a bind. Interpretations, like the text of Romans, take on living form. They are given human attributes (they are "humble," they "live") as does the text of Romans (when it "barely 'escapes' "). Absolutized reading must be avoided at all costs because it is costly to other interpretations; the interpretations, it appears, do the suffering. But who actually bears the cost in their bodies of destructive, absolutized readings? Interpretations or the targeted flesh and blood of Jewish and immigrant children? While we may speak figuratively of interpretations damaging other interpretations (as in the "conflict of interpretations"), in reality it is particular embodied men, women, and children who materially, not figuratively, suffer injustice when Romans and other biblical texts are weaponized. In my terms, where are the incarcerated children when exegetes debate the damaging readings of Rom 13 and interpretive validity and plausibility? It is all too ideational, impersonal, and immaterial for my liking.

This is why I much prefer the expression "sufferings of interpretations" (a subjective genitive) as an alternative because it provides a better grammatical perspective on material suffering and the actual sufferer in place of the interpretation and interpreter. The sufferings that result *from* interpretations challenge me to remember that broken bodies should not be subordinated grammatically to, or usefully categorized by, discourses about them. The better perspective is to see actual suffering bodies and textual interpretations dialectically and aporetically bound together, the way hermeneutical theory first engaged genocidal violence and interpretation. Like the dialectic created by holding up Bak's painting in one hand and Patte's commentary in the other. By keeping suffering in view each alters the other, suffering reality and concepts, caged children and Rom 13, in a negating, contradiction-filled process out of which suffering truth—not "one" or "the" interpretive truth—emerges in relation to the material suffering that Adorno insists is a condition of all truth (1992: 17–18). To turn Simic's phrase back against Patte in a way he might find unsettling: Does Patte's *idea* of inclusive reading risk becoming the "One and Only Truth" (Patte's capitalization) that dominates and does violence to life? Does the *idea* of a hermeneutic of "cause no harm to others" taken as a first principle for reading and responding to suffering not become a dangerous idea, a barbaric idea, that thinks of itself first as more than, better than life itself, more than, better than the suffering of children?

Life is more beautiful than ideas. But life is also more barbaric than ideas. Taken together both statements speak aporetic truth. This is more than an aesthetic judgment about beauty and barbarity; it is a critical and ethical recognition that when confronting the incomparable suffering of the Holocaust, discourse and ideas fail, and fail miserably. Paradoxically, to say that life is more beautiful and barbaric than words or ideas cracks open the door for hope in the possibility of a material change in thinking and acting that could transform barbaric culture. After Auschwitz, as Adorno writes and Bak paints, in the shadow of the Shoah as Patte writes and we read, the world is experienced contradictorily: beautiful/barbaric, life-giving/death-giving, aporetic/logical, incoherent/coherent, escape/nonescape. The experience of Auschwitz survivors, Bak included, is that the temporal and discursive distance between "life-giving" and "death-giving" collapses into the paradoxical elision of suffering-in-life/life-in-suffering. This is the aporetic condition of Langer's "death/life" that demands an Adornian aphorism or a Bakian ironic canvas to say and show, but in a negative, failing way, and only in the failing to succeed.

If Adorno and Bak are right, our critical and ethical condition, and by extension the aesthetic, philosophical, and theological domains of our lives after Auschwitz are better described in aporetic, paradoxical, and essentially negative terms. This is one consequence of living in the shadow of the Shoah. This is the "better perspective" Bak paints. Under the new moral imperative Adorno prescribes, after Auschwitz, the philosopher's, the artist's, and the biblical interpreter's first response to suffering must be bodily repugnance to actual suffering rather than marshal new hermeneutical interpretations, discourse, or questions. Our first reaction to the abhorrent suffering of immigrant children ought to be disgust that motivates the critical and ethical move to vacate them from their cages. This first motivation is material. Adorno reminds us that in our barbarous world "it is in the unvarnished materialistic motive only that morality survives" (1992: 365).

Life/death is more than my ideas, too. As I write this response, I recognize that I render the reality of suffering that confronts me in the electronic images of caged children (not the actual children) and image of Bak's painting (not the actual canvas) into ideas, discourse, and questions in the hope of making sense. Because I, too, find myself distanced from the reality of others' suffering; any effort on my part to describe and theorize it, too, is barbaric, and yet ethically and critically I am obliged to do so. As with Patte, I cannot escape the barbarism of a culture, at least not before biblical scholars' first response to the suffering of immigrant children is repugnance not discourse about the aesthetics or history of right interpretations. Not until a new arrangement of thought and praxis takes hold so that Auschwitz and other genocides will not be repeated will my own barbaric thinking and action change. My hope against hope—my skeptical utopian commitment—is for a new arrangement of thinking and action to end the suffering of caged children. Romans and its interpreters are not my first concern and never will be; biblical interpreters can take care of themselves and the texts they anthropomorphize and idealize. Freeing innocents from suffering detention centers and violent interpretations demands of me more than a better discourse and set of ethical reading questions. We need only remember it was Romans and its readers who helped put those children in cages in the first place.

We should be very grateful, but finally not surprised, that Patte's first motivation in writing his commentary was to *show* Samuel Bak's artwork, which I view as an ethical, aesthetic, and critical response—a skeptical utopic response—to Bak's suffering experience; it is an acknowledgment, literally *avant la letter*, of the facticity of Bak's suffering that precedes his discourse and questions, although Patte follows with them. Part of the tension, contradiction, and irony in Patte's effort as I see it is that in some important respect he does gesture to aporetic post-Shoah life. This partially explains the ambivalence in his use of Simic. He is less than completely certain that the categorical imperative to think and act first with categories that govern his historical and textual analysis is adequate to remedy the problem of violent readings of Romans. This is why he repeatedly hopes against hope to bring an end to the damage. Another way to say this is that Patte acknowledges the truth of Bak's suffering on his cover without the benefit of interpretation or a hermeneutic. It is also the case that Patte puts Bak's art in support of his own utopian vision of ethical reading practice and attributes that vision, metaphorically and unconvincingly, to Bak. It is an unresolvable contradiction he finds himself in; it is a barbaric interpretive act counter to his own ethical intuition and aspiration that he, like the rest of us, cannot escape.

Living/dying with Romans after Auschwitz will continue to be a contradictory and damaging experience, and inclusive exegetical discourse proves insufficient to address the deep hurt and brokenness of the world. Living/dying with Romans after Auschwitz is more than the *idea* of reasoning our way humbly through to inclusive interpretations and ethical discourses. It is a jolting, unhinging experience of concrete suffering. The revolting suffering and death of children in European ghettos and crematoria, Levinas reminds us, "thrusts us into the snake pit, into places that are no longer places, into places one cannot forget ... We have known such pits in this century" (1994: 85). Levinas refers here to his experience of the many genocidal and other catastrophes of the twentieth century that did not target only Jews. Lamentably, there are too many forms of violence that take after Auschwitz in our present century. The caging of immigrant children is but another snake pit that has emerged aided by Romans and its interpreters. Recognizing this and other snake pits means keeping the revolt and repugnance of suffering determinative of exegetical ideas and readings. This is what I think it means to make genocide or the shadow of the Shoah a condition for thinking about biblical texts as Patte challenges us to do when he holds up Bak's "Escape" and Romans to unsettle us. At least that is how I read him.

After Auschwitz, after the caged children, we experience ever more acutely the painful contradiction of living/dying at the hands of biblical texts that seemingly dwarf all means at our disposal to escape the violence, good intentions, and right interpretive strategies notwithstanding.[22] Child survivor Bak shows us past and present pits. So, too, do internet images of caged immigrant children. His art

---

22. Perhaps Rom 7:13-20 points to this type of aporetic experience where Paul laments Sin's power over his self, his interpretation of Torah, and indeed the world. This echoes in Patte's passionate, personal, and painful admission that scripture so central to his own teaching and scholarly writing career has been imprisoned to violence.

challenges us to attune our ears and eyes to this world's suffering and for that we stand to benefit from the "better perspective" his nonconsoling art provides us. We hear and see so that, as Adorno hopes, we arrange our thoughts and praxis to bring about an unbarbaric future, a *tikkun olam*. At least that is how I read them.

In the end we might be tempted to see the harsh reality of barbarous history, the aporia of post-Shoah life, and the ethical uncertainty related to it as morally quieting if not altogether defeating. I argue just the opposite. Adorno's aesthetic philosophy and Bak's artwork make abject suffering critically and ethically motivating. I mean by this that hearing the voices and seeing the bodies of hopeless suffering caged children triggers before all discourse and ethical questions a visceral repugnance, a critical and ethical disgust, a first response and movement that determines how to hear and see, to think and to act. How might we translate this into practical guidance for biblical interpreters? Perhaps this way: No credible discussion about hermeneutical interpretation, about discourse and questions, about the biblical text and Holocaust art, about Romans and valid readings, about Patte's commentary and my response to it dare happen outside the presence of incarcerated, suffering children.[23] When we make the material reality of their suffering determinative of thought and action in this way, we enable suffering to speak the truth. Finally, we learn from Patte that we stand in the shadow of the Shoah. We stand to learn from Bak and Adorno ways of critical thinking and ethical action that prioritize those who suffer and the truth they speak but refuse to let their suffering be the last word.

---

23. A recasting of Irving Greenberg's working hypothesis for theological reflection about the Holocaust: "no statement, theological or otherwise, should be made that would not be credible in the presence of burning children" (1977: 23).

Part III

ROMANS 1:16-18 AND 1:26-27

Chapter 7

A CHINESE CROSS-CULTURAL READING OF "ΔΙΚΑΙΟΣΥΝΗ ΘΕΟΥ" IN ROMANS 1:17: A PLAUSIBLE FOURTH EXEGESIS IN CONVERSATION WITH DANIEL PATTE

K. K. Yeo

Introduction

In his massive, five-hundred-page work on the first chapter of Romans alone, Daniel Patte has in fact offered readers his discussion of the "three exegetical interpretations and the history of reception," grounded in respect for multiplicity and in a choice—ethical responsibility to choose one appropriate interpretation for a particular context. Not only has Patte defended the validity of each of the three equally legitimate and plausible interpretations—forensic theological exegeses, covenantal community exegeses, and realized-apocalyptic/messianic exegesis—but also, for the first time in the Romans exegetical-commentarial tradition, we see how these three exegetical approaches stand on themselves yet in conversation via Patte's unique reception of Paul's Epistle to the Romans.

Summary of Patte's Work on Rom 1:17

It took me more than a month to completely read the 531-page work, mainly because I thought for years that Patte had been writing his Romans commentary. I was wrong. As I read through his work, I wondered why, if it were his commentary, he had to say so much about other scholars' views, and I could hardly find his own view on every verse of the Epistle to the Romans.

It was only in my second round of reading Patte's work that I found the "Contents" outline (Patte 2018: vii–xi) and the "Appendix: Threefold Interpretive Choices about Thirty-One Key Theological and Ethical Themes in Rom 1:1-32" (475–98) very helpful. For example, in considering the phrase "δικαιοσύνη θεοῦ" in Rom 1:17, Part 2 in the "Contents" guides me to locate where the phrase appears in the "triple commentary" (subheading) with which Patte is engaging: (i) go to pages 100–12 in Patte's discussion of the phrase regarding the interpretation of the "forensic theological commentary"; (ii) go to pages 172–91 in Patte's discussion of the phrase regarding the interpretation of the "inclusive covenantal community commentary"; and (iii) go to pages 271–92 in Patte's discussion of the phrase in the interpretation of the "realized-apocalyptic/messianic commentary." Before going to pages 100, 172, and 271 though, I find it helpful to read Patte's summary of these three exegetical interpretations regarding the phrase "δικαιοσύνη θεοῦ" in the Appendix (pp. 490–1).

So, there are at least three "legitimate and plausible" interpretations of this phrase (the following terms are those of Patte, but I summarize and arrange them in a different order).

The first interpretation, the forensic theological exegesis, basically understands δικαιοσύνη θεοῦ as "righteousness/uprightness of God" in terms of: (1) the end result of the gracious acquittal by God on individual sinners as innocent, therefore sinners are not condemned at the last judgement; or (2) such gracious acquittal of God has the ongoing effect on the present life, therefore fear of last judgement is erased; or (3) preaching of the good news of God's gracious acquittal (re)establishes upright/righteous relationship with God. The representative commentary Patte uses in this theological exegesis is that of Douglas Moo (also others, including Rudolf Bultmann and Joseph Fitzmyer).

The second interpretation, the inclusive covenantal community theological exegesis, basically interprets δικαιοσύνη θεοῦ as "righteousness/justice of God." That is, the faithful and covenanted God establishes righteous/just and inclusive communities of faithfulness/faith. The people of God then manifest the righteousness/justice of God in the world by carrying out the covenanted vocation/mission, thus participating in the gospel-story. The representative work Patte uses in this theological exegesis is that of Mark Nanos (but also others, such as the commentary of Robert Jewett).

The third interpretation, the realized-apocalyptic/messianic theological exegesis, basically reads δικαιοσύνη θεοῦ as "righteousness of God." That is, the rightful, sovereign power of God triumphs over all (especially evil) powers and intervenes in Jesus Christ being raised from the dead, and all those living by faith recognize such power, are recaptured by it, and live in freedom from bondage and evil powers. The representative commentary Patte uses in this theological exegesis is that of Ernest Käsemann (but also others, including D. Campbell).

Assessment

Many readers, such as me, who are used to reading the discussion of a biblical book in its canonical order and calling it "commentary," soon find out that there is something new here. The progression and layout of this work still looks like a standard commentary, but Patte is not giving readers his interpretation of Romans. I was frustrated at my initial reading because I was unable to find explicitly *his definite view* on every key phrase of Paul in Rom 1. There are some places where Patte gives his opinion, such as footnote 196 on page 172, where he writes, "I take the thesis to include 1:18, because Rom 1:17 and 1:18 should not be separated, as I (*Paul's Faith*, 257–8) and Elliott (*Arrogance*, 6–7) argue." Yet, one will not find *his commentary* on every key phrase of Romans; that is not his purpose, but instead his thesis of multiple interpretations of legitimate choices and plausible meanings guides him to write an "anti-commentary" work.

Patte's work here is "anti-commentary" not in the sense of rejecting traditional commentaries on Romans, but I suspect it has to do with not wanting to write his own interpretation as the normative reading of Romans—often such a normative reading that does not acknowledge every commentary has its own contextual character. With so many English and German commentaries on Romans on our bookshelves, I am glad that Patte's work can help us raise questions about: (i) how we should read all these commentaries; and (ii) what ethics are involved in writing a biblical commentary. I am as thrilled at Patte's great achievement as I am of the acumen of Paul to inspire us all because of the cross-cultural reading of Romans I am committed to. I have seen similar accumulative commentaries of the *Analects* (see Yeo 2008: 56–9) or the Ancient Christian Commentary on Scripture series (by InterVarsity Press), but none of these provides any analysis of the interpretations or any clarification of the ethical choice as well as of the context of the interpretations, while Patte's work is simply engaging and, thus, illuminating.

Ideally, Patte's choice of three exegetical interpretations could have been more culturally diverse and accentuated, so that the contrast regarding different contextual interpretations could be sharper, drawing on his wealth of experience editing the *Global Bible Commentary* (Patte 2004), the *Cambridge Dictionary of Christianity* (Patte 2010), and the Society of Biblical Literature Romans Seminars series (Grenholm and Patte 2000–5). Together with his colleagues, Patte has, in these projects, invited numerous contributors from outside the United States and Western Europe to enrich the reception of Romans globally. The cultural contexts of the three exegetical interpretations in Patte's work are mainly North American and European, though to be fair, this volume on Romans has incorporated multiple references to and deliberations on receptions of Romans in the East European, Latin American, African, and Filipino contexts, and a quick search on this falls under the "contextual/ethical" entry of "interpretive choices" in the subject index. Since this volume is not about cross-cultural interpretation per se, readers would have to use the index to locate various cultural interpretations within the text.

To be fair again, it is challenging to use context as one of the primary criteria for gauging an interpretation, especially in light of the multiple interpretive traditions and categories Patte works with. Attention to context not only makes it more challenging to assume ethical responsibility for an interpretation, since it involves crossing many cultural boundaries, but it may also perhaps make the already ambitious task even more daunting. In this essay though, while I do not intend to supplement Patte's work on Romans but to perhaps expand it, my purpose is twofold: (i) to determine how my cross-cultural approach can have a conversation with Patte's work to allow for deeper exploration (although he does discuss *pesher* interpretation on page 244, which may be similar to my cross-cultural reading) for the sake of readers beyond US and Western European contexts such as, in this essay, my Chinese cross-cultural reading of Romans; and (ii) to clarify the legitimacy and ethics of Patte's three exegetical interpretations as I bring in specifically my Chinese-Confucianist reading as a plausible fourth interpretation. I shall limit my work here to the understanding of δικαιοσύνη θεοῦ in Rom 1:17-18, the thesis statement of the Epistle.

My Cross-Cultural Critical Method

Daniel Patte and Cristina Grenholm's "scriptural criticism" is a comprehensive critical method of biblical interpretation that takes into consideration three frames or interpretive choices (analytical textual choices, hermeneutical theological choices, and contextual choices) based on three life-contexts (church in Bible reception, church in liturgy, and academy) of three kinds of readers (believers receiving the Bible as the Word of God, believers experiencing the Bible as Sacrament, critical exegetes studying the texts; see Grenholm and Patte 2000: 1–54; Patte 2018: 14–21, 225, 239, 242–3). From my student days through the early years of my professional life, I was preoccupied with the method of biblical study focusing on the following areas of cross-cultural hermeneutics: (i) the relationship between exegesis and hermeneutics; (ii) the relationship between biblical theology and cultures; and (iii) the relationship between the world of the writer, the world in the text, and the world of the reader—that is, behind the text, in the text, in front of the text. In the year 2000, I began to formulate the three interactive rhetorical planes of meaning contained and carried through the various media of writing, writer, and reader. A few years later, in 2004, I published an essay on Rom 7 discussing "culture and intersubjectivity as criteria of negotiating meanings in cross-cultural interpretations" (Yeo 2004a: 81–100; 2018: 16–24). I argue that, since the biblical text is historically situated and culturally conditioned, it is important to critically assess all the factors mentioned above that contribute to the meanings of the text. In his *Romans* work, Patte has paid much attention to several of these factors, such as "historical, cultural, sociopolitical situations" (2018: 19), individual-centered or community-base (33) in his "scriptural criticism" (14–21, 197, 225, 239, 242–3, 286).

First Plane: Cross-Linguistic Cosmology

Influenced by my classical Greco-Roman rhetorical study, my first rhetorical plane (illustrated by the triangle in Figure 7.1) depicts what is at work at the meta-spatiotemporal level of meaning production, that is, what the linguistic world as situated in the world signifies cosmologically in relation to the biblical author as the language(s) user.

Reality, language, and language user are the three angles that each interacts with the other two in the meaning-finding and producing process. For example, depending on what vernacular language one uses, the signified reality will be

signified (reality)

signifier (language)　　　　　　　　　　biblical author (rhetor as language user)

Figure 7.1 First plane of meaning-finding and producing process.

presented quite differently. And different rhetors have their own ways or grammars of comprehending and presenting the signified reality. There is no particular order of triangular interaction among the biblical author, the signified, and the signifier in this plane because all three angles are interacting with each other simultaneously. Let me explain using the book of Romans as an example. This plane gets very complex for interpreters because, though we work on the "same" Romans text, our understanding of Greek, Hebrew, Latin, and vernacular languages—such as Chinese for me—is different from that of Patte and from each other. Even for modern scholars who know koine Greek (or, in Patte's words, "Judeo-Greek … that evokes both a Greek/Latin identity and a Jewish identity" [2018: 248]; I prefer "Judeo-Greek" to koine Greek, as Judeo-Greek aptly describes the cross-cultural sense of Paul's languages) and biblical Hebrew well and use the same dictionaries, language is metaphorical and interpretation is cross-cultural (there is always a distance in space and time between the modern and the ancient world). All of these nuances are compounded by the languages themselves and the linguistic world of Paul. Therefore, the meanings of δικαιοσύνη θεοῦ in Rom 1:17 are fluid, polyvalent, and nuanced. That which makes a text "sacred" or "classic" has less to do with a sole authoritative meaning (its representation in terms of expression) and more to do with the textual power to utter meaning across time and space. This Ricoeurian understanding of textuality as the creation or re-presentation of meanings explains it well (Ricoeur 1979: 271–6).[1]

Let us see how the three angles of the first triangle work in the example of, say, the author Paul using the Greek word θεός to speak of the signified reality. English readers think of the cosmology of "God" and try hard to get back to the "Judeo-Greek" (Patte 2018: 248) semantic domain understanding of Paul's use of θεός, perhaps spelling out Paul's historical, eschatological, and christologically salvific meaning of this word. But can we assume that we know the linguistic world of the historical Paul well, if not completely? Or, has the historical Paul exhausted the meaning by using this Greek word θεός as his signifier? While we may *not*

---

1. With regard to textuality and what constitutes "sacred text," I am following Ricoeur's thesis: "Maybe in the case of Christianity there is no sacred text, because it is not the text which is sacred, but the One about which it is spoken … The critical act is not forbidden by the nature of the text, because it is not a sacred text in the sense in which the Qur'an is sacred" (1979: 271).

want to argue for "la mort de l'auteur" (Roland Barthes's phrase, "the death of the author," meaning that the author has no power to control the meaning of what he has written),[2] we certainly want to argue that this "sacred" text *invites* translator and interpreter to render its fuller meaning in other vernaculars. Thus, I want to illustrate this point by using the Chinese words for θεός.

Shen (God), *Shang-di* (Lord Above), *Tian* (Heaven),[3] or *Dao* (Way) are rich renditions of θεός in Chinese. *Shen* is a generic Chinese word that refers to a god, to a deity, or to divinity, and when used to translate θεός or *El* (singular)/*Elohim* (plural) in the (Chinese) Bible, it refers to God—though Chinese neither has capitalized letters nor numbers (the difference between single or plural can be understood in context only). Thus, some Chinese Bible translators, churches, and scholars prefer a more archaic and specific word, *Shang-di*, literally "Lord Above" or "Lord [of/on] High/Supreme." *Shang-di* is thought of by the ancient Chinese as a nonhuman deity/spirit who became the first, and thus most powerful, human ancestor of the Shang (dynasty, ca. 1600–1046 BCE) people. Did Paul's usage of θεός in Rom 1:17 assume such a relationship between God and humanity? Patte discusses the three exegetical interpretations, and though they understand the phrase "δικαιοσύνη θεοῦ" differently, they all relate this phrase to God and humanity. The "forensic" interpretation sees God as the Judge of individuals as sinners/guilty (Patte 2018: 100). The "covenantal" interpretation sees God as the faithful covenantal just One for community (176). And the "apocalyptic" interpretation sees God as the cosmic sovereign power to break through evil powers so that lives are transformed to live in the messianic sphere/age (279).

Did Paul's usage of δικαιοσύνη θεοῦ assume the political background of the Roman Empire, as the word *Shang-di* carries a political connotation? Patte's discussion of the "covenantal" and "apocalyptic" interpretations answers affirmatively (see 174, 285–7). For the Chinese semantic of *Di* (Lord), thus *Shang-di* also, the Supreme Lord is believed to be the Benefactor and Judge of the human world. Emperors in later Chinese history adopted the title of *Huang Di*, literally "King the Lord," as they believed that they had a divine right to be kings on earth mirroring that of the Supreme Deity in Heaven (*Tian*) in ruling, blessing, and judging. Ancient Chinese kings often communicated with *Di* (Lord) through shamans (*wu*), skillful craft-men (*shu*), and scholars (*shi*) in order to reign. *Ru*, referring to Confucianism ("*Ru-jia*" in Chinese—literally meaning "family/school of *Ru*"), was another class of scholars whose religious, political, and moral skills were employed by political rulers. Confucius's moral philosophy arose in response to this Shang context, and though he was not critical of the Shang religious belief regarding—and worship of—*Di*, *Shang-di*, and political rulers, Confucius's ethical teaching still is subversive to the Shang worldview and values. Perhaps then, the word *Tian* (Heaven) more accurately renders Paul's meaning of θεός?

2. Barthes (1977: 142–8).
3. The Chinese word "*tian*" can mean sky; when used as "*Tian*" it refers to Heaven, a metaphor for the Supreme Cosmic Power. On the translation of *Sheng*, *Shang-di*, and *Tian* in Chinese Bible versions, see the index entry "God" in Yeo (2021: 852).

Tian is the tribal god of the Zhou Dynasty (1046–256 BCE) people, and Confucius (551–479 BCE) lived in that era. Though *Tian* possessed all of the powers of *Shang-di*, *Tian* could also commission a human representative on earth with a *ming* (mandate or will) to do things on its behalf. Confucius's focus on *Tian* (Heaven) and *Tian-ming* (mandate of Heaven) comes closer to Paul's understanding of θεός and δικαιοσύνη θεοῦ (Yeo 2008: 129–30)—thus a Confucianist reading of Romans allows us to use the Confucian semantic beside Paul's "Judeo-Greek" semantic to understand him. *Tian* and θεός is the Creator and Being of a spiritual moral order. While Paul's emphasis is on Yahweh or Jesus and not on superstitious beings such as Jupiter or Zeus, Confucius likewise makes the similar interpretive move of stressing spiritual-moral *Tian* (Heaven) and not superstitious *Di* (Deity), stressing intellect (*zhi*) and sincerity (*cheng*) and not ignorance/fear, stressing righteousness (*yi*) and not wickedness (*è*), stressing propriety (*li*) and harmony (*yue/he*) and not violence/chaos, ethics/virtues, and superstitions.

The word *Tian*, when coupled with another Chinese character referring to the Supreme Deity, is used in ancient Chinese texts: *Tian-di*, *Tian-huang*, and *Huang-tian* refer to the Supreme Being, the ultimate order and source of all— and sometimes with the descriptions of this Being as the Judge and Rewarder of humanity. The question often posed to Chinese interpreters is: Is this *Tian* or *Huang-tian* theistic, as the One in the Bible? However, no one will ask the question: Given the Greek myths of polytheism, how can Paul use the Greek word θεός to signify the monotheistic God, Yahweh of Israel? The huge controversy over the Chinese term for God in Chinese church history is perhaps unfairly misplaced (Wang 2015: 140–60); so is the prohibition of some Muslim authorities against Malaysian Christians using the Arabic word "Allah" (which is pre-Islam) for "God" in the Bible. My point is that language does not exist in a frozen state, nor do specific expressions belong to any particular religion.

Another Chinese word "*Dao*" could also be used to translate θεός, but Chinese Bible versions have never done so, because the word "*Dao*" is reserved for translating λόγος specifically. I am arguing here though that the word "*Dao*" in both Daoist and Confucianist traditions has a meaning similar to *Tian*, for both words connote the universal Way or cosmic moral Principle. In other words, just like *Tian*, *Dao* is eternal in its existence and creative in its power, similar to the understanding of θεός in Rom 1, as the Creator whose "eternal power and divine nature" (ἀΐδιος δύναμις και θειότης in Rom 1:20) are revealed in creation, human conscience, and holy-cultural law (e.g., Jewish law called *torah*). The differences between the biblical θεός and Chinese *Dao* are: (i) θεός does not have beginning and ending (θεός is eternal), whereas *Dao* is self-generative, and it is the metamorphosis of a self-contained universe; (ii) θεός has personhood and, therefore, a narrative of creation and redemption whereas *Dao* is a spontaneous cosmic principle, one without personality but that has a textual meaning of giving birth to a myriad of things in the universe:

> There was something undifferentiated, and yet complete. Soundless and formless, it depends on nothing and does not change. It operates everywhere

and is free from danger. It may be considered the mother of the universe. I do not know its name. I call it *Dao*. If forced to give it a name, I shall call it Great. (Laozi, *Daode Jing*, chapter 25; see Chan and Rump 1979: 75-6)

Despite the differences, the word "*Dao*" corresponds to the Greek word λόγος (meaning word, reason, thing, logic, etc.). I would find it equally powerful to use λόγος and *Dao* to name θεός, so that both λόγος and *Dao* take on additional meaning from the signified they seek to render. This is in line with the missionizing purpose of cross-cultural interpretation: the vernacular (target language) takes on an expanded meaning from the host language it seeks to translate. This missionizing purpose is also demonstrated in the Judeo-Greek that Paul used in the Epistle to the Romans (Yeo 2004b: 1-28), because the hybridized language (Judeo-Greek) is the vernacular of the author (Paul) and the readers (Roman Christians).

Focusing on *Dao* in Chinese (Confucian and Daoist) semantic, one notices that the naturalistic cosmos worldview is the cultural assumption of the ancient Chinese. But that worldview does not imply a lack of understanding of transcendence, thus spiritual, in words such as *Dao* and *Tian*—transcendence as connoted in "eternal power and divine nature" (Rom 1:20). The ethical category in Confucian thought is transcendental/spiritual and therefore is a helpful lens for understanding Paul's use of δικαιοσύνη, for both Confucius's and Paul's languages render transcendence *aesthetically*—while Paul's emphasis is on God and Confucius's is on humanity. Let me explain.

In most classical cultures, such as Chinese, Greek, and Jewish, *Dao*, *Tianli* (cosmic order), λόγος, and *Elohim* were words used to designate the creative/first principle or primordial wisdom that generates a way of life that is harmonious, fulsome, and transcendental. Transcendence in Confucian thought is an aesthetic category in its ethical or virtuous sense, that is: (i) the awe one senses in encountering others or (ii) the charisma of a stylized interpersonal behavior called propriety or etiquette (*li*) and the delightful beauty of music or joy (*yue*). Paul's δικαιοσύνη θεοῦ in the Confucian language of *Tian* and *Dao* has the tenor of the dialectical relationship between *Dao* (Way) and *de* (morality), thus Romans' overarching theme of rectification (the word "justification" does not capture well the meaning below) of the union between *Tian* (Heaven) and *ren* (humanity), phrased in Confucian language (especially that of Mencius, the second grandmaster of Confucianism) as *Tianren heyi* (the aesthetic or spiritual union between Heaven and humanity).

But *Tianren heyi* is intertwined with the idea of "virtuous together with your neighbor" (*Analects* 4:25, see Yeo 2008: 261-82). For it is the transcendent *Tian* that compels human beings to be virtuous so that what is immanent (ethics) mirrors that which is transcendent (*Tian*)—similar to the δικαιοσύνη θεοῦ discourse in Romans about the "in-Christ" union of Jews and gentiles, Greeks and barbarians, the strong and the weak (in Rom 14). For Paul, growth in the process of sanctification (Rom 5-8) is directed toward the ultimate goal of realizing the glorious image of Christ in human beings. The process is initiated in the life of faith through grace. It is also a life of love toward one's neighbor (cf. Rom 13:8) as an expression of a life of faith and love toward God. While there is no explicit language of grace and Christ in Confucius (if there were, then this logic would be anachronistic), Confucian ethics has a holistic cosmology of seeing both heavenly and human realms as spiritually intersected. Thus Confucian ethics is the way to become fully human (*ren* 人), and to be human (*ren* 人) is to love (*ren* 仁) others (or to be *ren-ren* 仁人—a loving person).[4] The deep structure of the Pauline language of sanctification (ἁγιασμός) in the Confucian language is a process of human moral perfection achieved by means of fulfilling *Dao-de* (the Way of virtue), *Tian-dao* (the way of Heaven), *ren-dao* (the way of being human), and *Tian-ming* (the will of Heaven). The will of Heaven could be realized when everyone commits to *ren* (love), because what makes human beings human is *ren* (love). I am pleasantly surprised to read Paul, and therefore Patte's work here, that Paul's theology of God's love (see Patte's discussion in 2018: 108, 292–3, 439–51) and love of neighbor (37–42, 302–4, 441–5) parallels that of Confucius. The differences between Confucianism and Paul are: (i) in the distinctive understanding of the cruciform love of Paul and (ii) the different semantics and narratives of love in Confucius's and Paul's teachings.

In Western languages such as Greek and English—which draw an absolute distinction between the sovereign, transcendent God and sinful, earthly humanity and, thus, the absolute distinction between Creator and creation—perhaps the Confucian language and worldview of *Dao* and *Tian* can offer a corrective, though the Confucian language lacks an explicit narrative of a personal *Tian* or *Dao*. Transcendence in the Confucian language rarely involves encountering a *personal* Supreme Being outside the universe. Rather, it is the transcendence of the moral power within oneself as a way to relate to the Other (*Dao* or *Tian*). *Dao* is not a total mystery and, even though it is inexhaustible in being known, it embodies a self-generative and self-creative universe that is eternal. Its power is realized in the cosmic order (*Tian-li*) that generates morality in humanity—who has the ability to receive and imitate the Way of bearing virtues with such a self-generative and self-creative manner. The Confucian and Daoist understanding of *Dao* as the Way that originates in the ultimately timeless (cyclical) and inexhaustible knowledge is different from Paul's interpretation that God has been made known in Christ—but this difference has more to do with their respective views of time and space, namely cyclical against worldviews, respectively, for Confucius and Paul.

Language is fluid and dynamic; it keeps changing especially in translation and interpretation, which are the basic tasks of exegetical writing. It may be true that the work, the personality, and the revelation of *Tian* in ancient Chinese texts are either illusive or minimum, but Confucianist readers of the Bible do not have control of how cross-linguistic and cross-cultural interpretation of Rom

---

4. Note the English transliterated word "*ren*" is rendering two different Chinese words; one is *ren* (人) as a person and the other is *ren* as love (仁); and when the word is used together, *ren-ren*, it always means "a person who loves [others]" (仁人).

audience (context), e.g., Roman Christians

message (text), e.g., Romans   author (rhetor), e.g., Paul

Figure 7.2 Second plane of biblical exegesis.

1:17 would work—which I will explain in the second plane of my cross-cultural method. My point here is that, while Chinese Confucianist and Daoist cosmologies of *Tian* and *Dao*, respectively, are ahistorical (no beginning and no ending), the creativity of *Tian* and the open-endedness of *Dao* neither contradict nor prohibit Paul's understanding of θεός. Neither should Paul reject Confucianist reception of Romans and the Confucianist semantic world. At least the Confucianist moral world's emphasis is on the spiritual harmony between *Tian* and *ren* (humanity); thus, the ecological and communal aspects of the Chinese cosmology and semantic world are helpful and constitute a responsible choice we ought to make in more ecumenical/global interpretations of Romans.

Cross-cultural linguistics already exists in the first triangle, and interpreters ought to be aware of the limitation and creativity of their languages as they translate and interpret Romans. One language is always limited in the sense that it alone is unable to represent the signified with perfect clarity. Multiple languages offer us an expansive lens and a larger repertoire of the descriptive and creative functions of the languages used.

Second Plane: Cross-Historical Exegesis

The second plane of my cross-cultural method is traditionally understood as biblical exegesis, as preachers or scholars attempt to discern what Paul meant in the Romans text across historical contexts:

This triangle in Figure 7.2 represents a biblical utterance understood as the rhetorical communication of the biblical writer, Paul as rhetor, addressing the audience on contextual issues and expressing his messages in the indigenous cultures of the audience. In actual rhetorical communication process, there is no particular direction of the interaction among the three angles because they interact with each other simultaneously. Similar to cross-linguistic and cross-temporal-spatial factors in the first triangle, the second triangle is not simply a retrieval of Paul's world, of the Roman churches, and, therefore, of the message of Romans based on the Greek text alone. For just like the first plane, here exegetes are crossing from their own modern context to the first-century, premodern world. Let me list a few factors that complicate and pose challenges for us as we bridge the gap in this cross-historical exegesis:

1. We work with an eclectic Greek text of Romans, and textual criticism tells us that early on in the process of the copying, transmission, and reception of the manuscripts, various interpretations have already been made (Jewett 2007: 4–18).
2. Leaving aside the first triangle's concern of what Paul meant when he dictated or wrote Romans (and not what he meant after his dictation or writing—we can argue that the public reading and the canonizing process gradually remove the restrictive meaning of Paul's "first" meaning), we cannot be sure if his Greek usage in Romans is always consistent throughout Romans or with extrabiblical usage; therefore, we, the exegetes, find it challenging to pin down what Paul meant—because of the inconsistency in the way anyone uses language and the fact that language is changing all the time. When Patte writes, "With Fitzmyer, we have to be content (a) to demand consistency—keeping up with the same (forensic) interpretation of 'the righteousness of God' throughout one's reading of Romans (rather than implying that Paul used the same phrase with different meanings in different places)" (2018: 108), I have to disagree with Patte (and Fitzmyer) because we know that literary contexts often will change the meaning of the same word/phrase within a long document.
3. A similar concern regarding flux and change can be said of the Romans audience and readers as well. Exegetes reconstruct their situation differently, because we consider whether Paul is more Jewish or Greco-Roman in his use of particular words—such as πίστις, δικαιοσύνη, νόμος—or whether Paul has apocalyptic or eschatological cosmology, and deduce what the audience's situation could be. The fact that there are at least three possible readings of Romans in Patte's work proves the point.
4. As exegetes, many of us work with classical resources or dictionaries, such as *Theological Dictionary of the New Testament*, *New International Dictionary of New Testament Theology*, Loeb Classical Library, Josephus, Patristic writings, and so on in our reconstruction of Paul and his audience. We assume that this collection of resources gives us the best picture of Paul's world. Yet, few ever question the validity of our usage of these classical resources. For example, when we use Josephus to explain Paul, can we simply assume that the word or language or concept of both of them are the same or that they enlighten one another? Our assumptions will inevitably align or even twist the meaning of the biblical text we interpret. As Patte's work has demonstrated in the three exegetical approaches he used, "the Paul" that exegetes interpret turns out to be more often than not like them.

Because the second plane is also cross-cultural in understanding the *historical* meaning of Romans, the best we can do is to be self-reflective and critical of our entire reading process and forthright about our intentions and assumptions—neither demythologizing the first-century worldview and narratives nor assuming that there is no commensurability at all between Paul and our modern worlds. My rhetorical cross-cultural approach in the second triangle is clear in continuing the first triangle's bridging and dialogical task and in encouraging us all not to claim absolute meaning in a historical reading. Though many Romans scholars neither believe nor practice what H. G. Gadamer has shown to be true—the pre-understanding and fusing of horizons (see Patte 2018: 28; Gadamer 1989: 1–50)—I agree with Patte on the "ethic of interpretation" to be our accountable method of reading, thus being transparent about our interpretive assumptions. Gadamer's hermeneutics correctly accepts the finitude of human historicity, believing that human situatedness cannot be overcome by scientific method. Situatedness and historicity speak of the inevitable "pre-judgments" or "prejudices" that constitute the reality of an exegete's being (Gadamer 1989: 364; Thiselton 1997: 313–30). Thus, Gadamerian hermeneutics teaches us exegetes to be open to truth and to pluralistic interpretations. Reading Romans for me—such as the usage of δικαιοσύνη θεοῦ—will inevitably be filtered through my Chinese assumptions about *yi* (justice/righteousness), *Dao* (Way), *de* (morality). To quote myself from *Musing with Confucius and Paul*:

> Paul's discussion of divine self revelation and of the divine-human relation, found in Rom 1:18-32, is comparable to the Confucian understanding of *Dao* (Way) and *Tian* (Heaven), as well as to the dialectical relationship between the transcendent and immanent *Tian* (Heaven) and thus between *Dao* (Way) and *de* (ethics). In Rom 1 Paul explains that his gospel of Jesus Christ contains the power of God for salvation based not on works [obedience] but on faith. Paul argues that despite the revelation of God's (invisible) nature and the moral obligation of humanity arising from it, all people sin against him and fall short of his glory. According to Confucius, *Tian* (Heaven) is both transcendent and immanent: Creative *Dao* (Way) is transcendent, an elusive aspect of *Tian*; immanent *Tian* is the all-pervading life-force that expresses itself in virtue. For Confucius transcendence is best known in its immanence; it is virtue that reveals one's relationship with *Tian*. The mandate of *Tian* is to be moral selves, the free expression of oneness with *Tian*. While the cultural contexts and the issues addressed are different in Confucius and Paul, their arguments are similar. They include (1) the ethical quality of the eternal power and divine nature of God; (2) the ethical demand implicit in the self-revelation of God's righteousness; (3) the universality and clarity of God's self-revelation in creation (for which reason humanity is "without excuse" [Rom 1: 20]); (4) the criterion by which God judges humanity is its response to the universal self-revelation of God. (2008: 129)

Paul's usage of δικαιοσύνη θεοῦ in Romans connotes the revelation of θεός; therefore, his argument follows that humanity is "without excuse" (Rom 1:20) in responding to this revealed knowledge (1:19). In Confucian thought, Heaven can communicate, though it does not speak, or it does not *have* to speak—perhaps this is what Paul means with regard to nature as the first Bible/revelation of God (1:20). Heaven or God has will and does care for the creation, but, in Confucianism (and Daoism), Heaven acts *naturally* without intervention or disruption of human beings—whereas Paul's God "gave [them] up" (παραδίδωμι in 1:24, 26, 27, 28) without intervening in their godliness and wickedness. Since Confucius emphasizes morality much more than religiosity, a Confucian exegesis of Rom 1 inevitably understands the judgment of God as departing from the mandate of Heaven, that is, the will of God. For Confucius, "the true servant of Heaven should focus solely upon his virtue and leave its recompense to will/destiny/mandate [*ming*] (4:9, 4:14, 4:16, 11:18, 12:4-12:5, 14:36; 15:32)." *Tian-ming* (mandate of Heaven) is the *ming* (destiny), referring to the heavenly rules and moral principles with which one is obliged to comply. To reject Heaven's mandates that are communicated to us in creation is to disrupt the natural order of things. A Confucianist would find the God in Rom 1 too harsh and demanding in rendering judgment on humanity. For a Confucianist, one is able to accept the mandate of Heaven because *Tian* is the source of benevolence, and *Tian* is omniscient and thus cannot be fooled (*Analects* 9:12). Perhaps, a Confucianist Christian can read the sovereign will of God as a pre-horizoning (προορίζω or pre-place) sense of destination (Rom 8:28-30) but not predeterminism (Yeo 2004c: 259–89; 2002: 526–47).

Two more benefits of this cross-cultural exegesis of Rom 1 by a Confucian Christian are: (i) the way Confucius transforms the meaning of *Tian* and its mandate/will into a moral-spiritual principle of goodness and beauty allows us to see the aesthetic glory of God's eternal power and divine nature; (ii) the way Confucius transforms the mandate of Heaven from a political idea to a moral privilege of *all people* allows us to see if and how Paul critiques the emperor cult in his theology here. *Tian-ren he-yi* (union between Heaven and humanity) in Confucianism is not the only prerogative of the rulers over their subjects; it is now the prerogative of all people to cultivate virtues in fulfilling the will of Heaven. Confucius's *Tian-ming* (mandate of Heaven) is not exactly the same as Paul's "will of God" (cf. Gal 1:4): Paul's is christocentric in terms of Jesus's self-sacrifice as delivering of humanity from the present evil aeon. But in Confucius and Paul, Heaven (*Tian*) or God (θεός) has communicated his will, both of which have to do with saving and cultivating humanity *to becoming fully human*. To revere *Tian* in one's path toward becoming fully human is an explicit Confucian semantic but, in Paul's language, the common expression is to grant "glory to God" (Rom 1:23; 3:7, 23; 4:20; 5:2; 6:4; 11:36; 16:27; cf. Gal 1:5) to Christ's followers toward freedom (Rom 9:4, 23; 15:7)--that is, to be who they are as creatures made in the image of God (8:21).

Third Plane: Cross-Cultural Hermeneutic

The third triangle of Figure 7.3 is a necessary extension or re-figuration (Patte 2018: 240) of the first (Figure 7.1) and the second (Figure 7.2), because the fluidity of the meaning of the Romans text will want to free—rather than freeze—its utterance beyond the fixed text (script) for a modern audience. Biblical texts in their long history of reception have demonstrated that textual impact has influenced and will continue to influence (positively, negatively, or a mixture of both) outside its original context. This third plane (Figure 7.3) of meaning involves the interaction

kairotic message

modern audience   modern interpreter

Figure 7.3 Third plane of cross-cultural interpretation.

among three dimensions: a modern interpreter's understanding of the first two triangles, in interaction with her modern audience, and the configuration of her contemporary kairotic message:

The interactional process of the three angles in this third triangle, engaging with each other simultaneously, is often called "application" or sermon. For modern readers of the Romans text to assume that we can fully participate in the first, second, and third planes may be naïve, though diligence must be our work at every level of reading as much as possible; this, Patte's work has sought to include and demonstrate. We as interpreters play a significant role in the overall meaning-finding and meaning-producing process that is complex, because our readings will involve at least three planes (Figures 7.1, 7.2, and 7.3), each of which interacts and forms a confluence with the other two (thus becoming Figure 7.4).

Let me give an example. The word δικαιοσύνη is translated as *yi* (righteousness) in the Chinese Bible. *Yi* is the ultimate moral goal of *jun-zi*, literally "son of the lord." In Confucius's era, *jun-zi* as "son of the lord" is preoccupied with the power to rule over others, yet Confucius sees this vortex of power without virtue is corruption of power. Thus, Confucius's countercultural teaching is that *jun-zi* now should be impartial, that is, neither favor nor disfavor anyone under Heaven; they ought to "keep close to whoever is righteous (*yi*)" (*Analects* 4:10; also 7:31, 17:23). The righteousness of Heaven immanently engenders in those pursuing moral perfection—called *jun-zi* (refined by Confucius) and thus often translated in English as "[morally] exemplary persons" or "best moral selves" to make the meaning explicit (Huang 1997: 69). *Jun-zi* are "conversant with righteousness" (*Analects* 4:16), they care for the poor (*Analects* 6:4), they are trustworthy and calm (*Analects* 8:6), and they dissociate with those who behave unkindly (*Analects* 17:7; see Yeo 2008: 276–303, 339–47). *Jun-zi* have a sense of righteousness as their disposition, and they "have three kinds of conduct that they guard against: when young and vigorous, they guard against licentiousness; in their prime when their vigor is at its height, they guard against conflict; in their old age when their vigor is declining, they guard against acquisitiveness" (*Analects* 16:7; see Ames and Rosemont 1998: 198). In Rom 1, when Paul discusses the concept of δικαιοσύνη, it would be ideal if he would give also an expansive definition of virtues that are considered "righteous/just." Would the list of vices Paul gives in Rom 1 be much shorter if he had read the *Analects*? The *Analects* argues that *jun-zi*

7. A Chinese Cross-Cultural Reading of "δικαιοσύνη θεοῦ"

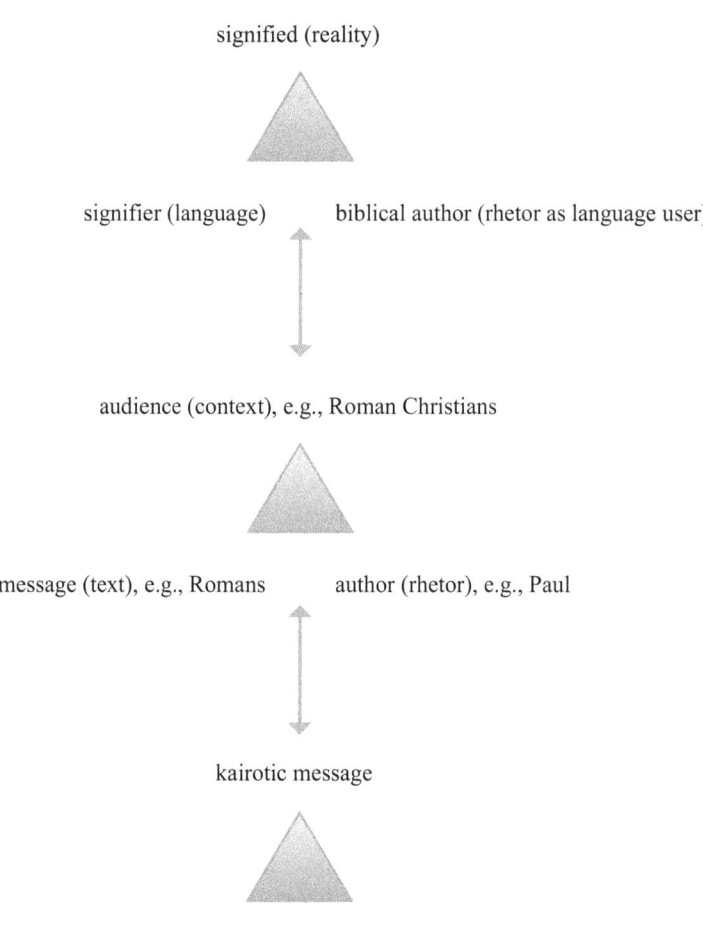

Figure 7.4 All three planes together form the whole reading process.

always keep nine things in mind: in looking they think about clarity, in hearing they think about acuity, in countenance they think about cordiality, in bearing and attitude they think about deference, in speaking they think about doing their utmost (*zhong*), in conducting affairs they think about due respect, in entertaining doubts they think about the proper questions to ask, in anger they think about regret, in sight of gain they think about [righteousness]. (*Analects* 16:10; see Ames and Rosemont 1998: 199)

While Paul did not engage with the *Analects*, Confucianist Chinese could, but unfortunately only few would.

Nothing and No One Has Absolute Control

To conclude, I wish to wrestle with my own questions along the way as I read Patte's work. First, differences and divergences in interpretation of a same text are positive, but what about conflicting or opposing views? My cross-cultural method seems to find Patte's claim of "legitimate until proven otherwise" to be overly cautious. I think languages change, the Romans text changes (see those textual variants), the Apostle Paul changed his thought from one setting to the next, and interpreters are multiple; thus, nothing and no one really has absolute control on *the* meaning of the Epistle to the Romans. This does not mean that "anything goes"; it simply means there are more interpretations than we are often allowed to have. Just because we cannot (positively) accept all interpretations as plausible and valid does not mean that we have to state (negatively) that some interpretations are disallowed. My recommendations on this point are fourfold.

First, putting the nine angles of the three triangles together, none are fixed or static. It is perhaps possible that the Romans text allows or encourages two opposing voices. For example, the ambiguity or semantic domain of different languages inevitably allows for multiple (and sometimes opposing) voices (cf. Patte 2018: 47). The idea of the inconsistencies/discrepancies/contradictions and tensions of Paul that need to be resolved is not a Chinese preoccupation, for even the biblical witnesses suggest multiplicity rather than singularity—multiplicity that is not only meaningful but, at times, even chaotic. Perhaps, more often than not, it is not the case that some interpretations are implausible or wrong but that all interpretations have their shortcomings and strengths—differing only in a matter of degree.

Second, putting the nine angles of the three triangles together (Figure 7.4) will encourage us to critically reflect and, ideally, keep us (although there is no fool-proof protection here!) from offering an interpretation that is counter to the salvation Christ has done for humanity—that is, the justice/righteousness of God (δικαιοσύνη θεοῦ). The ethic of biblical interpretation calls and judges interpreters to their task, and I recall:

> Every time I use the ten-volume lexicon entitled *TDNT* (*Theological Dictionary of the New Testament*) or simply called "Kittel," it is a painful reminder that some of the scholars and their best biblical scholarship—such as that of Gerhard Kittel and some of the contributors of *TDNT*—may have "willingly aided and abetted the Nazi movement" [according to Daley-Bailey 2012]. Kittel published a 78-page booklet entitled *Judenfrage* ("The Jewish Question") a month after he joined the Nazi party, proposing granting guest status to German Jews, in light of the other alternatives of extermination (he dismissed as impractical), forced exile to a Jewish state in the Middle East (he warned of hostilities from Arabs), and assimilation in Germany (he argued that was actually the problem, resulting secular liberalism). (Yeo 2018: 49)

Reading Romans today in the complex situation of modern Israel and the struggle of Palestinians calls for equal seriousness of caution. If the radical Zionist theology is used to exclude, dehumanize, or even demonize Palestinians, should that be called out as unethical interpretation? Patte raised a similar heart-wrenching question regarding the sociopolitical state of the United States: "Who is helped and who is hurt when one chooses one interpretation rather than another" (2018: xxv)? Will there be interpretations that we will lament and reject as implausible readings of Romans based on "ethic of interpretation"—those that go against the basic thesis of Romans to save *all* (πας)?[5] In other words, while contextual interpretations allow polyvalent readings of Romans, those readings that seek to destroy, rather than save, anyone will go against the meaning of the *gospel* of Christ as stated in Rom 1:16 (the gospel "is the power of God for salvation *to everyone* who believes"). But because doing biblical interpretation is such a complex and explosive business, let me further discuss two points that may help us to be sober about our work.

Third, my cross-cultural method does not simply want to explain why one interpretation reads the Romans text the way it does; my method calls for "crossing over" to other cultural interpretations (including contradictory ones) for greater meaningful interpretation that will garnish salvation, rather than damnation, of Jew or gentile, Greek or barbarian, and so on. I think Patte did write his volume on Romans based on his wisdom from scriptural criticism. If I am correct in my assumption, then scriptural criticism and my cross-cultural method have similar aspirations. For I see the ethics of biblical interpretations encompassing *humility and empathy* as we learn from others. I see the benefits of Patte's research on the three exegeses in helping us see the strengths and shortcomings of each one and gain the courage and faith for one culture to receive meanings beyond their own. In doing so, we will participate in a similar interpretive process of Romans that lives out its eschatological motif of Paul's resurrection theology—since both eschatology and resurrection point to a new openness of the human condition toward greater clarity of the future for all. This thinking is consistent with the open-endedness of the *Dao* (Way) in ancient Chinese philosophy.

Fourth, what would I do with Patte's three exegeses anti-commentary work (2018: 90)? For me, a Chinese Christian scholar, Patte's work is invaluable precisely in the understanding of the interrelationship among the three mutually engaging exegeses (88)—that is, their rhetorical interaction that continuously empowers readers to describe and shape the world in which we live. Paul's "horizon of faith" (55) in the "justice/righteousness/rightwising of God" vision speaks of individual forensic justification, covenantal community's inclusivity, and realized-apocalyptic/messianic vision of other-centeredness; all these demonstrate the gospel as the "power of God for salvation" for all. Interpreted in the Confucian moral framework and interrelational semantic (thus similarly to Patte's intratextual, intertextual; 236), the three critical exegeses can engage further with the goal (*telos*) of Confucius's moral world as harmony between Heaven (*Tian*) and humanity/humaneness (*ren*). According to Confucius, it is the ethical life that aesthetically actualizes the creativity and goodness of Heaven (*Tian*). Confucius sees being human as loving

---

5. Paul uses πας ["all, everyone"] sixty-one times; see Patte (2018: 205).

others (*ren-ren*) and, to him, loving others fulfills the will of Heaven (*Tian-ming*). Patte's discussion of three exegeses' movement from *individual* to *community* to *others* reminds me of the Confucian blueprint of the spiral process of life ("the organic structure of practical life"; 150): study the world, gain knowledge, have sincere intentions, regulate the heart/mind, cultivate yourself—then you can manage your family, govern the state, and bring justice and virtue to the world (*Daxue* or Great Learning). Each of the three exegeses, individually by itself, offers limited meaning (though plausible), so we can conclude that: (i) no exegesis can be true and complete in every time and in every place, and (ii) every interpretation will need to engage with others to become authentic, true, and complete. Patte closes his volume so beautifully: "Being ethically responsible—giving birth to the true-true—involves braiding our chosen interpretation with those of colleagues, making a hut with them" (474).

Congratulations, Daniel Patte, for such trailblazing work, and thank you for inviting me on the journey!

Chapter 8

A HISTORICAL ANALYSIS OF DANIEL PATTE'S STRATEGIES AND ETHICS OF READING WITH A FOCUS ON ROMANS 1:16-18 AND 1:26-27

Bernadette J. Brooten

This is a remarkable, densely argued, creative, and original study. I would like to address three areas. First, I will locate the study within the history of Christian reading strategies through the centuries. Second, I will take a closer look at Patte's three interpretations of Rom 1:16-17 or 16-18, usually understood to be the verses that signal the meaning of the letter as a whole. Third, in closing, I will say a few words related to Rom 1:26-27.

Reading Strategies: Daniel Patte and His Predecessors

In the late ancient Mediterranean world, the interpretive schools of Antioch and Alexandria competed with each other (for a survey of these interpretive schools, see Grant and Tracy 2005). In Antioch, scholars undertook grammatical-historical exegeses and were skeptical of allegorical interpretation, seeing it as fantastical and without boundaries. According to some classicists, the allegorical interpretive method extends far back in time, perhaps even to Homer himself, but certainly to Homeric interpretation in the Hellenistic and Roman periods. Allegorical interpreters saw the grammatical and historical meanings of the text as an entry point to the deeper, more spiritual, more significant meanings. The text thus meant something other than what it seemed to mean. Such Jewish philosophers as Philo of Alexandria, using this method, could interpret, for example, the biblical figure to Rebecca to signify a virtue. For example, in Philo's *On the Cherubim*, Rebecca signifies the virtue of "steadfastness in excellence" (*Cher.* 41). Origen of Alexandria exemplifies Christian allegorical interpretation. For Origen, the grammatical and historical level of the text represented the surface level, which for him was the Jewish level, the fleshly level, which one should take into account and then transcend. Well into the high Middle Ages and beyond, exegetes sought to discern the fourfold sense of scripture: (i) the grammatical and historical sense, in the wake of Origen understood to be the fleshly, Jewish, and thereby inferior level; (ii) the allegorical sense; (iii) the tropological or moral sense; and (iv) the anagogical or eschatological sense (Lubac 1998–2009). In short, a specific text had multiple meanings, not just one. Beyond this, any exegete who observed previous interpretations could see that the text was unstable, that it could be taken in multiple ways. One literary manifestation of this was the synoptic printing of multiple interpretations next to each other in one volume.

The Enlightenment introduced scientific skepticism, encompassing a demand for evidence and, eventually, peer review. Historians moved away from chronicles and toward evidence-based history, with its skepticism of the veracity of sources. Legal historians analyzed the Justinian Digest and other sources of Roman law to determine developments within Roman law and jurisprudence. German legal historians found many interpolations within the Justinian Digest (Savigny 1840: 257; Buckland 1924: 343–64; Röhle 2008: 671-2, 664–73). German Protestant biblical exegetes enthusiastically adopted Enlightenment principles. Like the legal historians exegeting the Justinian Digest, they found interpolations. Most significantly, they developed the Documentary Hypothesis for the Pentateuch and various hypotheses to explain the overlaps and discrepancies among the Synoptic gospels as well as theories about Paul and about competing theologies to that of Paul (Wellhausen 1927; Griesbach 1789; Baur 2003). As with the natural sciences, the goal was to arrive at one best interpretation: the truth will out.

In the United States, fundamentalism arose in response to higher biblical criticism and Darwin's theory of evolution, as well as to biblical debates over slavery. As Mark Noll has persuasively argued in *The Civil War as a Theological Crisis* (2006), US Protestants in the nineteenth century agreed both that the meaning of the Bible was plain for all to see and that law and public policy should be based on it. Profound disagreements over whether the Bible supported slavery, which was a central legal and policy question, led to a theological crisis. The abolition of legal slavery through military means meant that the theological crisis was never resolved. The theological debate over enslaving human beings has echoes in today's debates over the role of the Bible in law and policy and over passages of significance to law and policy, such as legal recognition of LGBTQ persons and their relationships and of the category of transgender and gender-nonconforming individuals. As this very cursory discussion of several modes of Christian biblical interpretation makes clear, fundamentalism is a thoroughly modern phenomenon. Rather than seeing a biblical text as having multiple meanings, fundamentalism seeks one meaning, the one correct meaning, the one plain meaning, the one historically and scientifically accurate meaning.

Biblical scholars, however, often overlook the commonalities between the historical-critical method and fundamentalism. Both seek one best meaning, the philologically correct meaning. Both listen for the clarity of the best meaning and try to block out the noise of extraneous, superfluous, and incorrect interpretations. Both appeal to science, historical critics in endeavoring to follow scientific methods and fundamentalists in claiming to put forth legitimate scientific theories, such as creationism or intelligent design.

Now a word about postmodern architecture, architecture being the discipline in which postmodernism first took hold (Venturi et al. 1972). In contrast to modern architecture, with its focus on form and function and its love of crystalline spare geometric shapes with little or no decoration, postmodern architecture returns to the past, incorporating traditional elements, which normally means some decoration, that is, forms with no other function than to please the senses of sight and touch. In addition, the architect uses all available materials and designs, creating something not only traditional but also thoroughly contemporary.

Enter Daniel Patte's *Romans: Three Exegetical Interpretations and the History of Reception, Volume 1*. Like postmodern architecture, Patte's *Romans* goes back to a time before the thoroughly modern historical criticism and fundamentalism, with their love of one clear, best meaning, to a time of interpretive multiplicity, of the inherent instability of the text. Rather than presenting one interpretation, Patte presents his readers, also understood to be communities, with three. Polyphony returns with all its musical complexity. As with postmodern architecture, Patte's *Romans* is also doing something very new, something contemporary. He reflects on the potential uses of each interpretation in time and space, arguing that each of the three interpretations may serve particular communities under specific historical circumstances. I do not know of that level of critical reflection about the potential for multiple communal uses of more than one interpretation in previous exegetical work. Christian theological interpreters, including myself, will often spell out the significance of their own interpretation for church and society, but that is quite different from what Patte does here, and I find what he does to be quite intriguing. Patte's *Romans* further resembles postmodern architecture in its incorporation of early Christian interpretations, as well as of interpretations with historical-critical roots.

While there is a postmodernity in the polyphony of the three exegeses, their being mostly historically critically based appears to me, however, not to be postmodern in the literary sense. The postmodern reader, as the co-signer to the text, is not constrained by historical meanings, which are, instead, without limit. Now, one might argue that these exegeses' origin in historical-critical interpreters does not, in itself, render them historical-critical. By presenting the three together, the meaning of the text becomes the meanings of the text. I personally admire historical criticism's boldness and its view that some interpretations are far more historically plausible than others, and I prefer interpreters who assume that the historical meanings of a text are not infinitely malleable. Beyond that, I critically seek historical meanings to texts, although with awareness of the plausibility of other construals. For these reasons, I see Patte's presentation of three historically plausible exegeses as a plus. His deep engagement with the history of interpretation, especially the earliest interpretations, resembles postmodern architecture's use of traditional elements, its simultaneous love of the past and of the present. For most of Christian history, Western theologians deemed it natural and essential to read the history of interpretation, but Protestants first and then Catholics gradually moved to a more presentist exegesis. By contrast, Greek and other Eastern

Orthodox Christians and Jewish interpreters maintained what I would like to call the humility of consulting earlier interpreters.

Historical-critical exegetes have often seen exegeses before the nineteenth century as shaped only by their own culture and of little interest for what the text might be about. And yet, anyone who seriously immerses themselves in the history of interpretation may come to see how difficult it actually is to say something genuinely new. I want to give two examples, both from Romans. When I researched the history of the interpretation of the name Junia (Brooten 1977), which most scholars at that time construed as an otherwise unattested male name, Junias, I discovered that I was saying nothing different from John Chrysostom, who praised Junia as being deemed worthy of the title of apostle. Beyond that, I found an eighteenth-century Leipzig dissertation by Christian Wilhelm Bose (Bose and Börner 1742), who said exactly what I was saying about the name Junia. Whereas I stressed the irony in rendering a name as male when there were no attested uses in inscriptions of the name Junias, Bose was outright sarcastic about it. In addition, one of the exegetical cruxes of Rom 1:26 is whether "their" women had sex with other women, comparable to the men of Rom 1:27, or whether they engaged in another kind of unnatural sex. The earliest commentators are evenly split on this question. Tertullian (second through third century) does not specify, but Ambrosiaster (fourth century) and John Chrysostom (fourth through fifth century) take it to refer to sex between women, and Augustine (fourth through fifth century) and Anastasios (date unknown) envision an unnatural form of sex between women and men.[1] Similarly, today, some take Rom 1:26 to refer to sex between women (Jewett 2007: 172–7; Brooten 1996: 239–53, 337–8, 353) and others to another form of unnatural sex (Bannister 2009: 569–90; Kuefler 2001: 383n; Fredrickson 2000: 197–222). We are not doing anything new in debating this point. Of course, discoveries of archeological remains, new papyri, codices, leather scrolls, and inscriptions provide both new readings of biblical texts and new literary and documentary texts that yield a better historical understanding of them. I am unable here to go into the details of the historical and contextual interpretations of Rom 1, upon which Patte draws to elucidate his three exegeses, but they will provide every reader with pause before dismissing a specific exegesis.

I see the ethics of exegesis to be the single most significant driving force in this book. What are the possible effects of each interpretation? The multiplicity of interpretations, so carefully spelled out, gravitates against both fundamentalism

---

1. Tertullian, *De Corona* 6 (Tertullian and Fontaine 1966: 86–7); John Chrysostom, *Homily on Romans 1:26–27* (PG 60.416bot–417mid) takes Rom 1:26 to refer to female-female sexual contact, as does Ambrosiaster (Vogels 1966: 50–1; Bruyn et al. 2017: 30–1). Note that Ambrosiaster changed his mind, as is evidenced by the manuscripts (Bruyn 2011: 463–83). Augustine, *De nuptiis et concupiscentia* 20.35 (Urba and Zycha 1902: 289), and Anastasios, tenth-century scholion by Arethas on Clement of Alexandria, *Paidagōgos* 3.3.21.3 (Stählin 1972: 337), take Rom 1:26 to refer to sexual contact between women and men.

and a type of historical-critical exegesis that pays no attention to how an interpretation functions in the world.

Rom 1:16-17 or 1:16-18

In *Romans: Three Exegetical Interpretations and the History of Reception, Volume 1*, Patte delineates three exegetical interpretations of Rom 1:1-32. As a mode of trying to condense this massive work, I will focus on Rom 1:16-17 or 16-18, which most interpreters see as the thesis statement or as setting up what will follow in the letter. Here are the three interpretations.

The first interpretation is a forensic theological one, which focuses on the individual in relation to God the judge, who can be both wrathful and the giver of grace. Patte sees such commentators as Frantz J. Leenhardt, Douglas Moo, Ulrich Wilckens, Peter Stuhlmacher, Joseph Fitzmyer, and Richard Longenecker interpreting Romans within a forensic theological framework. In this interpretation, Rom 1:16-17 summarizes not only Rom 1 but also the whole of Paul's theology:

> For I am not ashamed of the gospel; for it is the power of God for salvation to everyone who believes, to the Jew first and then to the Greek. For in it the righteousness of God is being revealed, from faith for faith, even as it is written, "The one who is righteous by faith will live" [Habakkuk 2:4]. (Rom 1:16-17, Moo) (Patte 2018: 101)

Paul's theology can be summed up in "justification by faith," derived from Romans and epitomized by Rom 1:16-17. How can an individual come into right relation with God? That question is at the center of the classical construals of Romans by Augustine and the Augustinian monk Martin Luther. God is indeed a judge, but one by whom an individual can be justified, not on the basis of good works but rather on the basis of faith.

According to this understanding of the rhetoric, the Jewish person in Rom 2:1 who condemns others is the target, and faith in Christ involves a separation from Judaism.

Second, a covenantal community interpretation of Rom 1 focuses not on the individual but rather on the community and the call for it to be inclusive. Exegetes in this line of thinking tend to see Paul behaving as a Jew in affirming Jesus as the Messiah/*Mashiach*/*Christos* and wanting to bring that Jewish message to Gentiles, challenging those Gentiles who seem to want to separate from Judaism. Relations between Christ-followers and Jewish communities and between Christ-followers and the Roman state are central to this line of thought. These interpreters aim to delineate the ancient group contexts and to select properly one or more contemporary context. Anti-Semitism, the Shoah, and empire (both ancient and modern) can constitute the context. Robert Jewett is Patte's main discussion partner in the covenantal community interpretation.

Patte's rendering of Rom 1:16-17 illustrates his view that a covenantal community reading is plausible and valid:

> For I am not ashamed of the gospel-story, for it is the power of the covenant God for salvation to the faithful, both to the Jew first and then to the Greek, for in it the justice of God is revealed through faithfulness for faithfulness; as it is written, "The one who is just shall live by faithfulness." (2018: 172)

Patte argues that these verses, so understood, challenge the honor-and-shame ideology, the power and practice of justice in the Roman Empire, and Gentile Christ-followers who may not understand the Jewish people and their covenant with God as God's people.

According to this construal, Paul is addressing Gentile Christ-followers, with Jewish Christ-followers as secondary addressees.

Finally, in the realized-apocalyptic/messianic vision interpretation, the commentator takes full account of Paul's embeddedness in Jewish apocalyptic in the sense that Jesus is the Messiah, that he was raised from the dead, that evil powers aim to separate humans from God, and that the promises of scripture are being fulfilled. Discussion partners include Ernst Käsemann, Leander Keck, and J. Christiaan Beker, but also postmodern philosophers and exegetes. Rather than looking at Romans as a compendium (Melanchthon) or as a story, commentators in this category look for themes, figures, typology, and surprises. Patte employs a typological apocalyptic hermeneutic.

In this view, Rom 1:16-18, rather than 1:16-17, provide insight into the letter:

> I am not ashamed of the gospel. It [the gospel] is the power of God for salvation to everyone who believes/has faith/vision. Because the righteousness of God is revealed in it [in the gospel] through faith/vision for faith/vision, as it is written: the righteous will live through faith/vision. Because the wrath of God is revealed from heaven against all impiety and unrighteousness of humans. (Patte 2018: 286)

To use Patte's own words, "What is revealed is a manifestation of the transformative power of God in the form of God's righteousness" (281). Patte seeks to show through figures why this is so. The revelation occurs not only in God's intervention in Christ but in ongoing revelation: powerful interventions will continue in the future.

Each of these three interpretations can have powerful communal and political effects. Seeing Romans as about justification by faith alone can free Christians plagued by a competitive society that measures success by what you do and accomplish and, particularly in the Western churches, can promote guilt for not doing enough good in the world. The individualistic focus can, however, also promote quietism, a tendency to neglect civil society and communal justice out of the view that individual salvation supersedes all other concerns. Exegetes employing the covenantal community interpretation are promoting Christian self-reflection on the long history of Christian anti-Judaism and its relation to anti-Semitism and challenging the ways in which Romans interpretations may have supported those phenomena. Their critical thought about imperialistic ideologies of domination in relation to both the earliest Christ-believers and to contemporary Christians can help Christians to contribute to more inclusive, equal, and cohesive societies. The realized-apocalyptic/messianic vision interpretation is well rooted within an important strand of the Jewish thought of Paul's time and is thus historically highly plausible. Reading Paul through an apocalyptic lens can be salutary for post-Enlightenment Christians because it preserves historical distance between contemporary rationalistic and scientific thinking and a Paul whose thought may not be compatible with that type of thinking. Seeing Paul as a strange and culturally distant figure can help readers to cultivate humility about how well one can actually understand the past and the scriptures composed in it. On the other hand, of course, a new form of apocalyptic thinking is alive and well, certainly in the United States today, within which an apocalyptic Paul is familiar and not strange at all. The challenge of any concept of revelation is how to discern it.

Rom 1:26-27

In closing, I will say a few words related to Rom 1:26-27 (on sex between women and between men) and point to an effect of a specific mode of reading the Bible, from which I will then return to Patte and to Romans. Recent social-scientific research of the level of fundamentalism in a pastor or among college students correlates with their acceptance of rape myths. In their article "Clergy's Attitudes and Attributions of Blame toward Female Rape Victims" (2002), Jane P. Sheldon and Sandra L. Parent describe their research with pastors, in which they measured Christian pastors' level of fundamentalism through a scale and presented pastors with three rape scenarios. In their study, the higher the level of fundamentalism, the more likely were the pastors to blame a rape victim (233–56). Another research study of 626 Christian college students resulted in a comparable result (Koch and Ramirez 2010: 402–10). The single most quoted verses of Rom 1 today in debates over public policy and law are Rom 1:26-27 on sex between women and between men and perhaps also on other forms of sexual behavior involving women that were deemed unnatural. Christians who oppose acceptance of LGBTQ people have in the past opposed domestic violence shelters receiving public funding if they served LGBTQ individuals and communities. This view often derived from Rom 1:26-27 and other biblical passages, as well as from church tradition. Might those who take these passages to mean that all forms of sexual love practiced by LGBTQ persons are unnatural also be more likely to blame the victim in cases of domestic and sexual violence? Domestic and sexual violence are major problems today among LGBTQ persons and desperately need addressing. Social scientific research works here with a blunt instrument, namely to measure the level of fundamentalism. Social scientists are not trained to ask about the interpretations of specific passages, such as Lev 18:22 and 20:13, Rom 1:26-27, the Household

Codes, and so on. What if biblical scholars, who know which passages are the most influential in church discussions about gender and sexuality, were to conduct such research, asking pastors and other Christians their interpretations of those passages that play the greatest role on the questions of female subordination, acceptance of LGBTQ individuals, and the like? I strongly encourage such research. Comparable research attempting to correlate each of these exegeses or others with potentially harmful attitudes relevant to the specific passages could be a way of actualizing Patte's concerns about dangerous effects. Former US attorney general Jeffrey Sessions used Rom 13 to quench dissent about the Trump administration's immigration policy on the border with Mexico (Zauzmer and McMillan 2018). Systematic investigation of how specific interpretations of Rom 13 might correlate with tolerance of political dissent could be very fruitful. I greatly look forward to Patte's exegeses of Rom 13. Maybe by that time, a biblical scholar, perhaps collaborating with a social scientist, will have established correlations that he can incorporate into his study.

Thank you, Daniel Patte, for such a stimulating and uplifting book.

Part IV

FUTURE APPLICATION AND PAST INFLUENCE

Chapter 9

PATTE'S *ROMANS* IN THE CLASSROOM: CAN THE INTRODUCTION AND CHAPTER 1 PROVIDE STUDENTS AN ENTRÉE INTO POSTMODERN HERMENEUTIC THEORY AND PRACTICE?

John Jones

Introduction

This is a brief report on an early experiment: a reading assignment and classroom discussion drawn from the introduction and chapter 1 in volume 1 of Daniel Patte's *Romans* (2018: 1–45).

La Sierra University, a comprehensive denominational (Seventh-day Adventist) institution in Riverside, California, enrolls a highly diverse student body of under three thousand students in four schools. The H. M. S. Richards Divinity School, composed of four departments (biblical studies; theology, ethics, and history of Christian thought; pastoral ministry; and religious studies) offers baccalaureate programs in religious studies and in Near Eastern archeology, plus a pre-seminary curriculum. Its graduate programs are the master of theological studies (MTS), master of divinity (MDiv), and master of arts (in religious studies or Near Eastern archeology).

As is typical, our MTS and MDiv curricula have provided exposure to the traditional scholarly approaches to hermeneutics plus over the past two decades and more, increasing engagement with postmodern approaches. Krister Stendahl's classic essay "Biblical Theology" (1962) has provided the conceptual grounding for readings and exercises relating to the former perspective. Elisabeth Schüssler Fiorenza's Society of Biblical Literature (SBL) presidential address on "The Ethics of Biblical Interpretation" (1988) has launched the students' exposure to rhetorical considerations that provide for diversity of interpretations from overtly positioned readers.

The Quest

In a sustained quest for a third focal essay that could complete a trilogy of readings to anchor our MTS/MDiv students' understandings of the background and evolution of scriptural interpretation, the biblical studies faculty has considered several options. Such a third document, it was felt, should provide a broad accounting of the developments in hermeneutical theory that underlie and carry forward the paradigm shift hailed by Schüssler Fiorenza. It should set forth something of how the worlds "in front of" the text are being brought into conversation with the scholar's traditional focus on the worlds "behind" and "within" the text. It should indicate the impact of current insights into meaning-production via the encounter between text and reader, thus taking account of the conditioned character of all exegetical endeavors. It should acknowledge the selective nature of interpretive choices as these are made by each reader. And it should provide some treatment of issues of controls, as deriving from (i) latent potentials within the text and (ii) the reader's openness to discern messages that, while necessarily perceived as addressing the reader's thought-world, may indeed counter previously held convictions.

Obviously, each of these angles requires further unpacking through additional readings and exercises. The intent has been to first tap a single integrative treatment that can help the student discern the whole. In so doing, such a discussion would show how these emerging trends bear upon the two integral acts of reading and interpretation. The act of reading thus locates itself as an ethical act with regard to those with whom its outcomes might be shared. And the exegetical act becomes one of conversation among equals, as the *pro me/pro nobis* quality of each interpreter's engagement with the text is allowed full voice.

Patte's Romans as Candidate

The committee's attention was particularly drawn to the essays appearing in the introduction and chapter 1 of Patte's *Romans*, which provide the combination of completeness and substance that we in the Biblical Studies Department have been looking for. While these opening sections launch a comparative exegetical commentary on a particular text, Patte's tracing-out of the text's reception by three types of interpretive communities over the centuries calls forth his opening essays that could equally well set the stage for comparable work across the canon. In a context of preparation for pastoral ministry, this treatment sets up the rationale for reading with one's congregants as their fellow disciple, rather than either to or for them (i.e., in authoritarian or presumptuous ways)—a vital consideration today.

Additional aspects that attracted the committee's attention include the following:

- An engaging eleven-page foreword (Patte 2018: xv–xxv) that locates the entire endeavor in today's cultural context of increasing relativism as a way of reckoning with the connotative force of language (Paul's and his interpreters');
- in the introduction (4–9), a pair of pointed illustrations of how the interpreter's choice of interpretive frames, in any given reading context, sets up issues of ethical accountability to fellow readers;

- an interweaving of the formative role, over a decade and a half, of very probing seminar sessions of the SBL, involving theologians, church historians and exegetes, as recounted by its central energizer;
- a "pilgrim's progress," so to speak, of Patte's own journey of insight in the company of these fellow pilgrims—a communal course remarkable for its shared rigor and integrity across diverse competencies; and
- a helpful section of pedagogical suggestions (39–45).

The Trial Run

The Divinity School's schedule of course offerings did not provide an opportunity in the autumn 2018 quarter to try this selection in an exegesis course on the graduate level. Less satisfactorily, an initial trial run was made that term with a fourth-year undergraduate course in the history of early Christian thought, enrolling religious studies majors, pre-seminary students, and general education students, of which I was the instructor. The majors had already received some initial exposure to traditional and postmodern hermeneutic theory and practice; the others had not. The Patte reading assignments were divided into two: (i) the introduction, followed by (ii) chapter 1. Coming during the seventh and eighth weeks, these followed upon examples of early Christian diversity in engaging various cultural contexts with early divergences in Christian thought and practice. So while the reading assignments did not engage the three streams of reception of Rom 1 as adduced in this volume, they did build on an evidentiary base of emerging disparities among early Christian communities, including their variations in readings of Christological texts in the early ecumenical councils.

Given the mixed enrollment and the undergraduate level of the course, this was bound to be a stretch for the students—in terms of both content and length. Accordingly, I devoted the two previous weeks to considerations of how circumstances in the first three centuries of Christian life set up the various questions that shaped early Christian discourse. This entailed thinking together about the thought-worlds not only "behind" and "within" the canonical and early post-canonical texts but also "in front of the texts," as we considered indications of how various groups of early Christians may have read through their respective eyeglasses. This step provided a natural entrée into the rise of postmodern approaches as presented in the two Patte assignments, devoted to implications for how we shall read today. I then took the first half of each of the two 100-minute sessions devoted to the Patte readings to "talk through" the issues involved, followed by free discussion in the second half. The discussions sparked lively engagement, involving both the religion and general education students.

I expected that the hermeneutic of encounter between text and reader might trigger more resistance than it did; the students seemed variously accepting of that dynamic model. More problematic was the concern on the part of a couple of the pre-seminary students that they would face backlash from their congregations over the resultant loss of univocal significations as presented in section II of chapter 1. While this was expressed as a pastoral concern, it clearly reflected some sense of personal challenge.

The ensuing discussion proved helpful, particularly with regard to the criteria of "plausibility" and "legitimacy." The fact that meaning-effects inevitably address tacit perspectives of receivers of a text (whether positively or negatively) helps provide a certain self-evident coherence to the readers'/hearers' perceived message. The students' discussion converged around the insight that semiotic structures within any semantically rich discourse can work to generate varied meaning-effects among varied recipients. The criteria of "value" and "validity," however, needed more help from the instructor. While uniformly affirming the picture of equally privileged voices around the interpretive table, the students parted ways over what to do in the event of incompatible applications. The ethic of accountability to others seemed self-evident to some students, while others understandably confessed a need "to think about this some more." Clearly, deeply ingrained assumptions about the singular demands of what is regarded as a prescriptive text (as a "Word-to-live-by") are not lightly reconsidered, for some. My recourse to semiotic theory went too far afield. In retrospect, I believe I should have found clearer, probably less theoretical ways to help address this criterion.

Results and Evaluation

These points comprised the gist of my report to the biblical studies faculty of the Divinity School in their first subsequent departmental meeting (January 31, 2019). Discussion led to consensus that we may be able to focus on some shorter portions of Patte's introduction and chapter 1 in our two upper-division courses on theory and practice of Old Testament/New Testament interpretation. It is also possible that some consultation with faculty in English literature (with whom we are happily on collegial terms) might help establish common frames of reference for our baccalaureate students. Even so, we continue to regard these essays of Patte's as better suited as a whole to the graduate level.

Accordingly we agreed to continue experimenting with Patte's essays in combination with those of Stendahl and Schüssler Fiorenza to provide a core set of readings to which each of our MTS/MDiv students would be exposed. Our two graduate courses in interpreting Old Testament/New Testament texts provide the most obvious venues for considering these three. Additionally, these could be well followed by illustrative examples of positioned readings.

Ultimately, we anticipate that even as the SBL seminars on postmodern hermeneutic theory and practice engaged theologians, historians, ethicists, and pastoral practitioners, so we may find ourselves increasingly exploring with colleagues of the other departments in the Divinity School the potentials for their involvement in the shared agenda to which Schüssler Fiorenza summons us:

> Such an approach [not only descriptive but also evaluative] opens up the rhetorical practices of biblical scholarship to the critical inquiry of all the

disciplines of religious studies and theology. Questions raised by feminist scholars in religion, liberation theologians, theologians of the so-called Third World, and by others traditionally absent from the exegetical enterprise would not remain peripheral or nonexistent for biblical scholarship. Rather, their insights and challenges could become central to the scholarly discourse of the discipline. (1988: 17)

Thus we regard the adoption of the proposed trilogy of focal essays as a possible shared action that could be taken, ultimately, by the entire Divinity School faculty, to be reflected throughout our MTS and MDiv curricula.

In sum, Patte's essays in his introduction and chapter 1 provide valuable insights into both the theoretical groundings and the historical development of postmodern perspectives as applied to biblical texts. His treatments of rhetorical implications for reader response and of the fruitfulness of multidisciplinary approaches are especially helpful. His carefully formulated paragraphs reflect the insights gained through years of vigorous, open-minded engagements with colleagues in a variety of academic disciplines. This comes through especially in his treatment of the criteria of plausibility, legitimacy, and validity in interpretation. The single greatest challenge in the Patte materials is their total length of forty-five substantive pages—doubtless necessary, but a particular demand under a quarter system of ten weeks per course. The need for efficiency will require considerable preparatory set-up by the instructor. At this time we are prepared to continue experimenting with this for the sake of the solid grounding these three selections in combination have to offer.

Chapter 10

THE TAPROOT OF MY PERCEPTION OF ROMANS AS NECESSARILY MULTIVALENT AND CONTEXTUAL

Daniel Patte

The comments of my colleagues are very generous, rich, and constructive. I greatly appreciate them and take them carefully into account in my future work. But as the title of the present essay expresses, my response does not prolong the comments of my colleagues. It goes in the opposite direction. It digs into my own experience to find the origins of *Romans: Three Exegetical Interpretations*. It asks: What initially motivated me to abandon a quest for "the (single) true meaning" of Paul's text and to recognize the contextual character of any given interpretation? What initially led me to acknowledge that no interpretation, including the most sophisticated ones, can ever be viewed as absolute?

For me, this issue arose out of the interpretation of Rom 1:16-17 and 3:21-24 by my Huguenot church and family since my youth. This is a long story—after all I wrote *Romans: Three Exegetical Interpretations* when I was in my seventies! So, it took me more than sixty years to reach the point where I could write this book. The "taproot of my perception of Romans as necessarily multivalent and contextual" goes deep into my life experience when I was a four-/five-year-old child. So be patient with me as I follow the twists and turns of my experience since childhood (in interaction with many others)—it is this multifarious experience that grounds this work.

I cannot remember when I became aware that Rom 1:16-17 and 3:21-24 should be read as proclaiming "justification and salvation by faith alone." It was simply self-evident in my Huguenot/Protestant context. Indeed, it would be better to say that I cannot remember a time when, for me, "justification and salvation by faith alone" was not the appropriate understanding of these verses. Already as a four-year-old and five-year-old child, I "felt" this was the proper meaning of these verses.

Of course, at that age, I did not read these verses by myself. Yet I "knew" these verses and their meaning—in the same way that Wole Soyinka, the future Nobel laureate of literature, knew/felt many things about his Yoruba culture already when he was a toddler.[1] These verses were among those that at bedtime my parents

---

1. I am alluding to Soyinka (1981), the first volume of his biography. In it, Soyinka brilliantly describes his progressive coming to consciousness, beginning with the description

read to me and my siblings and among the biblical texts on which I practiced my progressively improving reading skills. I had, of course, no clear understanding of the words "justification," "salvation," and "by faith alone."[2] But for me, as a child during World War II (especially when German troops occupied our small farm!), these words were a balm calming my fears and anxiety. We had faith in Jesus Christ. Therefore, God was with us, protecting us.

Yet, I soon recognized that these verses had at least one other meaning with a very different meaning-effect. In my first year in primary school, as a nearly five-year-old, I walked back and forth from school—a two or three mile hike—with Patrick, a schoolmate and neighbor, who soon became a good friend. New in Chabeuil (where we had just moved in 1943—it is a village in Drôme at the foot the Vercors, a mountainous Alpine plateau, which was an important location for the resistance during World War II), we did not know much about Patrick's family. They lived on a small farm that stood in between our farm and the village. So, at first, it was convenient for our mothers to alternatively accompany us. And Patrick quickly became my good friend and playmate. But this arrangement did not survive an incident.

Once, as we were coming back from school, my friend's mother stopped at a (Catholic) "church," asking us to play in its fenced courtyard while she was "going to confession."[3] For Patrick and me, this was not a problem. As four-/five-year-old boys, we were passionate marble players. So, we pulled out marbles from our pockets and began playing in the sandy walkway in between blooming bushes. Of course, as a Protestant, I had never entered the courtyard of this Catholic *église* (church), let alone the sanctuary. With my parents, we were attending services at the "temple" (as Protestant church buildings are usually called in France) a few blocks from there. And of course, I did not know what it meant to "go to confession." So, back home, I asked my mother. She was visibly upset that we arrived quite late, and even more so that we had stopped at this Catholic church. She took me aside and went on in a long explanation, telling me in substance, using words she hoped would be understandable for me, a child:

> Catholics believe they need to go and confess their sins to a priest in order to receive "absolution," that is, the assurance they are justified/forgiven by God. But for this, they must do the proper "penance" ("good works"). They believe

of the sounds and odors he first perceived in his Nigerian village of Aké—"sounds and odors that are still part of the memory of our own children, with whom we lived at the edge of the tropical forest in the Congo Brazzaville"—and then progressively discerning more and more abstract traditions and values that governed the life of his family and village ... and yet at each of these stages his views were and remained distorted by his fears of the unknown and turmoils that surrounded him.

2. As I understood "justice de Dieu par la foi en Jésus-Christ pour tous ceux qui croient" (Rom 3:22), the translation by Louis Segond that we were reading.

3. The church of Paroisse Saint Martin in Chabeuil, located not far from our school.

that it is because of the good things/good works they do that God loves them, protects them, and stays with them. They believe in justification/salvation by good works—works of the law; doing good things in order to be loved by God. This is totally ignoring the teaching of Paul and of the entire gospel. Instead of worshiping God and instead of having faith in Jesus Christ, they worship idols—statues. You saw in front of the church, the big statue of the Virgin Mary.

I was puzzled by my mother's strong reaction. Okay, we were late. But she was making a very big deal of the fact that I played marbles in the courtyard of a (Catholic) church. But apparently this was quite serious: from now on, I was actually forbidden to go back and forth from school with Patrick and his mother. From now on, since Patrick and his family were Catholic (something we did not know because we were new in the neighborhood), my mother would each time bring me to school and come and get me, and if she could not do it, my father or Mademoiselle Bé[4] (our Protestant neighbor and usual babysitter) would pick me up from school.

This was baffling for me. What! I had lost a friend because of Rom 1:16-17 and 3:21-24 and "justification and salvation by faith alone!" This teaching, which was a source of comfort and reassurance in times of anxiety, had also become a puzzling instrument of division and separation from my young Catholic neighbor. I wondered: Why do Catholics fail to read these verses of scripture? Indeed, it seems that their beliefs in confession and penance demonstrated that Catholics did not read their Bibles. Otherwise they would understand what Paul says so clearly in Rom 1:16-17 and 3:21-24. In short, I could not imagine that the same scriptural texts might be understood in different ways. But as a child I would soon learn about "conflicts of interpretations" (as Paul Ricoeur called them) regarding each given text of scripture.[5]

I progressively learned about "conflicts of interpretations" not only at home but also and mainly from annual "picnics" (for us, kids) and "memorial ceremonies" (for our parents) at the houses of our martyrs, such as the farm of the Huguenot pastor Pierre Durand and his sister Marie Durand—a farm-museum, le Bouschet de Pranles, a few miles from the homes of both of my grandparents. This museum carved in my young mind the graphic renderings of their sufferings at the hands of Catholic authorities: Pierre's imprisonment (in 1730) and his hanging (in 1732); Marie's imprisonment for thirty-eight years (from 1730 to 1768) in the Tour de Constance (near Nîmes). This tower/jail was another museum that we also visited regularly, on our way to the other annual picnics/memorial ceremonies at Le Mas Soubeyran (of the Camisard Roland [Laporte], 1675–1704, leader of

---

4. I guess her actual name was Béatrice. But despite fond memories, I never knew her full name, as she simply disappeared from my world as a child.

5. Ricoeur (1974). Paul Ricoeur was also a Huguenot; I attended, a generation after him, the same high school in Valence (Drôme).

an armed resistance fighting for the restoration of the Edict of Nantes),[6] and its Musée du Désert, presenting the long period (1685–1789) of active persecutions of Huguenots—the "Desert" period, during which our ancestors survived only by being underground in remote areas of the Cevennes.[7] All these museums also included worn-out Bibles as a reminder that Pierre, Marie, Roland, and all the other Huguenots were persecuted because they claimed the right to read the Bible for and by themselves. Being discovered with a Bible was enough to be imprisoned, to be sent to the galleys and other labor camps (of the Catholic king of France), or to be hanged. And these Huguenots died or were imprisoned for most of their lives, even though they could have been freed by a simple "abjuration" of their Protestant faith based upon their personal readings of scripture. They could be freed (as quite a few did) by simply adopting the pope's authorized interpretation of scripture. But they did not, as they viewed this teaching as a demonic "papist" misinterpretation. The Huguenots' reading was condemned as demonic by Catholics. And in turn, we, Huguenots, viewed the Catholic teaching as demonic.

In this way, Rom 1:16-17 and 3:21-24 and our (including my Protestant/Huguenot parents') understanding of it (as "justification and salvation by faith alone") became associated for me as a child with martyrdom, long-standing suffering, persecution, and hiding as refugees in mountains, such as those around le Bouschet de Pranles. Yes, it is and was a comforting text—a balm in time of anxiety—but it is and was also a dangerous text, bringing about suffering, trauma, loss, danger. It follows that such scriptural texts must be handled with great caution and respect. Thus, as a Protestant/Huguenot I was instructed that each of us should read scripture by and for ourselves. We should never simply adopt the interpretation by someone else—especially that of the pope. Then, as individual readers, each of us would see that Rom 1:16-17 and 3:21-24 proclaim "justification and salvation by faith alone."

Of course, I would soon learn that one never reads a text by oneself. As a child, was I reading these verses by myself? Of course not. Even as I deciphered the words in our Bible, my parents were telling me what they meant. And in

---

6. The Edict of Nantes (1598), while maintaining Catholicism as the official religion of France, granted rights to worship to the Huguenots. But it was revoked in 1685.

7. The heroic resistance by these Huguenot ancestors did not by themselves have much effect. Actually, they were quickly squashed by the Royal Army, by imprisonments, and by hangings. Yet, as we shall see, it is through their commemorations that they had long-time effects, including upon my generation. This is as in the case of the Stonewall gay riots. As the sociologists Elizabeth A. Armstrong and Suzanna M. Crage (2006) note in a study of what they call "the Stonewall myth," Stonewall was hardly the first and most powerful "gay riot." What gives Stonewall its stature, they argue, is that "Stonewall activists were the first to claim to be the first." Their point is that Stonewall is not commemorated because of its impact on the gay movement. Instead, it "made its impact on the gay movement through its commemoration." See also Appiah (2019). The Stonewall story is thus an achievement of gay liberation rather than an account of its origins.

turn they had learned this interpretation from preachers, who themselves were ultimately following the interpretation by Calvin, Luther, and other reformers. Our interpretation was/is embedded in an ecclesial tradition, as much as the Catholic interpretation was/is. As interpretations of scripture—that is, of texts viewed by believers as offering a Word-to-live-by—whether Protestant or Catholic (or anything else), our interpretations are necessarily contextual: they offer a Word-to-live-by in specific life contexts, including different ecclesial contexts. I could not understand this as a kid, although I soon would as a teenager from André Chouraqui. But already as a child, this contextual character of any reading of Scripture was front and center: the same scriptural texts were not understood in the same way in the context of Patrick's family and in the context of my family.

But from annual "picnics" (for us, kids) and "memorial ceremonies" (for our parents) at the houses of our martyrs, I already associated Rom 1:16-17 and 3:21-24 with the demonization of others. Thus, we, Huguenots, reject interpretations of scripture by anyone else as demonic. Everybody should read scripture on his/her own (this is why I was supposed to learn to read more fluently). In particular, the pope's authorized interpretation was demonic. Conversely, for Catholics, the interpretation by my Huguenot ancestors was viewed as demonic, and therefore it justified tortures, jail, hanging on the stake.

As a youth, I did not see this parallelism in the way Protestants and Catholics turned their particular readings of Scripture into destructive weapons against each other. Huguenots rejected the Catholic interpretation as demonic and idolatrous: such a "papist" misinterpretation could only be held by superstitious people, as Catholics are, who instead of praying to God and Jesus, address their prayers to saints (in front of statues of saints, including of the Virgin Mary); and instead of addressing their prayers directly to God, light candles. But vice versa: Catholics rejected the Huguenots' interpretation as demonic and idolatrous: Huguenots are heretics who should be killed or imprisoned; they are properly called "parpaillots"[8]—loonies with moth-filled heads, bound to think and say the craziest things; simplistic fanatical peasants; crackpots; stubborn like mountain dogs.[9] For Catholics, part of the process of rejecting the Huguenots' reading of scripture (including of Rom 1:16-17 and 3:21-24 as teaching "justification by faith alone") involved *demonizing these Huguenots* as heretic parpaillots.[10] Conversely, for Huguenots/Protestants part of the process of rejecting the Catholic reading of scripture (that denies "justification by faith alone") involved *demonizing Catholics* as gullible, superstitious, idolatrous followers of the papist interpretation and of its penitential rituals (confession to a priest, penance,

---

8. As Rabelais already called Protestants in 1535.

9. This is how Alexandre Dumas described the views that Catholics had of Huguenots in his historical novel *La reine Margot* (2009). See also Rouchy-Lévy (2008).

10. Thus, as an eleven-year-old, I was bullied by a group of Catholic boys who cornered me in the school yard, demanding that I show them my tongue. I was supposed to have a black tongue, as a sign that I was a "son of the devil."

and absolution). Consequently, at minimum, Protestants and Catholics should never truly trust each other. This was especially true in dangerous times—such as wartime, surrounded by German soldiers, with the constant danger that anyone around you could be a "collaborator."

This demonization of "others" because of their different interpretations of scripture is something that I first experienced as a child: I was forbidden to walk back and forth from school together with Patrick. I was even totally forbidden to play with him. Of course, for Patrick and me, this was silly. Therefore, at first, we disobeyed my mother's order, furtively playing marbles together, at least during school recesses. But this did not last. It soon became clear to me as a four-/five-year-old child that Catholics and Protestants do not mix and cannot really trust each other. I was sternly warned by my parents that I should never, in any circumstances, tell anyone—including Patrick—about the visitors who came to our home.

Being prevented from playing marbles with Patrick and losing a friend was not that consequential for me. Much more was going on in my young life. And I was far from being aware of the range of catastrophic consequences of affirming that only one interpretation—whatever it might be—is legitimate and plausible. Beyond the persecutions of "heretics" in the name of "orthodox" readings of Romans—with the catastrophic consequences illustrated for me by the Huguenots museums—I indirectly became aware of the catastrophic consequences such claims had for Jews.[11] What could be more benign than a belief in "justification by faith alone" based on a reading of Rom 1:16-17 and 3:21-24? But as soon as one realizes that this "faith alone" is a "faith *in Jesus as the Christ*," one can see that those who do not share such a faith, including Jews, are not among those who are justified and saved—they are excluded. Thus, this reading/teaching is anti-Jewish—or, more precisely, supersessionist—in that it relegates Jews to an inferior category of people (those who are not saved); it follows that such persons can be and actually are marginalized, ignored, and eventually demonized, persecuted, and even annihilated. Of course, as a child in 1943 and 1944, I was not aware of the Shoah/Holocaust and its systematic murder of Jewish people, which was in full swing in Germany at the time—in a largely Lutheran Germany abiding by justification by "faith *in Jesus Christ*" alone. But I soon became aware that Jews were in danger of being deported to concentration camps and Germany and needed to be protected and hidden. This protection was needed because in these dangerous times, too many people were exclusively concerned with their own security and that of their families, and therefore blocked out and ignored the fact that these "inferior people" were persecuted or worse.

I progressively learned all this from observing what my parents were doing and from meeting all kinds of "visitors" in our large farmhouse. The first visitors

---

11. I was not yet aware of other similar catastrophic consequences—such as the subalternization of all kinds of "others" (including women, gays and lesbians, less educated, barbarians, etc.).

I vividly remember were neither invited nor welcomed: for a couple of months in 1943 a platoon of thirty German soldiers camped in our barn, while the two officers (I guess, a lieutenant and a NCO) took over my large bedroom (on the second floor, next to my parents' and my sister's and brother's). I was relegated to a smaller bedroom on the third floor, next to that of Daniel Loupiac (a seventeen-year-old "farmhand" who soon became my accomplice/elder brother). I did not mind and gladly remained on the third floor, where I was more independent. But there were a lot of anxious tensions; with my sister (and baby brother) we had to play most quietly! And I was warned not to tell anything to my friends at school about what the German soldiers were doing or not doing[12] and who was in the house (especially, I was not to tell anything about the presence of Daniel Loupiac).[13]

As soon as the soldiers were gone, we had an ongoing stream of visitors. Some friends (including Monsieur and Madame Rochet) arrived on their bicycles from Lyon (for me, a faraway mythical city in the north!), sometimes spending the night (my former bedroom had become a guest room) and leaving with a load of fresh vegetables. Conversely, from time to time, my father was biking to Lyon, accordingly to bring food to Monsieur and Madame Rochet.[14] Strangely

---

12. I later learned from my parents that the presence of these Wehrmacht soldiers was a kind of protection; since they were here, the SS would not come. Therefore (as I was told much later), my father had meetings with members of the resistance at night in the cellar (while the officers slept upstairs and the soldiers were in the barn)!

13. After the war, Daniel Loupiac finished his studies at the Collège Cevenol (1952), where he came back to teach math (1958–60 and 1963–74), before becoming director of Sauvegarde 42—a large (more than two hundred staff members) and very active nonprofit organization helping through its several homes, shelters, and programs the youth at risk in Saint Étienne. He died in 2014. See "Daniel Loupiac, professeur de mathématique" (2009).

14. Since at any time one might have to explain one's movements to the French/Vichy or German police (and risk being arrested if one could not provide convincing explanations), with his bike loaded with vegetables he would simply say that he was bringing these from our farm to friends in Lyon—then simply coming back. Similarly, he was going from our farm to the Maquis du Vercors by foot following small steep trails. Yet, as a cover, he often went to the head of the trails with our oxen team, so as to be able to claim that he simply went in the forest for wood for our fireplace. And if asked why he was not in a labor camp in Germany (or a POW camp) where most men of his age were, he always had with him papers showing that he served in the French army as a nurse/ambulance driver and that as such he was not kept as a POW by the German (although he actually escaped in the chaos of the defeated French troops by simply driving away with his ambulance carrying a few wounded soldiers, accordingly in search for a hospital!). He also carried with him other papers showing that he was no longer required to serve in the Vichy French army because he had several children. Carrying with oneself all this paperwork at all times was a necessity back then! See Koreman (2018: 3–27 and passim). As a child I was aware of these "most important papers" that I was strictly forbidden to touch.

enough, after the visit of these friends or after my father's trip to Lyon, my father disappeared for a full-day up in the mountain, bringing back wood for our fireplace. I was sternly warned to say nothing to anybody about these friends and about my father's comings and goings. I later learned that they were serving as couriers between resistance headquarters in Lyon and the Maquis du Vercors.[15]

In addition, there was another stream of very different visitors. We kids were told these were aunts, uncles, and cousins. We have a large extended family. So, for me, it was not surprising that I did not yet know them. This happened to me all the time. But these visits had a different pattern that left me wondering. My mother left early in the morning and came back with these "family members" late in the afternoon. My role as the eldest was to show these visitors around the house and to lead them to their bedroom—my former bedroom—while my mother cooked and took care of my younger siblings. The next morning, before I woke up, they had disappeared—and so had my father. The first time did not raise questions for me. But when this happened again and again, I began asking questions. And I learned that, early in the morning, my mother went to see my grandparents—a twenty-five-mile trek on her bike crossing the Rhône river—and brought back with her these "family members," walking with them and carrying their bags on her bike. And the next day, when I woke up, they had disappeared with my father, who later came back with the oxen team carrying logs of firewood. My parents never explicitly identified these visitors for me. But, at night, as we were preparing to go to bed on the third floor, Daniel Loupiac explained to me that these visitors were Jewish refugees, whom my parents were helping escape persecution, by leading them in the Alps mountains where they could hide (on their way to Switzerland). This did not make much sense. But my parents refused to give any explanation. Still it was puzzling: Jews were in our home. This did not make any sense! Simply because Patrick was a Catholic who believed that one needs to do "good works" in order to be "justified," I was not allowed to walk to even play with him. And now, Jews—the very kind of people whom the gospels and Paul describe as hypocritically doing works of the law in order to gain favor from God[16]—were sleeping in my former bedroom! My parents' activities contradicted all the teaching they imparted to me. This was my first awareness of the "convictional contradiction," which characterized their lives as Protestants who read Rom

---

15. The Maquis du Vercors with its 4,000 maquisards kept the Germans away from the plateau of Vercors by guarding its difficult road accesses. Following orders from London, in July 1944, they rose up defiantly declaring the entire plateau and nearby villages to be a free French territory. They were finally defeated a month later—at the cost of 650 dead maquisards and 200 dead civilians—and dispersed by heavily armed German troops arriving by gliders and parachutes. A bitter defeat. Yet they achieved something else: they immobilized the entire German 157th Reserve Infantry Division (with its 10,000 soldiers, its 60 planes, and heavy artillery), even as the Allied troops landed on relatively poorly protected beaches in the south of France.

16. With my parents, I had already read texts to that effect in the Gospels and Paul.

1:16-17 and 3:21-24 as teaching that it is alone by "faith *in Jesus Christ*" that one is justified and saved—believing it while contradicting it in their lives … in the same way as Bible-pounding, *freedom-loving* Christians while contradicting it by being *slave* owners (as we will discuss).

My own puzzlement, while on target, was actually ignoring the most important part of what was going on: my parents were putting their lives (and those of their children) at risk. When she left in the morning to go "to see my grandparents," my mother was taking enormous risks and might not have come back! My grandparents lived on the other side of the Rhône river in Ardèche, at the foot of the Massif Central. Therefore, my mother had to go through several checkpoints on the way: checkpoints by the Vichy police at several places; but also, and more dangerously, through checkpoints when she crossed the Rhône river. The very few bridges still standing were guarded by Germans, with a much stricter control. Going to my grandparents was a good excuse—that she could justify with authentic papers (for a woman, it was enough to have her identity card showing her address), and the gifts of vegetables that she was bringing to them. Yet, this was a most dangerous journey. Although she carefully chose the bridge with the softer checkpoint, one never knew how the guards would react: for the Germans (and/or Vichy police), everyone was under suspicion. And coming back with Jewish refugees was much more dangerous. Of course, they did not have authentic papers! They had forged documents, giving them a non-Jewish identity and an address near the farm of my parents. So, they were "simply" going back to their home together with my mother, who simply helped them carry their luggage on her bike. But would their forged documents be good enough?[17] If they were caught, they would be deported to death camps or shot on the spot … and my mother with them. Furthermore, if there was a perquisition by the Vichy police or the SS when these Jewish refugees were in our home, the entire family might be killed and the house burned down—as unfortunately happened too often in our region during the German occupation. And, of course, the risks piled on when the next day my father guided these Jewish refugees up in the Vercors to the resistance—although as a cover they did part of the trip in the cart pulled by the oxen to "help" my father get wood for our fireplace.

Were my parents fearless? Not realizing the danger involved, and this for the entire family, including us, kids? (And this, even as they contradicted their basic conviction!) Of course, I was far from understanding what was going on. But one night in the summer 1944, a dangerous time when the Germans felt threatened by allied landings in Normandy and in the South of France, it became very clear to me, a five-year-old, that the presence of these people in our house was indeed very dangerous for all of us. I was woken up by my father screaming at a couple of "visitors." My father screaming! It never happened! I stood invisible at the top

---

17. See the excellent description of the ever-changing and very different identification papers required in occupied France (and also Belgium and the Netherlands)—especially for men of the age where they had to be in labor camps. See Koreman (2018: 3–27 and passim).

of the staircase, wondering what was happening. My father was furious. He was screaming to our visitors, because instead of staying hidden in our house while waiting to be on their way in the Alps, they went in town to see a movie! "Don't you realize there are collaborators and even Germans in town! If you want to be arrested, I don't care. But we are taking a lot of risks to help you. And, by your careless behavior, you, Jews, are putting all of our family in danger. This is not acceptable!" For the first time what Daniel Loupiac had told me was confirmed: these visitors were not members of our extended family … they were Jews. And it became very clear that their presence in our home was dangerous for us.

Actually, for us kids, this became the beginning of a great adventure! We went camping! We slept in grottos in the sandstone hills above our house; we played hide and seek in the woods; we foraged for food, finding berries and mushrooms. My parents had indeed been denounced, learned it, and we went "camping." And during that time, our house was shelled—although the shells hit and exploded in front of the house, destroying huge trees. So, when we came back, what is a young boy to do! I had new toys: pieces of shrapnel that I avidly collected, using them as soldiers and tanks in my armies!

From my perspective as a young child a lot of things were simply part of a puzzle called life, which I simply integrated together in my own childish way. A new toy. Someone ready to play with me for a short while—as many of these visitors did— and then suddenly disappeared. Another case in point was the twelve-year-old cousin, Rose, who often played with me, a four-/five-year-old, in the summers 1943 and 1944, when visiting with her parents and her four teenaged brothers (who did not pay any attention to me). So, I was very close to Rose. But after the war I never saw her again. Was she a real person I remembered? … or a phantasm of my dreams? Four- and five-year-old kids are easily confused. But recently, in 2017, this mystery was resolved: the name of the little girl was not Rose, but Rachel. She was a Jewish girl whom my great-uncle and -aunt were hiding (under the name Rose), pretending she was their daughter.[18]

How did these Jewish refugees reach my grandparents, great-uncles and great-aunts—before coming to our home on their way to the Alps and Switzerland? Actually, my family was part of a Protestant underground escape line for Jewish refugees on their way to Switzerland from the plateau of the Massif Central. This mountainous plateau (three thousand feet of elevation) in the center of France

---

18. After the war, in our family nobody spoke about Rachel/Rose—as was the case for everything else that happened during the war! Similarly, after settling in Israel, Rachel/Rose did not speak of this part of her life, even with her daughter. But finally, in 2016 Rachel/Rose told her story to her teenaged granddaughter, Faran; and the intrepid teenager followed through, found the family in which Rachel/Rose was a "daughter" and the "brothers" she had for three years. Faran reported the story to *Yad Vashem*. To cut a long story short, a "Certificate of Honor" as Righteous Among the Nations was posthumously awarded to my great-uncle and great-aunt; and in 2017 Faran gave it personally to Jean Claude, one of the "brothers" of her grandmother, Rachel/Rose, a lifetime earlier.

was a natural hiding place for all those threatened by German troops and the Vichy police—this is where, centuries before, Huguenots hid from soldiers of the Catholic king. It is indeed difficult to access and easily defended because roads to the plateau go through narrow gorges with many small bridges that often were blown apart to prevent any passage by Germans troops. So, with the help of the Protestant communities in the villages on this plateau—including Le Chambon sur Lignon—many Jewish refugees trying to escape death camps were hidden in the villages and the farms around them.[19] Of course, these exhausted refugees were fed and given time to rest, regain strength, and sleep in a secure place.[20] But, they were too many to stay there. So, provided with false papers—carefully crafted for them so that they would withstand the scrutiny of the German police and the Vichy police[21]—they were guided to security (usually to Switzerland but

19. Thus, in 1990, Yad Vashem built a stele in Jerusalem and set a commemorative plaque in Le Chambon, giving to "Le Chambon and neighboring villages" a "Certificate of Honor as Righteous Among the Nations" for rescuing "thousands of Jews"—at least five thousand, claim books and movies. This number seems impossible. How could Le Chambon and its surrounding villages rescue five thousand Jews, while altogether these villages had less than five thousand inhabitants!? Of course, it is because they had a lot of help from other people. Under the leadership of their pastors (including André Trocmé in Le Chambon), inhabitants of the plateau gave shelter to those who were too weak to travel: the elderly, the handicapped, families with young children, and also the many children separated from their families (creating for them already in 1938 a boarding school, later named the Collège Cévenol). Quite a large group, but not five thousand. For all other refugees (the vast majority), Le Chambon was simply a transit point. See Hallie (1979) and the 1987 documentary movie by Pierre Sauvage, *Weapons of the Spirit* (Sauvage was born in Le Chambon as his parents took refuge there during the war). See also Grose (2015) and, minimizing the role of the pastors, Moorehead (2014). With Aline, my wife, we knew many of the people interviewed by Philip Hallie and Pierre Sauvage for the simple reason that for one year (1960/1961) we worked at the Collège Cévenol (that continued as an international school emphasizing nonviolence until 2014).

20. This was possible because Le Chambon and other surrounding villages were strictly pacifist, and consequently the German occupation was very light, except for "rafles" (rounds-up), when a larger contingent of German soldiers were coming up the small roads to check everyone and eventually to capture young men who should have been in labor camps in Germany. But everyone was warned in advance, and most everyone that Germans were looking for—including the refugees—had usually the time to scatter, finding temporary refuge in out-of-the-way farms and in the surrounding forests.

21. Mr. Darcissac, the director of the public school in Le Chambon, soon created a well-equipped workshop (with cameras, copies of "official" stamps, and original blank forms for ID cards, ration cards, and certificates showing that men had fulfilled their military duties and were exempt of labor camps in Germany) where he worked with a group of "artists" to produce for each refugee false papers that would withstand the control by the Germans and the Vichy police—and in the great majority of cases these papers were accepted as "true papers."

also to Spain) through all a series of underground lines. For security sake, these underground lines were exclusively made up of Protestants.[22] Refugees were led by guides from a (Protestant) safe house to the next—and "family lines" (such as that from my grandparents to my parents) were particularly secure. And pastors actively organized and participated into such underground lines, often hiding Jews in their parsonages.

Yet it remained that, as a five-year-old, I was puzzled by the contradictory behavior (a convictional contradiction) of my parents; it was okay to have Jews in our home (in my bedroom!) and to take enormous risks to protect them, even as a strict separation from Catholics (including my friend, Patrick)[23] was demanded, because they did not follow "Paul's teaching"—justification/salvation by faith in Christ alone ("the only possible understanding of Rom 1:16-17 and 3:21-24")—the teaching that implicitly condemned Jews who sought to be justified by "works of the law." This is supersessionism: we are superior to Jews, we are justified, and we will be saved, because we, Christians/Protestants, believe in Jesus Christ; we are justified by this faith alone. But not the Jews. Then, even as a child I became aware of the convictional contradiction which was involved: My parents risked their lives and ours to help Jewish refugees even as they held supersessionist, anti-Jewish convictions. How does one live with this contradiction?

But there is more. Much later, in 1960, I brought Aline as my fiancé to my parents. They were very disturbed and objected: "But, she is Jewish!" … Wow! It hurt! What? Aline, who since her youth had been very active in the church, who was a student with me in seminary preparing for a Christian ministry. What? Aline was Jewish? Then it became clear that it was no longer a matter of anti-Judaism, as a religion. It was anti-Semitism—she belonged to the Jewish race. My immediate response was: Yes, she is a member of the chosen people! (And indeed she soon became my mother's favorite daughter-in-law.) A darker aspect—"a hidden figure" (to use Volney Gay's phrase discussed below)—of the rescue of Jewish refugees by Protestant rescuers became clear: these rescuers of Jews were

---

22. Catholics had their own underground lines to guide Jews to safety—especially from Lyon and its region to Switzerland. Sometimes the lines crossed and help each other (Rachel/Rose arrived at my great-uncle and great-aunt from a Catholic underground line). But Protestants and Catholics did not trust each other—as discussed above.

23. For sure, we were no longer in the time of the religious wars when Protestants were persecuted (until the fall of the monarchy in 1789), but there were plenty of active remnants of it. For instance, when I was kindly given the permission to use the Jesuit library in Lyon in the 1960s, I discovered that books written by Protestants were in a special section of the library called "hell" (kept under key until Vatican II)—something for which the Jesuits apologized to me. The separation of Catholics and Protestants was (and still is) a reality. Relatively recently I happened to be in St. Peter (Rome) on a weekday while a service was going on. As I inquired, I discovered it was a service for the beatification of three counter-Reformation priests who had led persecutions of my ancestors. Of course, sixty years later the wall of separation between Catholics and Protestants has largely crumbled.

not simply anti-Jewish; they also held strong anti-Semitic views. Hence this knee-jerk reaction against Aline, even though she could have been one of those that my parents hid and helped to safety.[24]

My puzzlement (with the anti-Judaism/anti-Semitism of my parents even as they risked everything to rescue Jews) faded as I grew up as a young boy, without any interactions with Jews. But it came back in full force when, as an early teenager, I was a boarding student (as a seventh and eighth grader) in a small church school led by pastor Louis Dallière (le Cours Isaac Homel, in Charmes sur Rhônes). This sophisticated pastor with excellent linguistic skills[25] was closely associated with our family and Le Chambon—during World War II, the Dallière's parsonage was one of the safe houses in one of the Protestant underground lines.[26] Yet this scholarly and charismatic pastor[27] remained a fiery preacher. I still hear his booming voice, repeatedly preaching sermons like this:

> "Woe to you scribes and Pharisees" (Mt. 23:13), Woe to you Jews, and woe to you who are hypocrites like them. [And, pointing at us,] Woe to you if you become like them … Woe to the Jews! They will not be saved, as long as they do not have faith in Jesus Christ.

For me, such sermons reinforced the teaching I had learned from childhood.

But at the school we had several visits from one of the Jews who had been hidden during the war in the Dallière's home. This Jewish refugee (who, after a

---

24. Actually, this was literally the case. Indeed, I learned that, during the war, Aline was hiding in the Alps with her parents and her two sisters, not very far from where my father was bringing refugees. As a Jewish family—her father was a Jew—they had to hide and found a house to rent in a small hamlet in the Alps, La Gorge. There, they were directly or indirectly protected by the farmers in the hamlet, who were themselves young French people hiding to avoid being drafted for forced labor in Germany. There was no big intentional organization, as in Le Chambon. But no one asked questions. No one denounced as suspicious Aline and her family to Germans or the Vichy police. This was the passive resistance of many people during the war—which involved much risks. If the Germans found refugees in a village, there were stiff punishments for the villagers—people being killed on the spot; entire villages being burned down. Aline and her family survived the war in this way. But her aunt, Reine, and thirteen other members of her family perished in death-camps.

25. Pastor Louis Dallière had degrees in philosophy and theology from both Paris and Harvard Divinity school; together with his wife, he gave me a good start in English, Latin, classical Greek, and French literature. Later, he made me read Gabriel Marcel (the cousin of Mrs. Dallière!) and other existentialist philosophers.

26. Indeed, our math and science teacher (Anne Trachtenberg, aka Doucia) was a Jewish refugee who stayed on and "converted."

27. Pastor Dallière was also the leader of a charismatic movement within the traditional Protestant church.

stint in the Maquis, arrived from Le Chambon in 1944) was André Chouraqui, who had studied law in Paris (in preparation for becoming a judge), even as he pursued rabbinic studies (becoming a biblical scholar, who also served the Israel government).[28] No wonder that André Chouraqui quickly became a good discussion partner and friend of Pastor Dallière, whom he visited from time to time after World War II. One of these visits happened while I was a thirteen-year-old student at the school. We students had a freewheeling conversation with Chouraqui around a huge fireplace. Following stories about his youth in Algeria and his studies in Paris, he told us how he had been saved during the war, hidden in the Dallière's home.[29] Then jokingly Chouraqui said: "I am one of these hypocrite Jews who are *not* justified and will *not* be saved because I do *not* believe in Jesus." We students laughed, in response to Chouraqui's attitude. But Pastor Dallière did not take it as a joke. Visibly embarrassed, he began talking to us about the "mystery of Israel": Israel remains the people of God and one day all Jews will believe in Jesus as the Christ and be saved (Rom 11:25-26).

In the presence of Chouraqui, Dallière had to acknowledge the *convictional contradiction* involved in, on the one hand, his reading of Paul and, on the other hand, his rescue of Jewish refugees. By responding to Chouraqui's joke as he did, Dallière acknowledged that his empathetic involvement in protecting Jews—welcoming them with open arms in his home, an attitude that could have been very costly, not only for him but also for his wife and their daughter—was in contradiction with his supersessionist views and preaching according to which Jews are inferior and excluded, because they refuse to have faith in Christ.

The many instances in which the *actions* of these Protestant Huguenots are in contradiction with their *beliefs* are best designated as "convictional contradiction." In his book *On the Pleasures of Owning Persons: The Hidden Face of American Slavery* (2016), Volney Gay presents a revealing "analysis" of the "convictional contradiction" involved in the case of American Christians who were also slave owners.[30] As a psychoanalyst Volney Gay powerfully unveils the contradiction involved in the practice of slavery by Christian slave owners: on the one hand, they were freedom-loving (American) Christians, and yet they owned slaves, and indeed found all kinds of "pleasures" in that practice (insisting that "sexual abuses" of slaves—a reality—was only a very small part of the pleasures involved in "owning persons"). Using all his tools and experience as a psychoanalyst, Volney Gay brings to light the fundamental contradiction involved in slavery: (i) the pleasure

---

28. Among many other publications, André Chouraqui published annotated French translation of the Hebrew Bible, New Testament, and the Koran. This amazing work is still available; see Chouraqui (1990; 2019).

29. Louis and Marie Dallière posthumously received Medals of the Righteous by Yad Vashem (1990) for hiding Chouraqui and other Jewish refugees.

30. Gay (2016). Actually, the present essay recasts a lecture I gave in honor of Volney Gay as he retired in 2018, in which the emphasis was on his book. In that lecture, I expressed how his book helped me understand what I experienced as a child during World War II.

of owning slaves (that can be compared with the much more limited pleasure of owning a thoroughbred horse) (ii) even though American Christians were also freedom loving and emphatically affirmed that part of their faith involved loving their "neighbors" as themselves.

I was at first tempted to focus my attention on Volney Gay's concluding chapter (chapter 10) which, by contrast with the rest of the book, discusses people who objected to and resisted "slavery" of all kinds. This chapter (Gay 2016: 306–46) is a quest for "a universal ethic" that explores the differences between slave owners (such as Bishop Polk, the brother of the president) and people who resisted slavery (including the Grimké sisters and the Quakers, Mother Ann, and the Shakers). In the middle of this argument (316–22), Volney Gay reviews the rescue of Jews in France in Le Chambon during World War II. Following three other books (Henry 2007; Block and Drucker 1992; Fogelman 1994), Volney Gay examines the psychological makeup of the rescuers, arguing that they had particular personality traits: independence of thought and action; empathy; deep and sustained relationships with others; and the ability to see Jews as human beings identical to themselves. This psychological analysis is much more sophisticated than the discussion by the ethicist Philip Hallie and his followers who sought to understand "How Goodness Happened in Le Chambon" (a part of Hallie's title, "*How Goodness Happened There*" [1979]). But it needs to be noted that all these studies—including Volney Gay's chapter 10—posit that the rescuers of Jews during the Holocaust were models of goodness and righteousness. By focusing on the "goodness" of the rescuers, these studies fail to recognize that the rescue of Jews by these Protestant Huguenots was itself framed by a fundamental contradiction … a contradiction as fundamental as that of the ownership of slaves by Christian masters, which Volney Gay analyzes in the preceding chapters. Therefore, it is the entirety of Gay's book that should be a good guide for the present discussion.

The contradiction displayed by Protestant/Huguenots—"saving Jews while being anti-Jewish and even anti-Semite"—is the reverse of that displayed by "good Christians who were slave owners." This is no longer the contradiction between "unrighteous" slave owners who were also "freedom-loving Christians" but the contradiction between "righteous" Protestant/Huguenots ("Righteous among the Nations," as Yad Vashem claimed) who risked their own lives and that of their families in order to help save Jews, even as these Protestant/Huguenots "held anti-Jewish/anti-Semite convictions." While the "hidden face" of the Christian slave owners was the "pleasures of owning persons," the "hidden face" of Protestant rescuers of Jews was their "anti-Jewish/anti-Semite convictions."

Philip Hallie, Patrick Henry, and other analysts failed to recognize this contradiction. It is indeed a puzzle. How could Protestant rescuers of Jews hold the very same beliefs that framed the Nazi final solution and its death camps (where six million Jews died)? These "righteous" rescuers cannot be anti-Jewish/anti-Semite, can they? My own experience showed that they were actually anti-Jewish (and even anti-Semite)—an ongoing attitude deeply rooted in their belief in "justification/salvation alone through faith in Jesus Christ" (a conviction that, for them, was "the only possible understanding of Rom 1:16-17 and 3:21-24"). Were they unaware of this tension/contradiction between their actions and their beliefs? It soon appeared that they did "feel it" and that they were constantly striving to find ways to overcome the contradiction involved in being Protestant/Huguenots urgently struggling to rescue Jews from deadly persecutions.

It follows that it is the preceding chapters of *On the Pleasures of Owning Persons* (and not chapter 10) that provide insightful categories to recognize how Protestant/Huguenot rescuers of Jews dealt with the contradiction involved in their lives. Parts I and II of Volney Gay's book are less directly helpful here, because they are dedicated to very instructive presentations of the institution of slavery (part I, chapters 1–3) and of the political and economic struggle to justify the institution of slavery (part II, chapters 4–5). It is therefore part III (chapters 6–9, each dealing with a specific type of "Response to Contradiction") that is the most helpful for shedding light and resolving the contradiction involved for Protestant/Huguenots who rescue Jews despite their supersessionist reading of Scripture (including Rom 1:16-17 and 3:21-24). This section of Volney Gay's book is most helpful because in it he successively analyzes the different ways in which people strove to resolve the contradiction involved in their practice of slavery even as they were freedom-loving Christians. While all the strategies of "Response to Contradiction" do apply to the cases of Protestant rescuers of Jews, the first two—"splitting" (chapter 6) and "spiritualization and empathy" (chapter 7)—most directly apply to the case of Protestant/Huguenots who rescued Jews.[31]

---

31. I do recognize that "Protestant rescuers of Jews" may have made uses of the two other types of "Response to Contradiction." But "Exposing Legal Fiction" (chapter 9) hardly applies to the case of Protestant/Huguenot rescuers of Jews, while of course it was an effective response to contradiction in the case of slavery. By contrast there are clear examples of the use of "Narrative Fiction" (chapter 8). Indeed, there has been many "narrative fictions," rumors whispered in the village of Le Chambon, portraying Pastor Trocmé as a saint from whom all the rescue movement started; these rumors gave rise to the books and movie—"narratives"—about Le Chambon. But these narratives were centered on Pastor Trocmé's preaching, and forgetting that the Temple as a building could contain only a small percentage of the people of the village. Most people never heard Trocmé preach—and often belonged to other churches or were atheists. These narratives seek to overcome the contradiction involved in "anti-Jewish Protestant rescuers of Jews" by insisting that the Jewishness of Jews was respected. Indeed, none converted to Christianity in Le Chambon (actually, a Christian converted to Judaism). Fine. Admirable. But, why did Jews not go to the Temple on Sunday morning and to Bible studies during the week? The narratives forget to raise this question, which would reveal that Jews were *not invited/welcomed* in these Protestant worship services; these services exclusively gathered those who believed in justification/salvation "through faith in Christ alone." In the following comments, I choose not to emphasize the response to contradiction by narrative fiction, because it would lead us away from my primary concern: the significance of conflicting interpretations of Rom 1:16-17 and 3:21-24.

Volney Gay names "*splitting*" (chapter 6) the first strategy for responding to contradiction. As he explains in nontechnical terms, splitting involves "locating one's experience and memories in different parts of the mind" (Gay 2016: 206). "Owners split their psychic space, their minds, into compartments: one labeled *Christian*, the other labeled *Master*" (206; emphasis original). This splitting was demanded from slave owners because, as Christians, they could not (readily) admit "the pain that such treatment [slavery, being possessed, lynching, etc.] induce in the victim" (224). While splitting is effective, it is not perfect. "Every so often—through doubts, dreams, and moments of insight—people sense something wrong with the maneuver since the mind aims at unity, at knowing who we are fully … [It remains that] splitting is common, if not universal" (206). As Gay exemplifies, this was the defense mechanism that the perpetrators also used to overcome the contradiction involved in the practices of the Spanish Inquisition, the Nazis, the Afrikaners, and people practicing lynching (205–24). For instance,

> Hitler described a contradiction: Aryans are superior to Jews, as the lion is superior to the rabbit, yet inferior Jews have trumped superior Aryans. Jews, he pronounced, were weak, the group least likely to survive the inexhaustible laws of nature. Yet, Jews have persisted for thousands of years and continued to threaten Aryan-Germans … [and therefore it is right for Aryan-Germans to eliminate Jews]. (210)

Huguenots/Protestants also practiced "splitting." How? When exhausted Jews, desperate for their lives and for that of their families, fleeing their persecutors who wanted to send them to death camps … When such people knocked on the door of Protestants, what were they to do? Actually, they felt they had no choice: "their impulse to help persons caught in need was 'spontaneous, as though they were no other kind of action available to them' " (in Henry's words). As Magda Trocmé (the wife of the pastor of Le Chambon) responded to the desperate Jewish refugees knocking on her door: "Of course, come in!" As she later explained: "We had no time to think. When a problem came, we had to solve it immediately … There was no decision to make" (Gay 2016: 318). When Jews needed to be brought to safety in Switzerland by crossing the heavily guarded Rhône valley, there was only one thing to do: of course, my grandparents would welcome them in their home; of course, my mother would guide them across the Rhône valley, offering lodging and dinner for them in our home; and of course, my father would serve as their guide in the Alps to lead them to members of the resistance … and so on and so forth, hopefully all the way to Switzerland, although many would remain hidden in small remote villages in the Alps (as Aline and her family did).

What happened? *Splitting!* Protestants/Huguenots did not see "Jews" in these people who were knocking on their door. Protestants/Huguenots saw "persecuted people." These are persecuted people, as we, Protestants/Huguenots, have been persecuted through the centuries. These people are "like us." The yearly commemorations of our martyrs kept this identity alive and fresh in our memories. Because of their identity as "persecuted people," Protestants/Huguenots could not but help these "other persecuted people." And for Protestants/Huguenots this was a spontaneous response: "no decision to make." Indeed, they kept their anti-Jewish convictions: since Jews do not have faith in Jesus Christ, they will not be saved. But for the time being, these beliefs are suspended. The lives of these persecuted people are at risk and therefore we cannot but urgently intervene to help them, as other people in earlier times intervened to help us when we were persecuted. Indeed, we were hidden in remote villages in mountains (Cevennes; Massif Central), from the (Catholic) king's soldiers—and we were hidden by people who put on the line their own lives and the lives of their families. It is our turn to do so for these refugees. Thus, in one corner of their mind, these people were refugees in desperate need of help—as we have been, once upon a time. Therefore, helping Jewish refugees, despite the risks, was the only appropriate response. It remains that Protestant/Huguenots kept in another corner of their mind the fact that these people were Jews, not saved/not justified by God, because they did not have faith in Jesus Christ—indeed, Jews are those who crucified Christ—and therefore people with whom they should not associate. But the other corner of their mind was prevalent: these were persecuted people—indeed even if they were persecuted precisely because they were Jews. This splitting between "persecuted people" and "Jews" was/is effective for the vast majority of Protestants/Huguenots around Le Chambon and along the Protestant underground escape line—as it reaffirmed their own identity as "persecuted people," an identity kept alive by the yearly commemoration at their martyrs' homes. But this splitting is never perfect. Many people sensed something wrong with this splitting maneuver, and therefore sought additional justification for their interactions with these Jews. For some (such as Pastor Dallière and my parents), another response to this contradiction was needed.

In chapter 7 of *On the Pleasures of Owning Persons*, Volney Gay describes another way in which people responded to the contradiction involved in the practice of slavery by freedom-loving Christians: by "spiritualization[32] and empathy." This involves "self-reflection, thinking about thinking that offers a single, coherent narrative about contradictions and puzzles in our emotional lives … [Such] self-reflection, thinking about thinking, is superior to splitting because it increases the amount of information" (Gay 2016: 246–7). "However, because self-reflection, even in the most refined of novelists and theologians, emerges out of specific cultures and evokes specific feelings it cannot demonstrate to skeptics that the causes it champions, even anti-slavery, are inherently better than its competitors" (247). Volney Gay illustrates in great detail these points through a discussion of this strategy as presented in (among others) Harriet Beecher Stowe's *Uncle Tom's Cabin*, Carter Godwin Woodson's *The Miseducation of the Negro*, and Joseph Conrad's *Heart of Darkness*. For instance, Conrad's opening scene describes English vessels, dedicated to colonial dominance in Africa, preparing to leave the

---

32. Volney Gay uses the term "spirituality." But he discusses a process. So I prefer the term "spiritualization."

harbor on the Thames. But he soon introduces the hallucinating dream that the English sailor, Marlow, has. Marlow envisions the feelings of a commander of a Roman vessel who, centuries earlier, was entering the harbor on the Thames with its legions in order to bring about the Roman dominance of British tribes ... as the British sailors would in turn conquer Africa, bringing British dominance to African tribes. But by contrast (in Marlow's reverie), British sailors would also bring British civilization to the dark continent of Africa. The feelings of the Roman sailor were shaped by the terror involved in entering the "darkness" of the British Isles and their detestable savages who only deserve to be conquered by brute force. Therefore, "they grabbed what they could get for the sake of what could be got." Indeed, the British sailors would also conquer darkness in the African continent. But in his dreamlike perspective (his *spiritualization*), Marlow envisions that "in contrast [to the Roman conquerors], the European conquerors of the dark continent told themselves they represented something noble: they brought civilization to the uncivilized and Christianity to heathens" (245; cf. Murfin 1996).

Spiritualization as a response to the contradiction of Protestants rescuing Jews despite their anti-Semitism is well illustrated by Pastor Dallière's response to Chouraqui's joke: "I am one of these hypocrite Jews who are *not* justified and will *not* be saved because I do *not* believe in Jesus." As noted above, Pastor Dallière was visibly embarrassed. Then, addressing us (students in the school) he began talking at great length about the "mystery of Israel"—namely, the mystery that all of Israel will be saved (Rom 11:25-29). In sermons and in presentations to the members of the charismatic movement that he led in the region of the Rhône valley,[33] Dallière developed at great length this theology of "the mystery of Israel."[34]

In brief (I follow the transcript of a sermon that Dallière preached in 1941), according

> to this "theology," Jews will ultimately be saved, despite their present lack of faith in Jesus Christ and their belief that they will be justified by works of the law. They ultimately will be saved, because Israel remains the people of God. How will they be saved? In brief (according to Dallière's interpretation of Rom 11:25-29): one day *all Jews will believe in Jesus as the Christ—as the Son of God and the king of Israel*. Consequently, they will be saved. But, as Paul says, this is a "mystery," and therefore something which does not make sense for us.[35]

---

33. This movement is still active today and is called *Union de Prière de Charmes sur Rhône*.

34. This "theology of the mystery of Israel" was developed in a book-length study by Lovsky, a historian and Dallière's close friend and collaborator. See Lovsky (1955).

35. See Dallière (1941); emphasis original. In this sermon, he makes clear that this mystery is that at one time all of Israel will recognize Christ as the son of God: "à un moment donné, le peuple juif, dans son ensemble, reconnaîtra en JESUS-CHRIST le FILS de DIEU et le Roi d'Israël."

In Volney Gay's perspective, this is a spiritualization of the fact that Jews do not believe in Christ (do not have faith in Jesus Christ): while this is true, the mystery is that, one day, they will believe in Christ, and therefore will show themselves for who they have been, are, and always will be, namely, the people of God. Therefore, now, in the present, they have to be respected as members of the people of God; they must be helped as one would help brothers and sisters: one day they will believe in Christ.

Spiritualization is effective. In that evening at the boarding school with Dallière and Chouraqui, I became aware that this was the way in which my parents resolved the contradiction involved in putting their lives (and our lives as children) at risk for the sake of rescuing Jews, despite their strong supersessionist/anti-Jewish views based upon the conviction that one can only be saved/justified if, and if *only*, one has faith in Jesus Christ. *Spiritualization* is effective, as I saw in the case of my parents and other members of the charismatic movement led by Dallière. But it is not perfect. Of course, this strategy does *not* work outside of this charismatic movement (or eventually a similar charismatic movement), which provides the necessary frame for this understanding of the "mystery of Israel."

As the long evening around the fireplace continued (while we were sipping cups of warm apple cider), it was clear that this "theology of the mystery of Israel" did not make sense for André Chouraqui. Pensive, he stood up, went to pick up two wood logs, added them to the fireplace, and spent a long time rearranging burning logs with a poker. Then he sat down again. Now it was his time to speak and to teach us (the students sitting around him and Dallière). This is what he told us in substance.

> To begin with, let me emphasize that I am deeply grateful to Pastor Dallière and his theology of the mystery of Israel. This theology allowed his wife and him to overcome the wall of separation between Protestants who believe in "justification by faith in Jesus Christ" and those—including Jews like me—who do not share this belief. You have noted that your families commonly invite Protestants for dinner or for family reunions in your homes. Similarly, other Protestants are always welcome in your homes; they are part of your extended family—of your tribe. By contrast, your parents never invite Catholics for dinner or other family celebrations; Catholics are not part of your extended families; and of course, there is no wedding between Protestants and Catholics. Of course, Catholics and Protestants constantly interact at work, at school, in shops, and so on. Of course, in case of emergency Catholics might be brought in your homes—for instance, if they need help after an accident. But these remain interactions with outsiders. Catholics and Protestants do not share the same faith—Catholics do not share your belief in "justification by faith in Jesus Christ alone." It would be contradicting this faith to treat Catholics as parts of your extended family.
>
> I was thinking of Patrick, who was my friend, until we discovered he was Catholic. ...

And the same applies to Jews, even though in this part of France you rarely meet Jews ... at least since WWII. Jews remain outsiders to your extended Protestant/Huguenot family: we, Jews, do not share your faith in Jesus Christ. And therefore, Jews have no place in your individual families. But what happened during the war was quite extraordinary. Pastor and Mrs. Dallière welcomed me, a Jew, as a member of their family, taking enormous risks to hide me in their home for several months. And they tried to make me welcome at their table, by providing me with ample vegetable servings—to allow me to avoid at least the major food prohibitions of my faith. And they did so in contradiction with their own convictions about justification by faith in Jesus Christ alone. It is because they accepted to live with this convictional contradiction that I am alive today—together with several other Jews who also took refuge in their home. Pastor Dallière recognized this contradiction and strove to overcome it through his theology of the mystery of Israel, his interpretation of Rom 11:25-29. According to it, Jews remains the people of God, because one day all Jews will "believe in Jesus as the Christ—as the Son of God and the king of Israel."

André Chouraqui got up once more, taking the poker and slowly rearranging burning logs in the fireplace. He hesitated to continue, but finally did.

Once again, I am deeply grateful to Pastor Dallière and his theology of the mystery of Israel. This way of resolving the convictional contradiction involved in opening his home to a Jew who do not share his faith in Jesus Christ saved my life. But I have several problems with his theology of the mystery of Israel. To begin with, I have a great deal of difficulty with interpreting Rom 11:25-29 to mean that Israel, the people of God, will ultimately be saved *because Israel will have faith in Jesus Christ*. These verses have been interpreted in quite different ways through the centuries.[36] But for me, nowhere in these verses Paul says anything about Israel being saved because Israel has faith "*in Jesus Christ*." Rather Paul affirms that *Israel is and remains the people of God because of the covenant*—an eternal covenant to which God is faithful. Paul's words are: "the gifts and the calling of God [i.e. God's covenant with Israel] are irrevocable" (Rom 11:29).[37]

After another long hesitation, André Chouraqui continued:

Because of my decade-long close friendship with Pastor Dallière, I feel that I can say something that I told him earlier, even though I know it hurts his feelings.

---

36. I would become fully aware of the diversity of interpretations of Rom 11:25-29 much later (in 1998) through the remarkable SBL paper by Joseph Sievers, "God's Gifts and Call Are Irrevocable," published in Grenholm and Patte (2000: 127–73).

37. Chouraqui makes this clear in his French translation of Rom 11:25-36 in Chouraqui (2019: 2203–4).

You see, I am deeply offended by Pastor Dallière's interpretation of Rom 11:25-29. His theology of the mystery of Israel posits that, in order to be saved and to be a member of the people of God, we, Jews, must abandon our Jewishness, our Jewish faith. We have to renounce being the covenantal people of God. This is why I am deeply offended. According to his theology of the mystery of Israel, when all Jews will believe in Jesus as the Christ, the Son of God and the king of Israel, *there will no longer be any Jews*. It hurts! Then, at last Hitler would have won! Sorry! But after the Holocaust/the Shoah, this is a very emotional issue for me and all other Jews. The death of 6 million—6 million!—Jews at the hands of Germans and their minions was rooted in the supersessionism embedded in their faith. During World War II, many Germans were Lutherans; as such they grounded their faith in the interpretation of Rom 1:16-17 and 3:21-24 as justification/salvation by faith in Jesus Christ alone. This interpretation excludes Jews; it is anti-Jewish. These Lutheran Germans had the same interpretation of these verses as you Protestants/Huguenots have, following your pastors, including Pastor Dallière. And the majority of Lutheran Germans accepted, at the very least passively, that Jews be sent to death camps; and of course, many of them were German soldiers.

I shivered. What! These dreadful German soldiers, who filled me with terror when they were in our home and whom I feared so much, might have been Lutherans, with the same convictions we have about "justification by faith in Jesus Christ alone"! I never thought of them as Christians. For me, they were terrifying monsters. Nothing else! But Chouraqui was continuing:

What was the difference between Lutheran Germans and Pastor and Mrs. Dallière and the many Protestants/Huguenots who hid Jewish refugees in their homes (as your parents might also have done)? Lutheran Germans did not dare to contradict the basic conviction of their faith. "Justification by faith in Jesus Christ alone" also meant "and damned be the Jews." So, what happened to Jews was not their business. By contrast, and happily, many Protestants/Huguenots squarely contradicted their faith, opening the door of their homes to threatened Jews: "Of course, come in!" (using welcoming words similar to those of Magda Trocmé in Le Chambon). This was in contradiction with their conviction about "justification by faith in Jesus Christ alone." But "vive la contradiction"—"long live the contradiction." It saved my life. It saved the life of thousands of Jewish refugees during World War II. I have a similar admiration for the Catholics who contradicted the basic conviction of their own faith—a sacramental and liturgical understanding of the teaching of Rom 1:16-17 and 3:21-25, that emphasizes "the redemption that is in Christ Jesus, whom God put forward *as a sacrifice of atonement by his blood*, effective through faith" (3:25, NJB). Generally speaking, for Catholics, outside of participation in the Mass (in which Christ's sacrifice of atonement by his blood is reenacted) following confession and penance, there is no redemption, no justification. Therefore, those who do not participate in the

Mass are excluded—and this means that all of us (you, Protestants, and us, Jews) are excluded. Like Lutheran Germans, most Catholic Germans did not dare to contradict the basic sacramental conviction of their faith: what happened to Jews was not their business. Yet happily, as you know, many Catholics also contradicted their basic convictions, by participating in Catholic underground escape lines and opening their homes to hide Jewish refugees. As in the case of Protestants, I have to say: *vive la contradiction* (long live the contradiction). Through it, Catholics saved the lives of many Jews. Of course, Catholics felt the contradiction involved in betraying the basic conviction of their faith. And they found their own ways of justifying this betrayal of their faith, as Protestants/Huguenots also did. But, let me focus on the Protestants/Huguenots who saved my life. Of course, Protestants felt the contradiction between their actions and the basic convictions of their faith—justification by faith in Jesus Christ alone. They felt uneasy about it, and found different ways to justify this contradiction. Pastor Dallière teaches and preaches the mystery of Israel. As I said, I have my reservations about this first type of response, although I appreciate it: it saved my life. A second type of response to this contradiction—the response most commonly adopted by Protestants/Huguenots—was to recognize that, after all, these Jewish refugees, who desperately needed help, were *like them*, Huguenots who, once upon a time, were also refugees and persecuted. And of course, this is true of me also: I am also constantly contradicting my Jewish faith—for instance, tonight by sharing a meal with my friends, Pastor and Mrs. Dallière, knowing that this meal would not be kosher. But in each case, it is essential to avoid rushing to resolve these contradictions, especially if they are contradictions of our basic convictions. You see, this is another mystery: these contradictions might actually manifest the fundamental truth of our convictions.

Your basic convictions are based upon an interpretation of Rom 1:16-17 and 3:21-24. Okay. And this interpretation and these convictions must be respected. But paradoxically, the truth of this interpretation fully appears only when it is contradicted "for a good cause." Saving Jewish refugees. Reaffirming an ongoing deep friendship. These convictions—these interpretations of Rom 1:16-17 and 3:21-24—are *true only when you feel free to contradict them for a good cause*. That is, when you do not hold tightly onto them, as the only possible truth. Because in such a case this truth becomes a demonic and destructive idolatry—as the absolutization of "justification by faith in Jesus Christ alone" by (many) Lutheran Germans engendered the catastrophe (Shoah) that the Holocaust was. By contrast, contradicting this basic conviction by welcoming Jews in your homes was expressing the truth of this interpretation—the real truth about your basic conviction fully appears when it is contradicted for a good cause.

For me, as I sat around the fireplace with André Chouraqui, all this did not make any sense. So, I looked at Pastor Dallière's face, expecting to see negative reactions. But I did not find any in it. And now, as I write this chapter, I find a strikingly similar statement by the Kurdish/Iranian poet Behrouz Boochani, who writes from prison, even as he thought he had at last reached a land of refuge: "Truth is a contradiction."[38] But Chouraqui was continuing:

> There are several possible and plausible interpretations of Rom 1:16-17 and 3:21-24: the Protestant one which read these texts for their theological teaching; the Catholic one which read these texts for their sacramental and liturgical teaching; and so on and so forth, including my own poetic reading of these texts seeking to discern the "religious vision" that Paul's texts convey, as the prolongation of the vision embodied in the Hebrew Bible, and as a basis for the vision embodied in the Koran.[39] Of course, for believers, their particular reading of these texts as Scripture is each time "held as true," proposing a way to walk,[40] worthy of directly or indirectly guiding their lives. But each of these interpretations is *"true" only in so far as it is regularly "contradicted"* and thus brought down to size, thus making room for other true interpretations, which can in turn be contradicted so as to make room for helping people in need. This is part of the Jewish tradition, in which for instance a Midrash presents side-by-side contradictory interpretations. This is also part of the New Testament teaching. Thus, contradicting one's basic convictions in order to respond to the needs of others (who are hungry, thirsty, stranger, naked, sick, in prison, Matt 25) is actually doing all this to Christ—a Christ whom one is surprised to find among people in need. The Jewish scholar, Emmanuel Lévinas, makes the same point by insisting that any face-to-face encounter with another—a neighbor—is each time an encounter with the Other (*l'Autre*), the mysterious, holy Other, to whom we are accountable and for whom we are ever responsible for all what we do. Such a face-to-face encounter is the foundation of ethics ("you shall not kill"), which trumps and eventually contradicts any theological convictions.[41]

---

38. See Boochani (2019: 61). This extraordinary work—which has been appropriately compared with *The Man Died* by Wole Soyinka and *Letter from Birmingham Jail* by Martin Luther King Jr.—was written from jail by the Iranian Kurdish refugee and poet Behrouz Boochani (in jail in Manus prison, Australia, because he was/is an illegal alien). His line "Truth is a contradiction" is part of a poem pondering the interactions of other desperate refugees in a crowded small boat during a perilous journey from Indonesia to Australia—this journey would end for him in his incarceration in Manus prison, from where he is writing. Boochani describes what a bright moon reveals to him regarding the truth of his situation in the middle of the sea in a small boat crammed with refugees, which led him to conclude: "Recognition of the truth of any situation conjures up a kind of fear of anxiety deep within … But the truth has another face, a form of comfort … Truth is a contradiction."

39. At that time Chouraqui was at work on his translation of the Hebrew Bible, the New Testament, and the Koran—a translation that brings out the poetic character of these texts.

40. Much later I understood Chouraqui was alluding to the Haggadah (vision) and the Halakah (the way to walk) that scripture conveys according to Midrash.

41. I found later that Chouraqui was referring to the 1946–7 lectures by Emmanuel Lévinas, published in Levinas (1985). And to other early essays by Levinas (see Levinas

That amazing evening—a very long evening (I guess we, students, did not have classes the next morning!)—with André Chouraqui deeply marked me, the thirteen-year-old that I was, especially because it revealed: (i) that, like my parents, Pastor Dallière had hidden Jews during World War II; and (ii) that, as I did as a child, Pastor Dallière uneasily felt the contradiction between his basic convictions ("justification by faith in Christ alone," based upon his reading of Rom 1:16-17 and 3:21-24) and his welcoming of Jews as brothers and sisters in his home. I had previously heard about Dallière's theology of the mystery of Israel, but without paying much attention to it. Now it became clear that this theology was developed in order to resolve the contradiction between his/our basic convictions (about justification by faith in Christ alone) and his actions (most appropriate actions, including hiding Jews in his home!). This implied that no single interpretation of scripture should be viewed as absolute, something that Chouraqui had clarified for me by insisting that we always have a choice among several interpretations (illustrated by his own translation of the Bible) and that our choice of an interpretation (or its suspension) should always be *contextual*, and therefore should be an *ethical choice*.[42] In order to recognize that we do have such a choice, it is necessary to treat with respect each of the very different interpretations of scriptural texts that believers make as they identify in these texts a Word-to-live-by (a way to walk),[43] which they strive to implement in their lives.

But, as my parents and Pastor Dallière demonstrated, we always can—and, indeed, always *must*—respond to the needs of others around us, even if it means suspending our beliefs based on our reading of a scriptural text. And we should never hesitate to do so. As Chouraqui insisted, this is our ethical duty—a duty ever grounded in our interactions with others in each of our contexts, since each of these interactions is the occasion of a face-to-face encounter with the Other (Lévinas). As a thirteen-year-old, I felt I could take to heart Chouraqui's teaching: Pastor Dallière had not objected in any way! Thus, as I look back, I have to acknowledge that this long evening around a fireplace with André Chouraqui became, through many vivid flashbacks along the years, the "taproot of my perception of Romans as necessarily multivalent and contextual."

1990), particularly the first essay, "Ethics and Spirit," which is a good and concise introduction to Levinas.

42. What I would have called as a thirteen-year-old a "moral choice." Pastor Dallière would not have agreed with this provisional conclusion I was reaching. But, far from preventing me to unpack it, Pastor Dallière and Pastor Paul Bechdolff—who was my mentor later on—gave me to read Gabriel Marcel and Jean-Paul Sartre (at first their plays, then their philosophical works), as well as Albert Camus (who wrote *The Plague* in Le Chambon during World War II!), Søren Kierkegaard … eventually leading me to Hans-Georg Gadamer.

43. I learned later on that Chouraqui was paraphrasing the rabbinic Hebrew הֲלָכָה, halakhah.

For me, as a teenager, this meant that I should constantly be open to different readings of scripture by others, and therefore never absolutizing my own, even as I should continue reading scripture for a Word-to-live-by, and indeed live by my reading. This is what I practiced during the four following years as I participated in a Lycée student group initiated by Pastor Paul Bechdolff (but meeting independently of him). This group became quite popular because, with a rotating leadership, we were discussing biblical texts together with novels and plays by Camus and Sartre, which Lycéens were avidly reading at the time.[44] An imperative principle that framed our discussions was that we would carefully listen to each other and respect each other's interpretations. Of course, there was plenty of leeway for interpreting Camus's and Sartre's novels. But this principle also applied to our interpretations of biblical texts. And because we were from very diverse backgrounds (Protestants from various contexts, but also a number of Catholics), our interpretations were most often very different. For sure, many of these interpretations were naïvely ignoring parts of the biblical text; so, during discussions, we "corrected" each other: "look again at the text!" But our sessions always ended with a plurality of plausible interpretations/teachings, and we were content with that … although we were always discussing the "believers' needs" that these teachings were addressing.

These last issues were stressed in the discussion because our group first started with five students who had accepted Pastor Bechdolff's invitation to join him in trying to help immigrant Muslim Algerians by teaching them how to read in French. For us, fifteen- and sixteen-year-old tutors, teaching thirty-year-old adult learners how to read French was quite a challenge. We had to undergo a training that emphasized that whatever exercises we chose, each time it needed clearly to address specific needs that the adult learner had. For instance, one of my adult learners was actually an educated man, who knew how to read and write Arabic. But he spoke only haltingly in French and did not know the Roman alphabet. Learning to decipher words in children's textbooks was necessary but tedious. So what? How will learning to read help him? So, part of each session involved talking about his daily life. Thus, I discovered that, in order to go to work by himself to one or another of varying construction sites where he was a carpenter, he needed to take a bus each morning. This trip was a source of daily anxiety for him. At the station there were several buses. Which one was going in the right direction? The only difference was a sign displaying the names of the stops where each specific bus would go. So, as he climbed in a bus, he tried to ask the driver if this bus was going to the area where he needed to go. But if there were many people climbing together with him, he could not do so … and therefore quite a few times he ended up on the wrong bus. So, for our next session, I came with the printed schedule

---

44. I should confess that, for teenagers, the popularity of this group was also due—no doubt!—to the fact that it was one of the rare places where girls and boys—from two different schools—could freely interact!

of buses and a map of the city. Then he became eager to learn how to decipher all these difficult words that represented bus stops.

The five of us brought with us this experience when we became the nucleus of the Lycée student group discussing biblical texts together with Camus's and Sartre's novels and plays. So, each of our discussions of a biblical text and its teaching always concluded by asking in very simple terms the broad question: What is the "problem" in the believers' life that your proposed interpretation of the text helps the believers to address? This was the same question we had learned to raise when teaching Algerian immigrants how to read in French, by identifying the "problem" they needed to address in their lives through learning how to read French. This context-centered question led us to discern families of interpretations that, despite other differences, addressed the same "problem." This was consistent with what I had learned from Chouraqui. Recognizing the different contextual values of various interpretations of a given biblical text—and thus the different "ways to walk" that these interpretations offered to believers ... Recognizing the different contextual values of various interpretations prevented the ever dangerous and tragic absolutization of any given interpretation (that unfortunately "fundamentalist" students practiced in their own biblical study group).

Asking each time "What is the 'problem' in the believers' life that this interpretation helps them to address?" engendered lively discussions, because our readings of scriptural texts clearly addressed *different "problems"* in our lives as believers. But, to our surprise, this was not the case when we discussed Rom 1:16-17 and 3:21-24: we could not truly see any difference regarding the "problem" that our respective interpretations of these verses sought to address. Indeed, we, Protestants/Huguenots, understood these verses as teaching "justification/salvation by faith in Jesus Christ alone," as we read these verses by focusing on their theological teaching. This was demanded by our understanding of "faith" as believing "something" about "Jesus Christ"—believing a particular Christological teaching. By contrast, in their interpretation (developed with the help of their priest), our Catholic friends emphasized a sacramental understanding of these verses. Thus, they maintained (i) that Rom 1:16-17 be read together with 1:18ff ("the wrath of God is revealed") and all the passages about the wrath of God in Rom 2–3 (e.g., "Do you imagine that ... you will escape the judgment of God?" [2:3]); and (ii) that Rom 3:21-25 be understood as presenting "Christ's death as a sacrifice of expiation/propitiation" (the basis of their sacramental understanding, implemented in the sacraments of Confession and Mass).[45] This Catholic sacramental interpretation is obviously different from the Protestant/Huguenot justification-by-faith interpretation. Catholics emphasize "Christ's death as a sacrifice of expiation/propitiation," while Protestants emphasize "faith in Christ." It was these patent differences that separated me, as a child, from my Catholic friend

---

45. Rom 3:24-25 is then understood and translated as: "Through the redemption [ἀπολυτρώσεως] that is in Christ Jesus whom God presented as an expiation/propitiation sacrifice [ἱλαστήριον] through faith in his blood."

Patrick. But these differences evaporated when we asked the question: "What is 'the problem' addressed for believers by each of these two interpretations?" To our surprise, we discovered that both types of interpretations address *the same "problem"* for believers. According to both Protestant and Catholic interpretations, "the problem" that urgently needs to be addressed is the "wrath of God." Because each of us has sinned and continues to sin against God, each of us feels guilty: each of us has betrayed God, and therefore God is rightfully angry at each of us. So, according to both the Protestant and Catholic understandings of Rom 1:16-17 and 3:21-24, each of us *needs to be saved from the wrath of God*—the "wrath of God [which, in the gospel,] is revealed from heaven against all ungodliness and wickedness" (Rom 1:18). Despite other differences between Protestant and Catholic interpretations, in both cases "the wrath of God" is what needs to be appeased—it is the "problem" that needs to be resolved so that humans can be in communion with God. God is angry with us. And this "wrath of God" is overcome by what Christ has done for each of us, by dying (instead of us) on the cross. The "problem"—being under "the wrath of God"—is resolved when each believer puts himself/herself to the benefit of the cross, either by having faith in Christ (faith that on the cross Christ has died instead of us) or by associating oneself to Christ's sacrifice (by participation in the sacraments of Confession and Mass).

The members of our group of Lycéens simply assumed that our agreement about the "problem" simply reflected what Rom 1:16-17 and 3:21-24 actually say. We had much to learn! For me, this learning process took place much later with colleagues in the SBL seminar "Romans Through History and Cultures" (from 1997 to 2011).[46] By studying the receptions of Romans through history and present-day cultures, we discovered that there are other families of interpretations of Romans that address fundamentally different "problems" in the believers' lives. This is what is presented at great length in *Romans: Three Exegetical Interpretations and the History of Reception: Volume I* in chapters 3, 4, 5, further emphasized in chapter 6, and summarized in pages 64–5. In brief, the various exegetical interpretations and various receptions address (i) either an *individual-centered* contextual problem[47] resulting from individual sins and ensuing guilt and fear of God's wrath; (ii) or a *community-centered* contextual problem, resulting from communal sins as rebelling against God (being "enemies of God"; 5:10) grounded in a wrong view of God's people (either conceiving of ourselves as being in a privileged position because we are included in God's people; or vice versa, conceiving of ourselves

---

46. A twelve-year-long seminar: the seminar was interrupted for two years, when the SBL did not meet with AAR (and its much needed theologians and church historians!). The proceedings of this seminar (with its ninety-three contributors) were published from 2000 to 2013 in ten volumes of the book series "Romans Through History and Cultures."

47. I use here the distinction that feminist theologians make among *three* modes of human experience: "Autonomy," "Relationality," and "Heteronomy." For an excellent summary presentation, see Grenholm (2019a: 89, 510–11, 1062) (and the bibliography for each at https://ir.vanderbilt.edu/handle/1803/3906) and Grenholm (2011).

as being excluded from God's people, which includes others and not us); (iii) or a *religious-centered* (*Other-centered, heteronomous*) contextual problem, resulting from wrong religious experiences—in brief, idolatry (1:22-25, 26a, 28)—through which humans find themselves in bondage to evil powers (including the "power of sin"), from which they cannot free themselves without divine interventions (such as *grace*, χάρις, as the gracious gift of a transformative divine intervention). And, of course, *Romans: Three Exegetical Interpretations* emphasizes and justifies that, far from being exclusive of each other, these three families of interpretations should be viewed as equally "true" even though—or actually *because*—they contradict each other. As Behrouz Boochani says, "*Truth is a contradiction*" (2019: 61; emphasis original).

This is what the epigraphs in *Romans: Three Exegetical Interpretations and the History of Reception* (volume 1) were supposed to signal ("supposed" because, unfortunately, several of these epigraphs ended up paraphrased in the text, by lack of proper permissions).

> INTRODUCTION: *"She [Mrs. Flowers] encouraged me to listen carefully to what country people called mother wit. That in those homely sayings was couched the collective wisdom of generations."* Angelou (2004: 79; emphasis original)

In the introduction, the first epigraph was supposed to be the above words from Maya Angelou's autobiography. She wrote these referring to her experience in the early 1950s. So, paraphrasing these sentences and her broader passages of her autobiography, I noted that we should follow Maya Angelou by refusing to reject offhand any interpretation, including those by illiterate people—opening the door to *all receptions* of Romans. Indeed, one should value such interpretations, because they are expressions of "mother wit."

> CHAPTER 1: *"The real meaning of a text, as it speaks to the interpreter, does not depend on the contingencies of the author and his original audience. It certainly is not identical with them, for it is always **co-determined also by the historical situation of the interpreter.**"* Gadamer (2000: 296; emphasis and bold original)[48]

The epigraph for chapter 1, from Gadamer's *Truth and Method*, emphasizes that "the real meaning of a text … is always *co-determined also by the historical situation of the interpreter*" (13; emphasis original). Since all interpretations are co-determined by the contexts of the interpreters, all of them need to be equally respected. It follows (as chapter 6 points out, without additional epigraph) that an essential part of the exegetes' task is to proceed to an excavation of the fossilized remains of different interpretations, so as to recognize both the collective wisdom

---

48. Note that it was first published in 1960—certainly written *after* Maya Angelou was taught to respect mother wit.

("mother wit") that these very different and conflicting interpretations still hold and the way they are related to different contexts and the issues these involve.

> CHAPTER 2: *As for that One and Only Truth, which many are searching for and others claim to have found, luckily for us poets and for everybody else, "La vie est plus belle que les idées."* Simic (2014: 53; emphasis original)[49]

As a step beyond the preceding epigraphs, the epigraph of chapter 2 by Charles Simic appropriately begins by emphasizing that the interpretive quest by philosophers (and biblical exegetes!) for the "One and Only Truth" is futile. But, "luckily for us poets and for everybody else, '*La vie est plus belle que les idées.*'" Indeed, philosophers want to strive to establish the "One and Only truth"—a nice and sturdy "idea." By contrast, poets strive "to remain in the midst of uncertainties, mysteries, and doubts, without reaching from some reassuring thought." "Uncertainties, mysteries, and doubts" characterize "life," the normal life of the rest of us, mortals. And far from being a problem, such a "life"—a concrete life in which we necessarily interact with others—is more beautiful than the "certitudes" of the philosophers' ideas: "*La vie est plus belle que les idées.*"[50] The concrete life contexts of the interpreters always shape the interpretations— thus, each interpretation reflects a certain context and the moral and ethical issues "braided" into it.

Of course, such a view of the interpretations of biblical texts fundamentally contradicts the various practices of the vast majority of the members of the Society of Biblical Literature (SBL), who most often still search for the "One and Only Truth" about the text.[51] And, unfortunately, the voices of these other biblical scholars are

49. The broader citation reads:

As Thoreau said, "The question is not what you look at, but what you see" … John Keats called "negative capability," the ability to remain in the midst of uncertainties, mysteries, and doubts, without reaching from some reassuring thought … As for that One and Only Truth, which many are searching for and others claim to have found, luckily for us poets and for everybody else, "*La vie est plus belle que les idées*," as the French say.

50. After "*La vie est plus belle que les idées*," Simic adds "as the French say." Far from being a French saying, as Simic claims, this line is a quotation from Wallace Stevens. Stevens continues by emphasizing that for the poet the only thing worth thinking about is "the world" (the "material for poetry"), that is, "reality" by contrast with the "ideas" of the philosophers (so poetry should "infuriate philosophers"). Stevens actually objects to Kant: "Kant says that the objects of perception are conditioned by the nature of the mind as to their form. But the poet says that, whatever it may be, *La vie est plus belle que les idées.*" See Kermode and Richardson (1997: 906).

51. As was exemplified by the bulk of the national SBL meeting that was taking place around us as we proceeded to the panel discussion of *Romans: Three Exegetical Interpretations.*

like those of Sirens that all of us are constantly tempted to follow. Therefore, as Odysseus did with his sailors (plugging their ears with beeswax), the subsequent chapters (3, 4, 5)[52] attempt to overcome these biblical scholars' temptation by plugging their ears with deconstructions of their own diverse interpretations (that I use as beeswax). These three chapters deconstruct the interpretations of Rom 1 proposed by respected critical exegetes, showing that, despite the fact that they are contradictory, each of these interpretations is as legitimate and plausible as the others. As I reviewed the interpretations by these prominent critical exegetes, I was led to present side-by-side three types of *different critical* interpretations of Rom 1, making explicit how these biblical scholars have, in each case, shown that each is exegetically *legitimate* and hermeneutically *plausible*, even though they are conflicting. Without going back to the differences between critical exegetical methodologies, it is enough here to note that these three kinds of different interpretations are hermeneutically framed by being either individual-centered, or community-centered, or religious/heteronomy-centered.[53]

It was necessary to complete this deconstruction and invalidation of the absolutist claims of existing critical exegeses (that seek to present the "One and Only Truth" about Rom 1) before turning in chapter 6 and 7 to the actual purpose of *Romans: Three Exegetical Interpretations* (as announced in the introduction,

---

52. With no epigraph for chapter 3, which presents the interpretations expected by most people in the West. For chapter 4, on the readings of Rom 1 "for Its Call to Mission of an Inclusive Covenantal Community," one reads Romans as a Haggadah by Paul the Jew; therefore I used as epigraphs a passage from Sifré 85a—"Do you wish to know Him who spoke and by whose word the world came into being? Study Haggadah: for through such study you can get to understand the Holy One blessed be He and to follow in his ways"—as well as Simic's modern expression of Haggadah in the poem "Stories" (from Simic 2015: 13), which includes the words "all things write their own stories No matter how humble." For chapter 5, on the readings of Rom 1 "for Its Realized-Apocalyptic/Messianic Vision" that presupposes (the need of) divine interventions in the present of the interpreters, I used an epigraph from Gench (2014: 143): "[Dedicated to] all who love and serve the city, bearing its daily stress, and are grounded in the conviction that the risen Lord is there, summoning us to join in at the cruciform places where God is already at work, bringing life out of death."

53. Someone may playfully ask: Why "three"? Why not "four"? Or "five"? A first answer is simply: because of the limitations of my mental capacities. I actually began with attempting to show the legitimacy and plausibility of four types of interpretation—as I did with the Sermon on the Mount (Patte 1999). But it was difficult for me to keep straight the differences among the interpretations—even though from the standpoint of semiotic theories I could identify six (a multiple of three!) different meaning producing textual dimensions. It remains that throughout my analysis of different critical interpretations of Rom 1, I was constantly guided by these semiotic theories—and in particular by Greimas's, as presented in Patte (1990). The clincher for me was the persuasive feminist analyses that distinguish *three* modes of human experience: "Autonomy," "Relationality," and "Heteronomy"—as mentioned above, I followed Cristina Grenholm's presentation of these.

chapter 1, and chapter 2). After exposing the equal legitimacy and plausibility of different/conflicting interpretations, chapter 6 could examine the contextual effects of choosing one type or another of interpretation—individual-centered, community-centered, or religious/heteronomy-centered contextual effects. Since human existence ("life") is complete, well-balanced, and thus "beautiful" (Simic) only when all three of its modes of existence (autonomy, relationality, and heteronomy)[54] flourish, chapter 7 concludes by reviewing the different choices of interpretations emphasized by receptions of Romans in different contexts through history and cultures. This examination brings to light the *positive and constructive* moral and ethical consequences of choosing to emphasize one or another type of interpretation, but also the far-reaching and destructive consequences—for instance, suicide, the burning of heretics, colonialism, economic and cultural devastations, the Shoah—when any one of these interpretations is absolutized. As André Chouraqui taught me, of course, as believers we necessarily live by (walk by) one of the many legitimate and plausible interpretations—and therefore we always emphasize one of them. But it remains that we should *not absolutize* that particular interpretation and disregard the other interpretations. This is the essential point that was supposed to be highlighted by the epigraph of chapter 7:

> CHAPTER 7: *"In what I tell you, there is the almost-true, the sometimes-true, and the half-true. Telling a life is like braiding all of that together … to make a hut. And the true-true comes to life out of that braid"*—as the storyteller, Marie-Sophie Laborieux, explains in *Texaco*. (Chamoiseau 1992; emphasis original)

In Patrick Chamoiseau's amazing postcolonialist novel *Texaco*,[55] the storyteller, Marie-Sophie Laborieux, stops many times to explain what she is doing as she tells the story of her family as well as her own. Although she acknowledges that at times she is lying, in most instances, she strives to tell the truth, as she explains, "In what I tell you, there is the almost-true, the sometimes-true, and the half-true." Following André Chouraqui I had learned to respect interpretations by others and their contextual character. Furthermore, in the SBL seminar "Romans Through History and Cultures," we learned to pay attention to the different kinds of "critical interpretations" (see chapters 3, 4, and 5) and thus to recognize that each of our interpretations of Romans is necessarily partial and limited. Each of

---

54. See the articles by Cristina Grenholm on each of these modes of human existence (*autonomy, relationality,* and *heteronomy*) in Grenholm (2019a: 89, 510–11, 1062). The distinction among these modes of human existence is an important contribution of feminist studies.

55. Chamoiseau (1992: 139). Rose-Myriam Réjouis and Val Vinokurov give an excellent English translation of the very difficult text mixing French and Martinican Creole, but I quote my translation of *Texaco* from the 1992 book above. The English translation hides important connotations of these sentences. Unfortunately, we could not receive the permission to put in epigraph these lines, because they were my translation!

our interpretations (including critical exegeses) is nothing more than "the almost-true, the sometimes-true, and the half-true." Is this a problem? No, says Marie-Sophie Laborieux. Each of these interpretations/storytellings is "telling a life." Exegetes "tell a life"—a contextual Word-to-live-by—as soon as they interpret Romans with the awareness that it is scripture for believers (whether or not they identify themselves as one). And this is *not a problem*, at the condition that one tells not a single story but a plurality of stories: "the almost-true, the sometimes-true, and the half-true." The essential is to hold on to this diversity. As Marie-Sophie Laborieux says: "Telling a life is like braiding all of that together [the almost-true, the sometimes-true, and the half-true] … *to make a hut*. And the true-true comes to life out of that braid" (emphasis original). In the same way that Marie-Sophie Laborieux is "telling a life," exegetes "tell a life"—a Word-to-live-by—as soon as we interpret Romans with the awareness that it is scripture for believers (whether or not we identify ourselves as believers). By interpreting we give shape to a Word-to-live-by that believers are expected to implement in concrete contexts (whatever these might be).

But, whenever we claim that our interpretation—which is always at best an "almost-true, sometimes-true, and half-true" interpretation—is absolute, then tragedy always follows, both for us and our neighbors. With Behrouz Boochani, who perceptively affirms "*truth is a contradiction*" (2019: 61; emphasis original), we have to remember that claiming to have the "truth" about anything (including the meaning of a biblical text) is indeed "a contradiction." As interpreters, we are *making an idol* (a false absolute) each time we are claiming for our interpretation (whatever it might be) an authority that it does not have—claiming that it is absolutely "true." This is far from being some inconsequential "personal sin"![56] When we absolutize any given interpretation—making an idol out of it—first, it gains power upon us and enslaves us by encasing us in its illusory world, then it tragically demands from us to create a "kyriarchal system" in its image. This is what Boochani illustrates by his most-powerful presentation and analysis of his experience as a refugee on Manus Island, showing the interlocking structures of power and oppression of its "kyriarchal system," which is perpetually reinforced and replicated, with the result of tragically dehumanizing *all* those who live in it—prisoners, refugees, but also the guards themselves, as well as all the enforcers of it (including the "benevolent" nurses and cooks on Manus Island, as well as all the inhabitants of the larger island, Australia).[57] Let me repeat it: Whenever we

---

56. From which we could easily be forgiven by confessing this sin.

57. Since Behrouz Boochani wrote *No Friend but the Mountains* in Farsi, he did not himself use Elisabeth Schüssler Fiorenza's term "kyriarchal system" (and "kyriarchy"). Schüssler Fiorenza defined "kyriarchal system" as a system "of interlocking structures of domination" (Schüssler Fiorenza 1992: 8, 122–5, passim). Boochani's translator, Omid Tofighian, gives credit to Schüssler Fiorenza for this concept (without explicitly referring to *But She Said: Feminist Practices of Biblical Interpretation*) that he as translator introduces in order to translate the Farsi phrase *system-e hâkem* ("oppressive system," "ruling system," "system of governmentality," "sovereign system"). Yet Boochani approved this translation.

claim that our interpretation is absolute—rather than acknowledging that at best it is an "almost-true, sometimes-true, and half-true" interpretation or rather than acknowledging that in all cases "truth is a contradiction"—tragedy always follows.

These tragedies did take place in the past—in the recent past with the Shoah as the most catastrophic example—but they continue to take place today with the multiplication of refugee camps/prisons throughout the world, including in the United States, and will continue to take place as there will be new waves of refugees throughout the world because of climate change. Of course, at first sight, these horrific dehumanizing systems do not appear to be related to an absolutization of an interpretation of Scripture. And yet … And yet … Why are evangelical Christians tacitly if not actively backing up this kind of practices in the camps/prisons along the southern border built by the US government?

Whatever might be the case, one thing is certain: *Today, we cannot but read Romans as a torn-apart scriptural text wounded by all its tragic misuses—as the bird of Bak's image (on the cover) with damaged wings.* But like the wounded bird of Bak's image (which is still flying, wrapped in the remains of its Jewish prayer shawl), Romans with all its wounds and scars can still fly. But now we can recognize that this "flight" is only possible if the plurality of its diverse interpretations is accounted for.

Of course, none of these diverse interpretations can claim to be "the truth." Each must acknowledge its limitations: it is nothing more than "almost-true, sometimes-true, and half-true." This is not a problem. Each of these diverse and conflicting interpretations should be valued as a strand that has a constructive and positive role to play in the construction of "a hut," *provided that it is braided together with the others.* In La Martinique—but also every place where a home is built—the construction of a hut is never done by a single person. One needs a community. In the present case, one needs a community of readers who accept to be challenged by each other and who respect each other, acknowledging that their different interpretations, in their differences, contribute to the process of "braiding" together these different readings of Romans in the process of building a "hut." Why do we need to respect these different interpretations? Because these different readings provide not one but several complementary Words-to-live-by. This diversity is not only useful but also necessary in order to address various life-contexts that reflect the diversity of the modes of our human experience.[58] Then, "the true-true comes to life out of that braid," as Marie-Sophie Laborieux/Patrick Chamoiseau says.

See the discussion between Boochani and Tofighian regarding the choice of this terminology for the translation (374–94—a part of the concluding chapter, "Translator's Tale," 359–98). This concluding chapter is a dialogue between Boochani and Tofighian, which opens with Boochani saying: "I just hope I wake up from this nightmare soon" (359)—indeed, tragically at the time of my writing, Boochani is still in "Manus prison."

58. As is illustrated in chapters 6 and 7 of *Romans: Three Exegetical Interpretations*.

REFERENCES

"AAR Calls on Institutions to Support Faculty in #ScholarStrike" (2020), *American Academy of Religion*. Available online: https://mailchi.mp/aarweb.org/aar-calls-on-institutions-to-support-faculty-in-scholarstrike?e=29d18273a5 (accessed July 22, 2021).

Adorno, Theodor W. (1981), *Prisms*, trans. Samuel and Shierry Weber, Cambridge, MA: Harvard University Press.

Adorno, Theodor W. (1992), *Negative Dialectics*, trans. E. B. Ashton, New York: Continuum.

Adorno, Theodor W. (1997), *Aesthetic Theory*, trans. Robert Hullot-Kentor, Minneapolis: University of Minnesota Press.

Adorno, Theodor W. (2003), "Metaphysics: Concepts and Problems," in *Can One Live after Auschwitz? A Philosophical Reader*, Rolf Tiedemann (ed.), Rodney Livingstone (trans.), 427–69, Stanford: Stanford University Press.

Adorno, Theodor W. (2004a), "Education after Auschwitz," in *Can One Live after Auschwitz? A Philosophical Reader*, Rolf Tiedemann (ed.), 19–33, Stanford: Stanford University Press.

Adorno, Theodor W. (2004b), "Commitment," in *Can One Live after Auschwitz? A Philosophical Reader*, Rolf Tiedemann (ed.), 240–58, Stanford: Stanford University Press.

Adorno, Theodor W. (2005a), *Minima Moralia: Reflections on a Damaged Life*, trans. E. F. N. Jephcott, New York: Verso.

Adorno, Theodor W. (2005b), *Critical Models: Interventions and Catchwords*, Columbia: Columbia University Press.

Albright, William (1947), "The War in Europe and the Future of Biblical Studies," in *The Study of the Bible Today and Tomorrow*, Harold Willoughby (ed.), 162–74, Chicago: University of Chicago Press.

Ames, Roger T., and Henry Rosemont, Jr. (1998), *The Analects of Confucius: A Philosophical Translation*, New York: Random House.

Angelou, Maya (2004), *The Collected Autobiographies of Maya Angelou*, New York: Modern Library.

Anti-Defamation League (2020), "Audit of Antisemitic Incidents 2019." Available online: https://www.adl.org/audit2019#executive-summary (accessed September 25, 2020).

Appiah, Kwame Anthony (2019), "Stonewall and the Myth of Self-Deliverance," *New York Times*, June 22.

Armstrong, Elizabeth A., and Suzanna M. Crage (2006), "Movements and Memory: The Making of the Stonewall Myth," *American Sociological Review*, 71 (5): 724–51.

Aymer, Margaret, and Laura Nasrallah (2018), "What Jeff Sessions Got Wrong When Quoting the Bible," *Washington Post*, June 15. Available online: https://www.washingtonpost.com/news/acts-of-faith/wp/2018/06/15/what-jeff-sessions-got-wrong-when-quoting-the-bible/ (accessed September 25, 2020).

Bak, Samuel (1983), "Samuel Bak: Escape/Flucht," *Art Archives*. Available online: https://www.kunst-archive.net/de/wvz/samuel_bak/works/escape__flucht/type/all (accessed July 22, 2021).
Bak, Samuel (2002), *Painted in Words: A Memoir*, Bloomington: Indiana University Press.
Bak, Samuel (2019a), Private email correspondence with Gary Phillips, August 4.
Bak, Samuel (2019b), "Samuel Bak: Catalogue raisoneé," *Art Archives*. Available online: https://www.kunst-archive.net/en/wvz/samuel_bak/works?v=grid&start=0&q=escape&group=type&filter=all&hpp=50&medium=&category= (accessed September 25, 2020).
Bannister, Jamie A. (2009), "Ὁμοίως and the Use of Parallelism in Romans 1:26–27," *JBL*, 128: 569–90.
Baranowski, Shelley (1996), "Conservative Elite Anti-Semitism from the Weimar Republic to the Third Reich," *German Studies Review*, 19 (3): 525–37.
"Barth in Retirement" (1963), *Time Magazine*, May 31. Available online: http://content.time.com/time/subscriber/article/0,33009,896838,00.html (accessed July 29, 2021).
Barthes, Roland (1977), "The Death of the Author." *Image, Music, Text*, translated by Stephen Heath, 142–8, London: Fontana Press.
Baur, Ferdinand Christian ([1845] 2003), *Paul the Apostle of Christ: His Life and Works, His Epistles and Teachings*, Peabody, MA: Hendricksen.
Beker, J. Christiaan (1980), *Paul the Apostle: The Triumph of God in Life and Thought*, Philadelphia, PA: Fortress.
Benhabib, Seyla (1996), *The Reluctant Modernism of Hannah Arendt*, Thousand Oaks, CA: Sage.
Bergen, Doris (1996), *The Twisted Cross: The German Christian Movement in the Third Reich*, Chapel Hill, NC: UNC Press.
Black, Fiona C., and Jennifer L. Koosed, eds. (2019), *Reading with Feeling: Affect Theory and the Bible*, Atlanta, GA: SBL.
Block, Gay, and Malka Drucker (1992), *Rescuers: Portraits of Moral Courage in the Holocaust*, New York: Holmes and Meier.
Bochenek, Michael Garcia (2018), "In the Freezer: Abusive Conditions for Women and Children in US Immigration Holding Cells," *Human Rights Watch*, February 8. Available online: https://www.hrw.org/report/2018/02/28/freezer/abusive-conditions-women-and-children-us-immigration-holding-cells (accessed September 25, 2020).
Boers, Roland (2009), *Criticism of Heaven: On Marxism and Theology*, Edinburgh: Haymarket.
Boochani, Behrouz (2019), *No Friend but the Mountains: Writing from Manus Prison*, trans. Omid Tofighian, Toronto: Anansi International.
Bose, Christian Wilhelm, under the direction of Christian Fredrich Börner (1742), "Andronicum et Juniam in Epist. Ad Romanos Cap. XVI Comm. 7 Commemoratos," Leipzig: Langenheim.
Bourdieu, Pierre (1991), *Language & Symbolic Power*, trans. Gino Raymond and Matthew Adamson, Cambridge, MA: Harvard University Press.
Boyarin, Daniel (2000), "Epilogue: Israel Reading in 'Reading Israel,'" in *Reading Israel in Romans*, Cristina Grenholm and Daniel Patte (eds.), 246–50, Harrisburg, PA: Trinity Press International.
Bray, Karen, and Stephen D. Moore, eds. (2019), *Religion, Emotion, Sensation: Affect Theories and Theologies*, New York: Fordham University Press.

Briggs Kittredge, Cynthia (2012), "Feminist Approaches: Rethinking History and Resisting Ideologies," in *Studying Paul's Letters: Contemporary Perspectives and Methods*, Joseph A. Marchal (ed.), 117–33, Minneapolis, MN: Fortress.

Brooten, Bernadette (1977), "Junia … Outstanding among the Apostles (Romans 16.7)," in *Women Priests: A Catholic Commentary on the Vatican Declarations*, Leonard Swidler and Arlene Swidler (eds.), 141–4, New York: Paulist.

Brooten, Bernadette J. (1996), *Love between Women: Early Christian Responses to Female Homoeroticism*, Chicago: University of Chicago Press.

Bruyn, Theodore de (2011), "Ambrosiaster's Interpretations of Romans 1:26–27," *Vigiliae Christianae*, 65: 463–83.

Bruyn, Theodore de, Stephen A. Cooper, and David G. Hunter (2017), *Ambrosiaster's Commentary on the Pauline Epistles: Romans*, Atlanta, GA: SBL.

Buckland, William Warwick (1924), "Interpolations in the Digest," *Yale Law Journal*, 33: 343–64.

Burke, Kenneth (1941), *The Philosophy of Literary Form*, Berkeley: University of California Press.

Butler, Judith (2004), *Precarious Life: The Power of Mourning and Violence*, New York: Verso.

Casey, Maurice (1999), "Some Anti-Semitic Assumptions in the 'Theological Dictionary of the New Testament,'" *Novum Testamentum*, 41 (3): 280–91.

Chamoiseau, Patrick (1992), *Texaco*, Paris: Gallimard.

Chan, W.-T., and Ariane Rump (1979), *Commentary on the Lao Tzu by Wang Pi*, Hawaii: University Press of Hawaii.

Chouraqui, André ([1985] 2019), *La Bible d'André Chouraqui*, Paris: Le Cerf.

Chouraqui, André (1990), *Le Coran*, Paris: Robert Laffont.

Daley-Bailey, Kate (2012), "The Curious Case of Gerhard Kittel," *Religion Bulletin*, May 31. Available online: http://bulletin.equinoxpub.com/2012/05/the-curious-case-of-gerhard-kittel/ (accessed June 30, 2020).

Dallière, Louis (1941), "Le mystère de l'Eglise composée de Juifs et de Païens," *Union de priere: Charmes sur Rhone*. Available online: http://www.uniondepriere.fr/articles.php?lng=fr&pg=115 (created February 12, 2016; accessed June 3, 2021).

"Daniel Loupiac, professeur de mathématique" (2009), *Collège Cévenol—70° anniversaire—Recontre*. Available online: http://pentecote2009.pasteur.ch/index.php/post/2009/01/30/Daniel-Loupiac%2C- professeur-de-math%C3%A9matique (accessed June 2, 2021).

Darden, Lynne St. Clair (2015), *Scripturalizing Revelation: An African American Postcolonial Reading of Empire*, Atlanta, GA: SBL.

Derrida, Jacques (1981), "Plato's Pharmacy," in *Dissemination*, Barbara Johnson (trans.), 63–171, Chicago: University of Chicago Press.

Detweiler, Robert, ed. (1985), *Reader Response Approaches to Biblical and Secular Texts*, Decatur, GA: SBL.

Dumas, Alexandre ([1845] 2009), *La Reine Margot*, Paris: Gallimard.

Dunn, James D. G. (2005), *The New Perspective on Paul*, Tübingen: Mohr Siebeck.

Elliott, Neil (2010), *The Arrogance of Nations: Reading Romans in the Shadow of Empire*, Minneapolis, MN: Fortress.

Fewell, Danna Nolan, and Gary A. Phillips (2008), "Genesis, Genocide and the Art of Samuel Bak: 'Unseamly' Reading after the Holocaust," in *Representing the Irreparable: The Shoah, the Bible and the Art of Samuel Bak*, Danna Nolan Fewell, Gary A. Phillips, and Yvonne Sherwood (eds.), 75–91, Boston, MA: Pucker Art.

Fewell, Danna Nolan, and Gary A. Phillips (2009), *Icon of Loss: The Haunting Child of Samuel Bak*, Boston, MA: Pucker Art.
Fogelman, Eva (1994), *Conscience and Courage: Rescuers of Jews during the Holocaust*, New York: Doubleday.
Fontaine, Jacques, ed. (1966), *Q. Septimi Florentis Tertulliani De Corona. Sur la couronne*, Paris: Presses Universitaires de France.
Fowler, Robert M. (2001), *Let the Reader Understand: Reader-Response Criticism and the Gospel of Mark*, Harrisburg: Trinity International.
Fredrickson, David E. (2000), "Natural and Unnatural Use in Romans 1:24–27: Paul and the Philosophic Critique of Eros," in *Homosexuality, Science, and the "Plain Sense" of Scripture*, David L. Balch (ed.), 197–222, Grand Rapids, MI: Eerdmans.
Gadamer, Hans-Georg (1989), *Truth and Method*, 2nd rev. ed., New York: Crossroad.
Gadamer, Hans-Georg (2000), *Truth and Method*, New York: Continuum.
Gay, Volney (2016), *On the Pleasures of Owning Persons: The Hidden Face of American Slavery*, Astoria, NY: International Psychoanalytic Books.
Gench, Roger J. (2014), *Theology from the Trenches: Reflections on Urban Ministry*, Louisville, KY: Westminster John Knox.
Gibbs, Robert (2002), "Unjustifiable Suffering," in *Suffering Religion*, Robert Gibbs and Elliott R. Wolfson (eds.), 13–35, New York: Routledge.
Grant, Robert M., and David Tracy (2005), *A Short History of the Interpretation of the Bible*, 2nd ed., Minneapolis, MN: Fortress.
Greenberg, Irving (1977), "Cloud of Smoke, Pillar of Fire: Judaism, Christianity and Modernity after the Holocaust," in *Auschwitz: Beginning of a New Era? Reflections on the Holocaust*, Eva Fleischner (ed.), 7–55, New York: KTAV.
Gregg, Melissa, and Gregory J. Seigworth, eds. (2000), *The Affect Theory Reader*, Durham, NC: Duke University Press.
Grenholm, Cristina ([2010] 2019a), "Autonomy," in *The Cambridge Dictionary of Christianity*, Daniel Patte (ed.), 89, Eugene, OR: Pickwick.
Grenholm, Cristina ([2010] 2019b), "Heteronomy," in *The Cambridge Dictionary of Christianity*, Daniel Patte (ed.), 510–11, Eugene, OR: Pickwick.
Grenholm, Cristina ([2010] 2019c), "Relationality," in *The Cambridge Dictionary of Christianity*, Daniel Patte (ed.), 1062, Eugene, OR: Pickwick.
Grenholm, Cristina (2011), *Motherhood and Love: Beyond the Gendered Stereotypes of Theology*, Grand Rapids, MI: Eerdmans.
Grenholm, Cristina, and Daniel Patte (2000–5), "Romans Through History and Cultures Series," in *Society of Biblical Literature Seminar Papers 2000–2005*, London: T&T Clark.
Griesbach, Jakob (1789), *Commentatio qua Marci evangelium totum e Matthaei et Lucae commentariis decerptum esse monstratur*, Jena: Stranckmann-Fickelscher.
Grose, Peter (2015), *A Good Place to Hide: How One French Community Saved Thousands of Lives during World War II*, New York: Pegasus.
Hallie, Philip (1979), *Lest Innocent Blood Be Shed: The Story of the Village of Le Chambon and How Goodness Happened There*, New York: Harper and Row.
Hanh, Thich Nhat (2007), *Living Buddha, Living Christ 20th Anniversary Edition*, New York: Berkley.
Harrill, J. Albert (2017), "'Exegetical Torture' in Early Christian Biblical Interpretation: The Case of Origen of Alexandria," *Biblical Interpretation*, 25: 39–57.

Henry, Patrick (2007), *We Only Know Men: The Rescue of Jews in France during the Holocaust*, Washington: Catholic University of America Press.
Huang, Chi-chung (1997), *The Analects of Confucius (Lunyu): A Literal Translation with an Introduction and Notes*, Oxford: Oxford University Press.
Jewett, Robert (2007), *Romans: A Commentary*, Minneapolis, MN: Fortress.
Käsemann, Ernst (1980), *Commentary on Romans*, trans. Geoffrey W. Bromiley, Grand Rapids, MI: Eerdmans.
Kelley, Shawn (2002), *Racializing Jesus: Race, Ideology and the Formation of Modern Biblical Scholarship*, New York: Routledge.
Kelley, Shawn (2015), "Hermeneutics and Genocide: Giving Voice to the Unspoken," *Palgrave Communications*, 1 (15031). Available online: https://doi.org/10.1057/palcomms.2015.31October (accessed September 25, 2020).
Kemp, Jonathan (2020), "After Auschwitz: Adorno and the Aesthetics of Genocide," unpublished paper. Available online: https://www.academia.edu/1357928/After_Auschwitz_Adorno_and_the_Aesthetics_of_Genocide?email_work_card=view-paper (accessed September 29, 2020).
Kermode, Frank, and Joan Richardson, eds. (1997), *Wallace Stevens: Collected Poetry and Prose*, New York: Library of America.
Koch, Jerome R., and Ignacio Luis Ramirez (2010), "Religiosity, Christian Fundamentalism, and Intimate Partner Violence among U.S. College Students," *Review of Religious Research*, 51: 402–10.
Koosed, Jennifer L., and Stephen D. Moore, eds. (2014), "Affect Theory and the Bible," *Biblical Interpretation*, 22: 4–5.
Koreman, Megan (2018), *The Escape Line: How the Ordinary Heroes of Dutch-Paris Resisted the Nazi Occupation of Western Europe*, Oxford: Oxford University Press.
Kotrosits, Maia (2015), *Rethinking Early Christian Identity: Affect, Violence, and Belonging*, Minneapolis, MN: Fortress.
Kotsko, Adam (2018), "The Political Theology of Trump," *n+1*, November 6. Available online: nplusonemag.com/online-only/online-only/the-political-theology-of-trump/.
Kuefler, Matthew (2001), *The Manly Eunuch: Masculinity, Gender Ambiguity, and Christian Ideology in Late Antiquity*, Chicago: University of Chicago Press.
Langer, Lawrence (1991), *Holocaust Memories: The Ruin of Memory*, New Haven, CT: Yale University Press.
Langer, Lawrence (2006), *Using and Abusing the Holocaust*, Bloomington: Indiana University Press.
"A Letter on Justice and Open Debate" (2020), *Harper's Magazine*, July 7. Available online: https://harpers.org/a-letter-on-justice-and-open-debate/ (accessed June 14, 2021).
Levi, Primo (1996), *Survival in Auschwitz: The Nazi Assault on Humanity*, trans. Stuart Woolf, New York: Touchstone.
Levinas, Emmanuel (1982), "Useless Suffering," in *Entre Nous: Thinking of the Other*, trans. Michael B. Smith and Barbara Harshav, 91–102, New York: Columbia University Press.
Levinas, Emmanuel (1985), *Time and the Other*, trans. Richard Cohen, Pittsburgh: Duquesne University Press.
Levinas, Emmanuel (1990), *Difficult Freedom: Essays on Judaism*, Baltimore, MD: John Hopkins University Press.
Levinas, Emmanuel (1994), *In the Time of the Nations*, trans. Michael B. Smith, Bloomington: Indiana University Press.

Linafelt, Tod (2000), *Strange Fire: Reading the Bible after the Holocaust*, New York: New York University Press.
Linafelt, Tod (2002), *A Shadow of Glory: Reading the New Testament after the Holocaust*, New York: Routledge.
Lovsky, Fadiey (1955), *Antisémitisme et mystère d'Israël*, Paris: Albin Michel.
Lubac, Henri de ([1959–64] 1998–2009), *Medieval Exegesis: The Four Senses of Scripture*, trans. Marc Sebanc, 3 vols, Grand Rapids, MI: Eerdmans.
Mack, Burton L. (1990), *Rhetoric and the New Testament*, Minneapolis, MN: Augsburg Fortress.
Magonet, Jonathan (2004), *A Rabbi Reads the Bible*, Norwich: Hymns Ancient and Modern.
Martin, Dale B. (1990), *Slavery as Salvation: The Metaphor of Slavery in Pauline Christianity*, New Haven, CT: Yale University Press.
McIntyre, Alasdair (1988), *Whose Justice? Which Rationality?*, Notre Dame, IN: University of Notre Dame Press.
McKnight, Scot (2019), *Reading Romans Backwards: A Gospel of Peace in the Midst of Empire*, Waco, TX: Baylor University Press.
Mill, John Stuart (2015), *On Liberty, Utilitarianism and Other Essays*, Oxford: Oxford University Press.
Moore, Stephen D. (2018), "Those Incommensurate Activities We Call 'Biblical Studies': A Future-Oriented History of Their Bifurcated Past," in *Present and Future of Biblical Studies: Celebrating 25 Years of Brill's Biblical Interpretation*, Tat-siong Benny Liew (ed.), 274–96, Leiden: Brill.
Moorehead, Caroline (2014), *Village of Secrets: Defying the Nazis in Vichy France*, New York: Harper.
Mullen, Lincoln (2018), "The Fight to Define Romans 13," *Atlantic*, July 15. Available online: https://www.theatlantic.com/ideas/archive/2018/06/romans-13/562916/ (accessed September 25, 2020).
Murfin, Ross, ed. (1996), *Heart of Darkness and Essays from Five Contemporary Critical Perspectives*, New York: Macmillan.
Nanos, Mark D. (2017), *Reading Paul within Judaism: Collected Essays of Mark D. Nanos, Volume 1*, Eugene, OR: Cascade.
Nanos, Mark D. (2018), *Reading Paul within Judaism: Collected Essays of Mark D. Nanos, Vol. 2*, Eugene, OR: Cascade.
Noll, Mark (2006), *The Civil War as a Theological Crisis*, Chapel Hill: University of North Carolina Press.
Nosthoff, A.-V. (2014), "Art after Auschwitz—Responding to an Infinite Demand. Gustav Metzger's Works as Responses to Theodor W. Adorno's 'New Categorical Imperative,'" *Cultural Politics*, 10 (3): 300–19.
Patte, Daniel (1990), *The Religious Dimensions of Biblical Texts: Greimas's Structural Semiotics and Biblical Exegesis*, Atlanta, GA: Scholars.
Patte, Daniel (1999), *The Challenge of Discipleship: A Critical Study of the Sermon on the Mount as Scripture*, United Kingdom: Bloomsbury Academic.
Patte, Daniel, ed. (2004), *Global Bible Commentary*, Nashville, TN: Abingdon.
Patte, Daniel, ed. (2010), *Cambridge Dictionary of Christianity*, Cambridge: Cambridge University Press. Reprinted as a two-volume set (2021), Eugene, OR: Pickwick Publications.
Patte, Daniel (2018), *Romans: Three Exegetical Interpretations and the History of Reception, Volume 1: Romans 1:1-32*, London: Bloomsbury Academic.

Phillips, Gary (2017), "Icons of Justice: Justice, Suffering and the Artwork of Samuel Bak," *Religions*, 8 (6): 108. Available online: https://doi.org/10.3390/rel8060108 (accessed September 25, 2020).
Raskin, Richard (2004), *A Child at Gunpoint: A Case Study of the Life of a Photo*, Aarhus: Aarhus University Press.
Ricoeur, Paul (1974), *The Conflict of Interpretations: Essays in Hermeneutics*, Evanston, IL: Northwestern University Press.
Ricoeur, Paul (1979), "Epilogue: The Sacred Text and the Community," in *The Critical Study of Sacred Texts*, Wendy Doniger O'Flaherty (ed.), 271–6, Berkeley: Graduate Theological Union.
Rogers, John (2000), "The Potential of the Negative. Approaching the Old Testament through the Work of Adorno," in *Rethinking Contexts, Rereading Texts: Contributions from the Social Sciences to Biblical Interpretation*, M. D. Carroll (ed.), 24–47, Sheffield: Sheffield Academic Press.
Röhle, Robert (2008), "Theodor Mommsens Verdienste um die Herausgabe der Justinianischen Digesten," *Zeitschrift der Savigny-Stiftung für Rechtsgeschichte, Romanistische Abteilung*, 125 (1): 664–73.
Rouchy-Lévy, Violette (2008), "L'image des protestants dans 'La Reine Margot' de Patrice Chéreau," *Bulletin de la Société de l'Histoire du Protestantisme Français*, 154: 163–73.
Runions, Erin (2014), *The Babylon Complex: Theological Fantasies of War, Sex, and Sovereignty*, New York: Fordham University Press.
"Samuel Bak," *Pucker Gallery*. Available online: https://www.puckergallery.com/artists#/samuel-bak/ (accessed July 22, 2021).
Savigny, Friedrich Karl von (1840), *System des heutigen Römischen Rechts*, vol. 4, Berlin: Veit.
Schaefer, Donovan O. (2015), *Religious Affects: Animality, Evolution, and Power*, Durham, NC: Duke University Press.
Schüssler Fiorenza, Elisabeth (1988), "The Ethics of Biblical Interpretation: Decentering Biblical Scholarship," *Journal of Biblical Literature*, 107 (1): 3–17.
Schüssler Fiorenza, Elisabeth (1992), *But She Said: Feminist Practices of Biblical Interpretation*, Boston, MA: Beacon.
Scott, Bernard Brandon (2018), "Romans 13 in Our Time," *Westar Institute*, June 25. Available online: https://www.westarinstitute.org/blog/romans-13-in-our-time/ (accessed September 25, 2020).
Sheldon, Jane P., and Sandra L. Parent (2002), "Clergy's Attitudes and Attributions of Blame toward Female Rape Victims," *Violence against Women*, 8: 233–56.
Simic, Charles (2014), "The Prisoner of History," *New York Review of Books*, August 14, 53.
Simic, Charles (2015), *The Lunatic: Poems*, New York: Ecco/HarperCollins.
Soyinka, Wole (1981), *Aké: The Years of Childhood*, New York: Random House.
Stählin, Otto, ed. (1972), *Clemens Alexandrinus*, vol. 1, Die griechischen christlichen Schriftsteller, 3rd ed., Berlin: Akademie.
Steiner, George (1967), *Language and Silence: Essays on Language, Literature, and the Inhuman*, New York: Atheneum.
Stendahl, Krister (1962), "Biblical Theology, Contemporary," in *The Interpreter's Dictionary of the Bible: An Illustrated Encyclopedia*, vol. 1, George Arthur Buttrick, Thomas Samuel Kepler, John Knox, Herbert Gordon May, Samuel Terrien, and Emory Stevens Bucke (eds.), 418–32, New York: Abingdon.
Stendahl, Krister (1982), *Scripture in the Jewish and Christian Traditions: Authority, Interpretation, Relevance*, Nashville, TN: Abingdon.

Stone, Ken (2005), *Practicing Safer Texts: Food, Sex and Bible in Queer Perspectives*, New York: T&T Clark.
Stubbs, Monya A. (2007), "Philippians," in *True to Our Native Land: An African-American New Testament Commentary*, Brian K. Blount (ed.), 363–79, Minneapolis, MN: Fortress.
Stubbs, Monya A. (2013), *Indebted Love: Paul's Subjection Language*, Eugene OR: Pickwick.
Thiselton, Anthony (1997), *New Horizons in Hermeneutics*, Grand Rapids, MI: Zondervan.
Ticineto Clough, Patricia, with Jean Halley, eds. (2007), *The Affective Turn: Theorizing the Social*, Durham, NC: Duke University Press.
Urba, Carl F., and Joseph Zycha, eds. (1902), *Sancti Aureli Augustini: De perfectione iustitiae hominis*, …, Corpus Scriptorum Ecclesiasticorum Latinorum 42, Vienna: Tempsky.
Venturi, Robert, Denise Scott Brown, and Steven Izenour (1972), *Learning from Las Vegas*, Cambridge, MA: MIT Press.
Vogels, Heinrich Josef, ed. (1966), *Ambrosiastri qui dicitur commentarius in epistulas paulinas*, Corpus Scriptorum Ecclesiasticorum Latinorum 81.1; Vienna: Hoelder-Pichler-Tempsky.
Wang Zi (2015), "How to Understand a Biblical God in Chinese: Toward a Cross-Cultural Biblical Hermeneutics," in *The Trinity among the Nations: The Doctrine of God in the Majority World*, Gene L. Green, Stephen T. Pardue, and K. K. Yeo (eds.), 140–60, Grand Rapids, MI: Eerdmans.
Weapons of the Spirit (1987), [film] Dir. Pierre Sauvage, USA: Chambon Foundation.
Wellhausen, Julius (1927), *Prolegomena zur Geschichte Israels*, 6th ed., Berlin: de Gruyter.
Wimbush, Vincent L. (2012), *White Men's Magic: Scripturalization as Slavery*, New York: Oxford University Press.
Wimbush, Vincent L. (2017), *Scripturalectics: The Management of Meaning*, New York: Oxford University Press.
Yeo, K. K. (2002), "The Rhetoric of Election and Calling Language in 1 Thessalonians," in *Rhetorical Criticism and the Bible*, Stanley E. Porter and Dennis L. Stamps (eds.), 526–47, London: Sheffield Academic.
Yeo, K. K. (2004a), "Culture and Intersubjectivity as Criteria of Negotiating Meanings in Cross-Cultural Interpretations," in *The Meanings We Choose*, Charles H. Cosgrove (ed.), 81–100, Edinburgh: Sheffield.
Yeo, K. K. (2004b), "Introduction: Navigating Romans through Cultures," in *Navigating Romans through Cultures: Challenging Readings by Charting a New Course*, K. K. Yeo (ed.), 1–28, New York: T&T Clark.
Yeo, K. K. (2004c), "Messianic Predestination in Romans 8 and Classical Confucianism," in *Navigating Romans through Cultures*, K. K. Yeo (ed.), 259–89, New York: T&T Clark.
Yeo, K. K. (2008), *Musing with Confucius and Paul: Toward a Chinese Christian Theology*, Eugene, OR: Cascade.
Yeo, K. K. (2018), *What Has Jerusalem to Do with Beijing? Biblical Interpretation from a Chinese Perspective*, 20th anniversary ed., Eugene, OR: Pickwick.
Yeo, K. K., ed. (2021), *The Oxford Handbook of the Bible in China*, New York: Oxford University Press.
Zauzmer, Julie, and Keith McMillan (2018), "Sessions Cites Bible Passage Used to Defend Slavery in Defense of Separating Immigrant Families," *Washington Post*, June 15. Available online: https://www.washingtonpost.com/news/acts-of-faith/wp/2018/06/14/jeff-sessions-points-to-the-bible-in-defense-of-separating-immigrant-families/ (accessed June 17, 2021).

CONTRIBUTORS

Robert L. Brawley is the Albert G. McGaw Professor of New Testament, Emeritus at McCormick Theological Seminary, USA. He is the editor-in-chief of the *Oxford Encyclopedia of Bible and Ethics*, and his most recent publication is *Luke: A Social Identity Commentary* (2020).

Bernadette J. Brooten, the Brandeis University Robert and Myra Kraft and Jacob Hiatt Professor, emerita, directs the Feminist Sexual Ethics Project. She is currently writing on enslaved and slaveholding women in early Christianity, gender variation in early rabbinic literature, Roman-period sources for woman-woman marriage, and new sources on female homoerotic desire in the Roman world. Publications include: *Women Leaders in the Ancient Synagogue: Inscriptional Evidence and Background Issues* (1982; 2020); *Love between Women: Early Christian Responses to Female Homoeroticism* (1996; 2020); and, with the editorial assistance of Jacqueline L. Hazelton, *Beyond Slavery: Overcoming Its Religious and Sexual Legacies* (2010).

Kathy Ehrensperger is Research Professor of New Testament in Jewish Perspective, Abraham Geiget College, University of Potsdam, Germany. She is the author of *That We May Be Mutually Encouraged: Feminism and the New Perspective on Paul* (2004), *Paul and the Dynamics of Power* (2009) and *Paul at the Crossroads of Cultures* (2013), in addition to numerous articles. She is also the executive editor of the *Encyclopedia of Jewish-Christian Relations*.

Timothy Gombis is an independent scholar living in Grand Rapids, MI, USA. He has published on Pauline theology and Paul's Letter to the Romans. His most recent publication is *Power in Weakness: Paul's Transformed Vision for Ministry* (2021).

James P. Grimshaw is Associate Professor of Religion at Carroll University, USA. He is author of *The Matthean Community and the World: An Analysis of Matthew's Food Exchange* (2008). He is coeditor of *Matthew* (2013) and editor of *Luke-Acts* (2019), both in the Texts@Contexts series. He serves on the steering committee for the SBL Contextual Biblical Interpretation section.

John Jones is Associate Professor of New Testament Studies and Phenomenology of Religion in the H. M. S. Richards Divinity School of La Sierra University, Riverside, CA, USA. Publications include "Humanistic Values in the Lotus Sutra" (2001) and "Flaming Fountain, Burning House: Upaya in the Lotus Sutra" (2002), both in *Hsi Lai Journal of Humanistic Buddhism*, and a chapter on Christianity and homosexuality, "In Christ There Is Neither: Toward the Unity of the Body of Christ," in *Christianity and Homosexuality: Some Seventh-day Adventist Perspectives* (2008).

Tat-siong Benny Liew is Class of 1956 Professor in New Testament Studies at the College of the Holy Cross, MA, USA. He is the author of *Politics of Parousia* (1999) and *What Is Asian American Biblical Hermeneutics?* (2008). In addition, he is the editor of the Semeia volume on "The Bible in Asian America" (with Gale Yee; 2002), *Postcolonial Interventions* (2009), *They Were All Together in One Place?* (with Randall Bailey and Fernando Segovia; 2009), *Reading Ideologies* (2011), *Psychoanalytical Mediations between Marxist and Postcolonial Readings of the Bible* (with Erin Runions; 2016), *Present and Future of Biblical Studies* (2018), and *Colonialism and the Bible: Contemporary Reflections from the Global South* (with Fernando Segovia; 2018). Liew is also the series editor of T&T Clark's Study Guides to the New Testament.

Daniel Patte is Professor Emeritus of Religious Studies, New Testament and Christianity at Vanderbilt University, TN, USA. Among his publications are *Early Jewish Hermeneutic in Palestine* (1975) and *Paul's Faith and the Power of the Gospel* (1982). He is the editor of *Global Bible Commentary* (2004) and *The Cambridge Dictionary of Christianity* (2010) and coeditor of "Romans Through History and Cultures" (ten volumes). He is also the author of *Romans: Three Exegetical Interpretations and the History of Reception: Volume 1: Romans 1:1-32* (2018).

Gary A. Phillips is the Edgar H. Evans Professor of Religion and dean of the College emeritus at Wabash College, IN, USA. Scholarship interests include the Bible's relationship to Western art, culture, and the ethics of interpretation after the Holocaust. Collaborative and individually authored publications include *The Postmodern Bible* (1995), *Bible and Ethics of Reading* (1997), and *Reading Community Reading Scripture* (2002). His most recent focus is on the artwork of Holocaust survivor Samuel Bak. Writings include: *Representing the Irreparable: The Shoah, the Bible, and the Art of Samuel Bak* (2008), *Icon of Loss: The Paintings of Samuel Bak* (2009), and *Just Is in the Art of Samuel Bak* (2018).

Monya A. Stubbs is a chaplain in the US Navy. She also serves as an affiliated assistant professor at Chicago Theological Seminary, Chicago, IL, USA. Stubbs is the author of *Indebted Love: Paul's Subjection Language in Romans* (2013) and coauthor of *A Contextual Introduction to the Gospel of Matthew and Its Readings* (2003). Her published essays include works on "Romans" in *Navigating Romans Through History* (2004), "Philippians" in *True to Our Native Land* (2007), "1 Thessalonians" in *Women's Bible Commentary* (2012), "1 and 2 Corinthians" in *Covenant Bible Study* (2014), and "John" in *Feasting on the Gospels* (2015).

K. K. Yeo is Kendall Professor of New Testament at Garrett-Evangelical Theological Seminary and affiliate professor at the Department of Asian Languages and Cultures at Northwestern University in Evanston, IL, USA. He has been a visiting professor to major universities in China and has authored or edited more than forty Chinese- and English-language books on critical engagement between Bible and cultures, including *What Has Jerusalem to Do with Beijing?* (2018). Yeo coedited the "Majority World Theology" series (2020) and *Theologies of Land* (2020). He is the editor of *The Oxford Handbook of the Bible in China* (2021).

INDEX OF AUTHORS

Adorno, Theodor 5–6, 53, 55–6, 59, 64–7, 69, 72–6, 78, 149
Agamben, G. 21
Albright, William 61
Althaus, Paul 60
Ames, Roger T. 94–5
Angelou, Maya 4, 31, 143, 149
Appiah, Kwame Anthony 118 n.7
Armstrong, Elizabeth A. 118 n.7
Austin, J. L. 40
Aymer, Margaret 62

Badiou, A. 21
Bak, Samuel iv, 5, 6, 18, 41, 53–9, 63, 64, 66–78, 103, 148, 158
Bannister, Jamie A. 102
Baranowski, Shelley 59
Barrett, C. K. 19
Barth, Karl 56
Barthes, Roland 86
Baur, Ferdinand Christian 100
Beckett, Samuel 66
Beker, J. Christiaan 3, 15, 21, 23, 104, 150
Benhabi, Seyla 3, 29, 150
Bergen, Doris 59
Black, Fiona C. 41
Block, Gay 129
Bochenek, Michael 60
Boers, Roland 55
Boochani, Behrouz 137–8, 143, 147–8
Börner, Christian Friedrich 102
Bose, Christian Wilhelm 102
Bourdieu, Pierre 35, 150
Bourke-White, Margaret 66 n.17
Boyarin, Daniel 39
Brawley, Robert L. v, 2–3, 7, 10, 17, 157
Bray, Karen 41
Briggs Kittredge, Cynthia 38, 150
Brooten, Bernadette vi, 1, 3, 6, 7, 8, 10, 99, 102, 157
Bruyn, Theodore 102

Buckland, William Warwick 100
Bultmann, Rudolf 15, 82
Burke, Kenneth 41
Butler, Judith 71 n.20

Campbell, D. 15, 21, 82
Camus, Albert 10, 139–41
Casey, Maurice 59, 61
Celan, Paul 66
Chamoiseau, Patrick 32, 146, 148
Chan, W.-T. 88
Chouraqui, Andre 9, 10, 119, 128, 133–9, 141, 146
Conrad, Joseph 132
Crage, Suzanna 118 n.7

Daley-Bailey, Kate 96
Dallière, Louis 9, 127–8, 132–9
Darden, Lynne St. Clair 4, 34
Derrida, Jacques 55
Detweiler, Robert 37
Dibelius, Martin 60
Dodd, C. H. 19
Drucker, Maika 129
Dumas, Alexandre 119 n.9
Dunn, J. 15, 19, 37

Ehrensperger, Kathy v, 3–4, 10, 27, 157
Elliott, Neil 20, 36, 83

Fewell, Danna Nolan 35, 69, 73
Fitzmyer, Joseph A. 15, 23, 82, 91, 103
Fogelman, Eva 129
Fowler, Robert M. 37
Fredrickson, David E. 102

Gadamer, Hans-Georg 92, 139 n.42, 143, 152
Gaventa, Beverly 15
Gay, Volney 126, 128–30, 132, 134
Gench, Roger J. 145

Gibbs, Robert 56
Gombis, Timothy 13, 1–2, 10, 13
Grant, Robert M. 36, 99
Greenberg, Irving 78 n.23
Gregg, Melissa 41
Grenholm, Cristina 27, 83–4, 135, 142–6
Griesbach, Jakob 100
Grimshaw, James P. iii–v, 1, 157
Grose, Peter 125 n.19

Hallie, Philip 125, 129
Hanh, Thich Nhat 4
Harrill, J. Albert 34
Henry, Patrick 129, 131
Hirsch, Emmanuel 60
Horkheimer, Max 64
Huang, Chi-chung 94

Jewett, Robert 15, 20, 82, 91, 102–3
Jones, John vi, 1, 8–10, 109

Kant, Immanuel 66, 144 n.50
Käsemann, Ernst 15, 21, 36, 82, 104
Keck, Leander E. 15, 104
Kelley, Shawn 59 n.7, 63
Kemp, Jonathan 65
Kermode, Frank 144
Kittel, Gerhard 7, 60, 61, 96
Koch, Jerome R. 105
Koosed, Jennifer L. 41
Koreman, Megan 121 n.14, 123 n.17
Kotrosits, Maia 41
Kotsko, Adam 40
Kuefler, Matthew 102
Kuhn, K. G. 61

Langer, Lawrence 57, 58, 66, 68, 76
Leenhardt, F. 19
Levi, Primo 72
Levinas, Emmanuel 22, 59, 72, 75, 77, 138–9
Liew, Tat-siong Benny v, 4, 10, 33, 158
Linafelt, Tod 59 n.7
Longenecker, Richard 103
Lovsky, Fadiey 133 n.34
Lubac, Henri de 100
Luther, Martin 18, 37, 41, 103, 119–20, 136–8

Mack, Burton 41

Magonet, Jonathan 4, 35, 41
Marcel, Gabriel 127, 139
Martin, Dale 37
McIntyre, Alasdair 18
McKnight, Scot 38
McMillan, Keith 106
Mill, John Stuart v, 4, 5, 43–51, 56, 58
Moo, Douglas 15, 19, 82, 103
Moore, Stephen D. 39, 41
Moorehead, Caroline 125
Mullen, Lincoln 60
Murfen, Ross 133

Nanos, Mark D. 15, 36–7, 82
Nasrallah, Laura 62
Noll, Mark 100
Nosthoff, A.-V. 56, 67

Parent, Sandra L. 105
Patte, Daniel i, iii, v–vi, 1–23, 27, 29–51, 53–9, 61, 63–4, 68–78, 81–6, 89, 91–4, 96–9, 101–6, 109–13, 115, 122, 135, 145, 158
Phillips, Gary vi, 1, 5, 10, 53, 66–7, 69, 73, 158

Rabelais, Francois 119 n.8
Ramirez, Ignacio Luis 105
Raskin, Richard 53, 68, 73
Réjouis, Rose-Myriam 146
Richardson, Joan 144
Ricoeur, Paul 85, 117
Riffaterre, Michael 21
Rogers, John 55
Röhle, Robert 100
Rosemont, Henry, Jr. 94–5
Rouchy-Lévy, Violette 119
Rump, Ariane 88
Runions, Erin 40, 155, 158

Sartre, Jean Paul 10, 139, 140, 141
Sauvage, Pierre 125 n.19
Savigny, Friedrich Karl von 100
Schaefer, Donovan O. 41
Schoenberg, Arnold 66
Schreiner, Thomas 15
Schüssler Fiorenza, Elisabeth 8, 29, 109, 112, 147
Scott, Bernard Brandon 62, 155

Searle, John R. 40
Seigworth, Gregory J. 41
Sheldon, Jane P. 105
Simic, Charles 64, 73–7, 144–6, 155
Soyinka, Wole 115
Stählin, Otto 102 n.1
Steiner, George 56
Stendahl, Krister 8, 36, 109, 112
Stevens, Wallace 144 n.50
Stone, Ken 36
Stowe, Harriet Beecher 132
Stubbs, Monya v, 4, 5, 10, 43, 45, 47
Stuhlmacher, Peter 103

Tamez, Elsa 20
Taubes, J. 21
Ticineto Clough, Patricia 41
Thiselton, Anthony 92
Thoreau, Henry David 144 n.49
Tofighian, Omid 147 n.57, 148 n.57
Tracy, David 36, 99

Urba, Carl F. 102 n.1

Venturi, Robert 101
Vinokurov, Val 144
Vogels, Heinrich Josef 102 n.1

Wang Zi 87, 156
Wellhausen, Julius 100

Wilckens, Ulrich 103
Wimbush, Vincent 4, 34
Woodson, Carter Godwin 132
Wright, N. T. 15

Yeo, K.K. vi, 1–3, 5–7, 10, 81, 83, 84, 86–8, 93–4, 96, 158–9

Zauzmer, Julie 106
Žižek, S. 21
Zycha, Joseph 102 n.1

Ancient Authors
Abelard 18
Ambrosiaster 102
Anastasios 102
Arethas 102 n.1
Augustine 3, 18, 29, 36, 102–3

Clement of Alexandria 18, 102
Confucius 6, 86–9, 92–4, 97

John Chrysostom 18, 102
Josephus 91

Laozi 88

Philo 100

Tertullian 102

www.ingramcontent.com/pod-product-compliance
Lightning Source LLC
Chambersburg PA
CBHW061840300426
44115CB00013B/2456